The Devil You Dance With

The Devil You Dance With

Film Culture in the New South Africa

EDITED AND WITH
AN INTRODUCTION BY

Audrey Thomas McCluskey

UNIVERSITY OF ILLINOIS PRESS
Urbana and Chicago

Manufactured in the United States of America
1 2 3 4 5 C P 5 4 3 2 1
∞ This book is printed on acid-free paper.

Library of Congress Cataloging-in-Publication Data
The devil you dance with : film culture in the new South Africa / edited and with an introduction by Audrey Thomas McCluskey.
p. cm.
Includes bibliographical references and index.
ISBN 978-0-252-03386-5 (cloth : alk. paper)
ISBN 978-0-252-07574-2 (pbk. : alk. paper)
1. Motion pictures—South Africa—History.
2. Motion picture producers and directors—South Africa—Interviews.
I. McCluskey, Audrey T.
PN1993.5.S6D48 2009
791.430968—dc22 2008021801

To the next generation of
Africa's descendants who,
having inherited a taste of freedom,
must not rest until it is won

Contents

Acknowledgments

Since my first visit to Cape Town, Pretoria, and Johannesburg, South Africa, in 2000 with the International Faculty Development Seminar, I have been captivated by the political volatility of South Africa and the rich culture and warmth of its people. The germination of this project began shortly after my second visit to Johannesburg. I have many to thank for their encouragement and helpfulness from the beginning of this project and all along the way to its completion. In 2004 I participated in the Indiana University Office International Programs' faculty exchange with the School of Arts at the University of Witwatersrand, a program initiated by Paula Girshick along with Patrick O'Meara, director of OIP. Without their generous support, this work would not have been possible. While at Witwatersrand, I was welcomed at every turn and treated graciously by faculty, staff, and students.

I want to acknowledge the support of Arnitra Nettleton, acting dean of the School of Arts, and the helpful assistance of professors Haseenah Ebrahim and Kgafela oa Magogodi Kgafela and staff member Matilda Nong, who provided guidance in facilitating my relationship with the Letsibogo Girls' High School in Soweto. On the custodial staff, "Sophie" always greeted me with a smile and a warm Xhosa greeting. I thank my driver, David N., for helping me to navigate the sprawling city and for answering my nonstop questions. I am forever grateful to Canadian filmmaker Peter Davis for providing contact information for many of the filmmakers I interviewed. Peter's various film works are in a special collection at the Black Film Center/Archive at Indiana University, and he regularly visits Indiana to update this important resource.

I am especially indebted to all the interviewees for interrupting their busy lives to make themselves available for interviews and for being gracious and supportive and introducing me to their colleagues in the industry. No one was more helpful in this way and in "schooling" me in the rich culture of the capital city than Palesa Letlaka-Nkosi. She literally took me by the hand and led me around Jo'burg—like the dear friend she became. Akin Omotoso facilitated my meeting with other filmmakers and gave me the idea for the title of this collection. A special mention goes to Motshabi Tyelele, a gifted actor, for her friendship and warm hospitality (that included a nice meal) during two of my visits.

Stateside, I extend a special thanks to Paul Heyde, the archivist at the Black Film Center/Archive, for all his good work and steady, dependable presence during the nearly four years that we worked together.

As a scholar in residence at the Institute for Advanced Study at Indiana University, I was provided with comfortable space and a supportive environment for my research and writing. I especially appreciated the support of Assistant Director Ivona Hedin who manages the day-to-day operations of IAS with efficiency and care. I won't forget Victor Kinzer, the very helpful receptionist at IAS, who responded to my numerous requests for technical assistance. I also thank Regina Nacole Barnett, a keen-eyed graduate student in African American and African Diaspora Studies, for proofreading a version of this manuscript and for her good work ethic.

I must also note that Joan Catapano, associate director and editor-in-chief of the University of Illinois Press, and her staff were good shepherds of this work from beginning to end—and I thank them.

Last but not least, I thank my extended family and a long, unnamed list of friends for their continuing support and belief.

Introduction

The recent rash of internationally distributed films from South Africa deals in some way or another with the country's tumultuous racial history. The ideology and legacy of state-sanctioned white supremacy and oppression are dealt with directly in *Catch a Fire* (2006) and indirectly in the Academy Award–winning *Tsotsi* (2005).[1] As is frequently the case today, both of these films had international or multinational backers. An increasing number of foreign film companies use this scenic country as a backdrop even when the subject is not about South Africa. It serves as an ideal location for film production because it is considered exotic but very accessible and relatively inexpensive. Providing location services is one of the current strategies used by industry professionals for establishing an international, South African presence in the lucrative global film market. Also, film production and the arts in general are an important part of the reemergence of civic and public life in the young democracy installed after the 1994 elections.

Although the celebratory glow of freedom festivals has long faded and the slow pace of addressing the accumulation of decades of racial oppression and displacement has deepened the tension over the government's priorities, that has not halted the debate over the role of the arts in the postapartheid state. South Africa is seen by many opinion leaders in the international community as a poster child for nonviolent democratic reform and among many as the titular leader of a hoped-for "African Renaissance" on that exploited and distressed continent. Scholar Paul Gilroy views the country and its lessons as the best hope for a politically realigned world: "It is my hope that, not Europe and the North Atlantic, but the post-colonial world in general, and

South Africa in particular, will in due course, generate an opposed and yet equivalent sense of what our networked world might be and become."[2] Such raised expectations acknowledge the lethal consequences of racial hierarchy applied to politics, as well as the magnanimous but practical vision offered by its first popularly elected president, Nobel Peace Prize laureate Nelson Mandela. His endorsement of a "politics of negotiated compromise,"[3] which created the historic Truth and Reconciliation Commission (TRC), chaired by another of the country's Nobel laureates, Archbishop Desmond Tutu, left unaddressed the troubling notion that truth itself was negotiated and left in place gross economic inequities. The international reputation of South Africa suffered some harm from the controversial stance of Mandela's successor, Thabo Mbeki, on HIV and AIDS that are ravaging the country.[4] However, his aggressive economic development initiatives and support of other African nations have helped the country become a leading tourist destination and an economic engine for the whole region.

Media culture, as one of the most salient expressions of the democracy, has found it difficult to avoid what Mandela called "the threat of one dimensionality." Rather than serving as an arm of a totalitarian state, all forms of media are expected to operate for the greater good and in the public interest. In this context, many people in the film community feel optimistic about South Africa's film culture, which, like the country as a whole, is experiencing the openness of this new era. But with a steady increase in film production and the emergence of a new community of filmmakers no longer confined by race, the questions grow sharper: What is the responsibility of the filmmakers to history, to nation, and to individual artistic calling? Do these questions impose complementary or competing demands on the filmmaker? Is there a national cinema or even a desire for one? Do the dictates of global market forces make such questions moot? These issues are addressed in different degrees by the filmmakers included in the current volume. They are concerned with the revitalization of film and media culture and the lasting effects of an industry that had been designed to purposely fracture the psyche of its people by using film to advance the dictates of a racist political order. Yet, bearing the weight of history and its legacy in South Africa can be a complicated dance that requires filmmakers to demonstrate deft footwork and to have many pivotal positions. That the new environment offers opportunities that are laced with recurring challenges as well as new pitfalls is to be expected. In the words of filmmaker Akin Omotoso, this is simply "the devil you dance with" in pursuing your passion to make films.

A Historical Context

The beginning of film in the 1890s coincides with European expansion into Africa and represents the height of modernist enterprise. The emergence of South African film production in 1896 was one of the earliest. Its development is linked to the period of the Anglo-Boer War (1899–1902) and was fueled by a demand in Britain for war images.[5] African film scholar Nwachukwu Frank Ukadike reminds us that electronic media have historically been used as an instrument for the consolidation of power and bureaucratic propaganda, rather than for transgressive political empowerment.[6] Part of that history parallels developments in Hollywood in which film facilitated and maintained racial hierarchies. In South Africa, one year after American pioneer D. W. Griffith directed his racist epic *Birth of a Nation* (1915) that posits white supremacy as the "natural" cure for black savagery and aggression, *De Voortrekkers* (1916) was produced by African Film Productions with the help of American I. W. Schlesinger.[7] This film burnished and popularized the so-called "Great Trek," the central myth of Afrikaner nation-building in which European emigrants laid claim to Zulu land and established a justification for white supremacy after they defeated the Zulus at the Battle of Blood River (Ncome River). Like *Birth of a Nation,* the film shows the fiercely independent Boers, like the Southern Confederates of the American Civil War, fighting nobly for nationhood and their threatened way of life. Also like *Birth of a Nation,* the film glorifies the establishment of white supremacy by violent means and at the expense of the black population. It is more than coincidental that before Griffith, the son of a Kentucky Confederate colonel, directed *Birth of a Nation,* he wrote and directed the short film *The Zulu's Heart* in 1908. It is reportedly the first American fiction film set in South Africa (although photographed in New Jersey with American actors) and the first to advance the Manichean binary of the "good" or "bad" African, as determined by whether the black served whites or threatened them.[8]

Solomon T. Plaatje, a well-traveled South African journalist, novelist, and founding member of the organization that became the African National Congress, is linked to the beginnings of black film culture in South Africa. A contemporary of W. E. B. Du Bois, Plaatje recognized parallels between the "New Negro" in America and the "New African" in his country. Plaatje was very aware of the power of the new medium and noted the harmful effects that Griffith's masterwork would have on race relations.[9] He personally introduced films brought back from his trips abroad that showed the achievements of African Americans. He used these films to inspire and uplift his fellow black South Africans.[10] Some of these biopics were given to Plaatje during his visits to places like Tuskegee University, founded by Booker T. Washington in Alabama.

Filmmaker Peter Davis, in his documentary and accompanying book on the history of South African film, *In Darkest Hollywood* (1993; 1996), argues that in the early 1900s, South Africa created a "little Hollywood" in its film industry.[11] It instilled a mythology of white conquest by producing Hollywood-style Westerns, with the Zulus replacing Native Americans as the suppressed group in the 1950s. Hollywood cooperated with South Africa by signing an agreement to distribute locally produced newsreels that directed propaganda to an international audience for the apartheid regime. It was the beginning of an economic and psychological dominance of American-style cinema that found a partner in South Africa because of that government's desire to use film as a vehicle of control and suppression. The Hollywood studio system gained dominance in South Africa in the post–World War II era when these films exported the American dream to the rest of the world. Through control of commercial cinema production, distribution, and exhibition, the dictum "trade follows film" gained hold.[12]

Another aspect of the Hollywood–South African nexus occurred when the black population in the urban areas adopted the sounds and images of American popular culture as their own. As noted in *Homelands,* Harlem and Hollywood American movies provided an escape for black South Africans that prompted their realization that the world is bigger than South Africa. As young adults, blacks copied the styles of their heroes, the American movie stars of the 1940s and 1950s—both black and white—including the music, clothes, and dance styles. Harlem, recognized as the capital of black America, held a special significance among urbanized blacks in South Africa. The zoot-suit, cabaret lifestyle that was a symbol of urban cool in the cities of black America resonated among young South Africans, especially during the "Sophiatown Renaissance" of the 1950s.[13] This fascination with being hip and defiant was documented on the pages of *Drum,* the influential publication featuring black writers Lewis Nkosi, Can Themba, Bloke Modisane, and others who countered white notions of "authentic" tribal Africans and offered a creative outlet. Among the average black moviegoing population of Johannesburg, the imported Hollywood films, although heavily censored, provided temporary escape from the crush of apartheid. Yet, blacks remained under a tight scrutiny that maintained racial hierarchies. Like their counterparts in the American South, who were confined to theater balconies or watched movies in makeshift or substandard facilities or were ushered through separate theater entrances from white moviegoers, there was no unfettered access to films by black South Africans.

Meanwhile, the local film industry sought to capitalize on that yearning for black stars as a marketing opportunity to produce homegrown films that featured black talent with whom the audience could identify. Films like *Jim Comes to Jo'burg* (1949), touted as the first feature starring a "native cast," and *Zonk!* (1950), which included an imitation of a white man in blackface makeup in the all-black cast film, were directed by Europeans. Both films recall the black-cast musical that was Hollywood's version of black life in the 1940s and early 1950s, such as the classic *Stormy Weather* (1946) starring Lena Horne. In South Africa, Dorothy Rathebe, who starred in *Jim Comes to Jo'burg,* became the rising star of that genre that few African intellectuals considered "African films."[14]

Ironically, these films that showcased black talent coincided with the 1948 installation of the National Party, the architects of "apartness." They passed a series of legislative acts that legalized and formalized the racial segregation that already existed and reduced blacks to the status of legal minors, citizens, not of the nation but of the government-mandated residential "homelands." Most of the all-white film industry continued its alliance with the government until the end of the apartheid regime. This included going along with government "studies" that supposedly showed that blacks were not intelligent enough to encounter adult-oriented cinema that might confuse them or raise their ambitions.[15] Such a political economy meant that blacks were not seen as a primary market for films, and, therefore, the domestic films that were targeted to them were of low production value and made mainly to gain access to lucrative film subsidies by white-owned film companies, not to address the needs of the black population.[16] Another example of this collusion is that the influential Producers Institute lodged a heated objection to the coverage of the cultural boycott that was waged to force the government to free Mandela.[17] The impetus to question the historical role of cinema in the country that presented apartheid as part of the natural order came from outside the country. It was energized at film festivals and by the international popularity of Jamie Uys's film *The Gods Must Be Crazy* (1980).[18]

Local resistance occurred on many levels. One of the most interesting examples of black resistance to cinematic indoctrination that has mostly evaporated from official history was the defiant and courageous attempt by independent black film exhibitors to screen banned films to black audiences. Independent distributors and theater operators, such as Shami Young of Cape Town, started showing films in homes and churches by exploiting loopholes in the censorship laws. Before he was forced out of business, his operation had expanded to thousand-seat cinemas.[19] Young relates how he maneuvered around the censors by maintaining two projectors—one with standard-fare American Westerns and another with the banned films starring black actors like Sidney Poitier and Harry Belafonte. "We had lookouts posted outside, down the road so that by the time the police would show up we would have already have switched the films over,"[20] he recalled. Young was part of the collective of black exhibitors forced to pay exorbitant fees by the distribution conglomerate Ster-Kinekor and cheated at every turn, eventually being forced out of business in the mid-1980s. He believes that such activities should not escape scrutiny: "I wish there had been a TRC for the film industry, because if that had happened people would learn the truth, how Ster and the others killed a whole culture of cinema in this country. My view is they acted in a criminal fashion, restraining trade, and denying our people a form of entertainment they had come to love."[21]

As apartheid tightened its grip on the country, its effects were brought to international attention through the film version of Alan Paton's 1948 best-selling novel, *Cry, the Beloved Country*. It became a Zoltan Korda–directed film in 1952, starring American actors Canada Lee and Sidney Poitier and South African newcomer Lionel Ngakane, an actor-filmmaker who would make a pioneering film *Jermina and Johnny* (1962) while in exile in England. The Darrell Roodt postapartheid remake of *Cry, the Beloved Country* in 1995 featured a cast of American, Irish, and South African actors, headed by James Earl Jones and Richard Harris, and was produced by South African Anant Singh, the leading film producer in the country. This film version of the novel, although well acted, was criticized for its inadequate indictment of the apartheid system and for revamping the "good African" stereotype. To my mind, the Christian stoic Reverend Stephen Kumalo bears resemblance to Harriet Beecher Stowe's long-suffering, iconic title character in the American classic *Uncle Tom's Cabin*. Both men are conveyed as nonthreatening paragons of virtue who earn white sympathy.

Considered a more progressive film of the apartheid era, American director Lionel Rogosin's highly regarded *Come Back, Africa* (1960) took a less-compromised view of the effects of apartheid on the black population. His film highlights the talents of a core group of young African writers and intellectuals who include Modisane and Nkosi. As the fractious apartheid regime began to crumble, *Mapantsula* (1988), a film by Oliver Schmitz, set a "threshold" for South African film by focusing on the interior lives of the characters in a way that parallels, rather than becomes subsumed by, the political.[22]

Filmmaker, poet, and scholar Kgafela oa Magogodi has been critical of the sexual objectification of black women in African films. He notes the possibilities invoked by *Mapantsula*, filmed in the waning years of the apartheid era, and Ramadan Suleman's *Fools* (1997), a postapartheid film. Magogodi argues that both films highlight the political marginality of black women without satisfactorily dealing with it.[23] Given the narrow purview of South African film under the racist regime, that threshold once reached—though incomplete and wanting—made the promise of an emergent film culture in the transforming nation more urgent and exciting. By the end of the apartheid era, blacks in South Africa had not yet amassed the skills, training, or opportunities to insert themselves into the discourse on film and media on the continent or to direct their own destinies in the industry. That would await future developments and the "open spaces" of a rapidly changing society.[24]

Addressing Critical Issues in African Cinema

South Africa, a pariah nation after independence movements ousted colonial rule in much of Africa, was for many decades out of synch with the rest of Africa. The insularity of apartheid depressed Pan African identity and locked its citizens into a dialectic of white supremacy and victimization until the last decade of the twentieth century. This was one of the factors that set South Africa on a different trajectory from the rest of Africa.[25] The country's geographic isolation, its isolation from political developments elsewhere on the continent, its multiracial population, its relative richness, and the triumphalism of the European-descendant Afrikaners and their ferocious attachment to the land all contributed to making South Africa a troublesome enigma.[26] The historical combination of economics, politics, and geography prompted realignment with core African interests within the new democratic government and necessitated burnishing its leadership credentials on the continent. While the political leadership looked to broaden its mandate, artists were looking inward at the history and structure of society. Frederic Jameson (1986) states that artists in transforming societies often engage in creating a "national allegory"[27] through their texts that seek to represent—collectively or individually—the embattled society.

In South Africa, films that engage the tensions of the society based upon its past are met with a combination of praise and scorn. A significant segment of opinion leaders view the engagement of film culture with weighty matters of history and national priorities to be fruitful and necessary, while an equally adamant group argues that the concern with historical reckoning perverts nationalism into a backward-looking project that stifles the local market.

This rift highlights the fragmentary nature of postapartheid South African culture—between those who want to exorcise the past and those who want to engage it beyond the tight boundaries proscribed by the TRC activities. Devotees of the latter see film as a site of resistance, while the former is focused on market-sensitive forces that usually favor the Hollywood formula. Similarly, Ukadike identifies four objectives of the postcolonial black African film: (1) to decolonize the mind, (2) to contribute to the development of a radical consciousness, (3) to promote a revolutionary transformation of society, and (4) to develop new film language to accomplish these tasks.[28] These postulates align with liberationist Third Cinema, which portrays a vision of social and cultural emancipation as it interrogates forces that perpetuate inequality and injustice in the Third World.[29] Although film has long been deployed for repressive purposes, as notably used by the racist white South African government, this reconceptualization anticipates a space for film to function in the Habermasian sense of a "public sphere," in which citizens or moviegoers, in this case, gather to debate critical public issues.[30] The Latin American–derived concept of Third Cinema[31] and the iterations that derive from its anticolonial, antiracist stance do not appear to register strongly in the South African context.

Yet, some believe that film can have a transformative effect and serve the integrative and creative function that politics cannot. According to Pan Africanist filmmaker Haile Gerima, "Our cinema should transcend [and] . . . demystify[y] . . . politics."[32] South Africa in particular owes the rest of Africa for support of the struggle against apartheid. The country cannot afford the arrogance of dissociation from the rest of Africa, even though its technical and economic resources may be superior. The most energized film industry on the continent comes from impoverished capitals such as Ouagadougou, Burkina Faso, which presents the biennial Festival Panafrican du Cinema de Ouagadougou (FESPACO).

Gerima contends that we are "all children of the same revolution"[33] and posits that film can be a bridge for Pan African healing and—given the developments in South Africa in the years since the collapse of apartheid—for recovering memory and consciousness among the disparate groups who share a fractured past and landscape. This is where the high theory of Sylvia Wynter meets the praxis of Gerima. It is this power to create and to own memory that, Wynter argues, gives the West its global hegemony. Film has been complicit in this enterprise by providing the image track and storyline that construct and equate humanity with Western values. In such a project, Africans are nonchanging and mired in primitivism. Film can offer the "redemption" referred to earlier by initiating what Wynter considers the primary issue of the time—"the recovery of memory and consciousness."[34] She proposes a reordering of historical memory, and Gerima calls upon Africans to "restore our individual humanity" and "energize each other."[35]

As a filmmaker committed to finding a "new vision" for African filmmakers, Gerima exhorts the energized filmmakers of South Africa to claim and invent new forms and not to be intimidated by conventions of filmmaking linked to Eurocentric hegemony. Instead, Gerima favors stories in which grandmothers, uncles, and cousins—people who inhabit the structures of everyday life—are central. By claiming the storytelling traditions of their forebears, filmmakers can help to redeem and reimage Africa and reconnect its people.

Moving between this general postulate for black filmmakers on the African continent to specifics on the ground issues in South Africa, one understands that the large ideas and new possibilities that the country seems to offer are lures to outsiders and a bevy of theorists, romanticists, opportunists, and sundry others. It is as if South Africa were a giant laboratory for the birth of a regenerated humanity. The other side of transformation is the manifestation of social disorder, corrosive nostalgia, narcissism, and the crass excesses of late-stage capitalism. These circumstances inspire filmmakers like Teboho Mahlatsi to ask what freedom really means and how filmmakers should capture it. Others raise questions about relations among Africans on the continent, a topic tackled in *God Is African* (2003), a film by Nigerian-born, Johannesburg-based filmmaker Akin Omotoso. While it is hoped that President Mbeki's call for a renaissance on the continent will undercut some of the xenophobia[36] and intergroup hostilities so evident in the country, the challenge of resolving such seemingly intractable issues still looms.

The Present State of South African Cinema

Despite intractable issues, the development of the South African film industry since 1994 constitutes a minirenaissance in itself. It has come about as a result of governmental involvement, private initiatives, and the country's emergence as one of the top-five production locations in the world. As noted earlier, South Africa attracts major Hollywood stars and production budgets that have added over a billion dollars to the economy.[37] "We have arrived,"[38] exclaimed Zola Maseko in his native Zulu upon being awarded the Etalon d'Or de Yennenga, the grand prize at FESPACO 2005. The award at Africa's largest film festival and cultural event included a cash prize of twenty million CFA (twenty thousand U.S. dollars) and marked the first time that South Africa had won in the festival's thirty-six-year history. *Drum*, based on the lives of a group of 1950s writers, earned Maseko the prize at the most prestigious festival on the continent, and he viewed this as confirmation of South Africa's rising status in the international film community. The award added to the growing list of international prizes garnered by South African films.

Even with international recognition, the South African film industry is having a difficult time developing an audience for its own products. The fragmentation of the moviegoing public can be traced to apartheid-era policies that attempted to serve white consumers while limiting access to black audiences. Today, there is still a void in opportunities for the majority black population to view movies. There are few facilities in their communities, and they do not have economic resources to indulge this costly leisure. Instead, the state-funded South African television (SABC) is the medium most available to the black majority. Television, the principal form of media consumption, replicates the fragmentation of the market by offering separate channels that target different demographics—youth and the many different language groups recognized by the government. Yet, the intermingling or "creolization" of cultures is an understated fact of life in South Africa that is observable on the street and reflected in popular culture, especially television.[39]

The burgeoning film industry has not yet experienced a similar creolization of its vertical structure. In the Western Cape and more generally throughout the nation, the rapid growth has not created employment and business opportunities for the majority black population. Blacks are less than 0.1 percent of all managers, technical crews, and service providers[40] in an industry that employs over 20,000 people and generates over 1.5 billion rand per annum (almost US$2 billion). This is true despite the government's efforts to invest public funds in the industry that it views as an engine for economic development. The National Film and Video Foundation (NFVF), created by government legislation in 1997 with state and private funding, provides financing for all levels of the filmmaking process—including training, development, production, marketing, and distribution that give priority to projects with local content. NFVF has coproduction treaties with other countries that enter into partnerships with South African producers and filmmakers. The funding requirements favor coproduction efforts because of the strained government coffers. The reported 250 million rand (over US$41 million) that the government's Industrial Development Corporation granted to finance film projects is hardly enough to generate robust independent production.

Another effort to import film production is the recently revised (April 2008) Film and Television Production Rebate first established by the Department of Trade and Industry in 2004. It promotes the production of big-budget foreign and local films made in South Africa or those under coproduction agreements. This initiative favors large companies, which can earn rebates of 15 to 25 percent on production costs.[41]

Although the regional film commissions all have different requirements for the procurement process, they are nevertheless advancing formulas to stimulate film production in their areas. Distribution is controlled by two conglomerates, Ster-Kinekor and Nu-Metro, accounting for 68 percent of the available screens in the country and showing mostly American products. The numerical breakdown shows the uphill climb that independent, socially conscious distributors like the Film Resource Unit (FRU) face. The report shows that South Africa's major distributors primarily function as sales and marketing arms for studios in the United States, with 70 percent of all titles. A lesser number of films comes from U.S. independent producers (25 percent), while 4 percent comes from Europe, and the remaining 1 percent includes 0.5 percent from South Africa.[42]

Despite such gloomy statistics, local efforts to promote an indigenous film culture are ongoing and achieving results. For example, the Newtown Film and Television School in Johannesburg has for years had the most successful program aimed at training young people from "marginalized communities" to become film and video professionals. Other programs and initiatives are starting to show promise but the process is slow, as is the availability of film products outside the arena of public television for this underserved but hungry market.

The Filmmakers

The film community of South Africa is as diverse as its people. The twenty-five filmmakers and cultural leaders whom I was privileged to interview represent the new and emerging as well as the established and prolific in film and performing arts. Although their work articulates different priorities and sensibilities, together and separately they view their work not only as personal statements of their artistic vision but also in line with an effort to (re)build a national cinema. Their shifting and unequal circumstances foster a context that has produced a range of aesthetic and political visions—and discontents. Filmmaker Ntshaveni wa Luruli, for example, acknowledging the service orientation of much of the South African film industry, points to the government's tepidness in nurturing and supporting native filmmakers: "It was the country's artists who kept pressure on the apartheid government by exposing it to the world and hastening its demise." He now feels that the new government has forgotten the essential role that arts play in the life of a nation. "The arts are treated like a stepchild," he told me in an interview. Although there are a National Film Board and a film policy that includes grants to filmmakers, the board's prominence does not approach the level of support and attention afforded athletics and sports.

As a visitor, one immediately notices that local filmmakers are not included in the mix of films at the local multiplex cinemas. Instead, Hollywood fare is ubiquitous. When I asked filmmakers where I could view his or her film or obtain a copy, the response was often, "It's not available right now," or "I'll make you a copy." Sometimes a reference to the Film Resource Unit, a Johannesburg-based distributor, was made, but more often, a foreign, usually American, distributor was mentioned. Distribution is the unglamorous part of filmmaking that most directors would rather not have to think about. Not thinking about distribution is a luxury that the independent filmmakers I spoke with admit they cannot afford.

Bhekizizwe Peterson, a screenwriter and professor of African literature at the University of Witwatersrand, put the issue into perspective by urging the black filmmaking community—denied artistic development under the apartheid regime—to imagine "new paradigms" for distribution as well as the filmmaking process itself. He advocates different ways to think about the formalities of filmmaking. For example, by imagining a collaborative process in which the arrangement of responsibilities gives the director what he or she needs to function, minus all the trappings of celebrity, creates new economies for a fledging industry and develops a sense of shared purpose and efficiency among everyone involved. Peterson and director Ramordan Suleman's recent film *Zulu Love Letter* (2004) is touted as the first historical feature film of the postapartheid era, even though it is set in the present day. It is the story of a mother, brutalized by apartheid, searching for her daughter, and shows in dramatic and wrenching form how "we live in history"[43] and how attempts to deny the past, a current vogue in much of South African life, are counterproductive.

I found this question of how to deal with the past an essential one for many filmmakers. How *should* film deal with recent history and memory, given the discourse of forgiveness and "moving on" that many equate with the completed work of the Truth and Reconciliation Commission? Certainly, it is a fruitful topic, as the 2004 film *Forgiveness* by Ian Gabriel shows. It follows a guilt-ridden apartheid-era policeman's search for forgiveness from the family of a young activist he killed. But Palesa Letlaka-Nkosi, a historian, filmmaker, and television producer, disagrees with the simplistic way that forgiveness is being marketed and counts on film to complicate and nuance, not flatten, the narrative of forgiveness: "[H]istory—it's not harmonious. It's about the different strands that are there, and I believe that people are caught in history, and history is caught in people." For that reason, she thinks that film can unlock the cultural resources of the country by telling silenced stories.

Filmmakers must be diligent about telling silenced stories, even though sizable segments of their fellow citizens are turning a deaf ear. As in the United States, many whites and an increasing number of young blacks are less willing to go to see films that deal with "political" subjects, and that includes many of Spike Lee's films. They will, however, flock to see blacks in noncontroversial roles, such as Will Smith in *Men in Black* (1997) and other fantasy action roles. Smith, according to *Parade* magazine (November 12, 2006), was perched to overtake Tom Cruise as Hollywood's most sought-after movie star. With the being-rich-equals-happiness message of his 2007 hit film, *The Pursuit of Happyness*, stripped of political context, Smith is now heralded as the most popular movie star in the world. But the political content that is vociferously disparaged in some quarters in South Africa is not required to be lacking in mass appeal or drab and humorless. Dumisani Phakathi, one of South Africa's young, rising filmmakers, uses a breezy, comic style to make a political point. His short film *Old Wives' Tale,* about an Afrikaner man who wants to be like his black worker and take on another wife, makes an important statement with an understated touch.

Another young filmmaker I interviewed, Khalo Matabane, whose recent films include *Story of a Beautiful Country,* decries that black filmmakers are castigated for dealing with political issues and notes that no other group is expected to forget what has happened to them, especially not the artists. Because of this pressure to make what he calls "ahistorical" films and because the funding sources often come from outside the country, black filmmakers cannot always make the films they want to make. This is a challenge that filmmaker Maseko attributes to not only funding but also to language, audience development, and distribution and that everything is so new: "We are creating a tradition."

This relative newness offers not only a great challenge but also a great opportunity for South Africans to define cinema for themselves through language, movement, styles of storytelling, and different selections of images without being intimidated by Euro-American formulas. While it seems too early to expect a definitive national cinema, the richness of South African life and its many diversities inform everyday life for blacks and whites and offer abundant subjects for young auteurs and their cohorts in the film industry. Although South African national television [SABC] was instrumental in realizing the concept of a multicultural democracy through its targeted cultural and generational channels on its three designated networks, it appears, to an outsider, to be weighed down by a steady diet of soap operas and syndicated American reruns.

Television, as the predominant visual entertainment source for most of the population, also helps to maintain defined gender roles and traditional expectations of women, as seen in programming and commercials. Perhaps this is linked to the comparatively low number of women filmmakers and executives in an industry still, with few exceptions, controlled by white men. Black women actors specifically and black actors in general are more likely to find work in television productions than film. The explosion of soap opera has given rise to several stars including the very committed actor-playwright Motshabi Tyelele. She remained in South Africa even during the turbulent times and despite opportunities outside the country. She did so because she views her work as an actor as part of a mission to empower others through the arts. A story largely untold is that of white filmmakers who were against apartheid. While some filmmakers left South Africa permanently, others such as Ingrid Gavshon, founder of a well-respected film production company, left the country and returned as apartheid was ending. Others including Kevin Harris and Angus Gibson committed acts of resistance inside the country on their way to becoming major players in the emerging film industry.

The path for black women in the film industry has been especially difficult. Even today, they are more likely to be producers than directors. Letebele Masemola Jones, an accomplished producer, views her job as an opportunity to help develop young black talent. Bridget Pickering, a producer, also acts and directs. But when asked why she did not do more directing, Pickering's response was essentially that so much is on the line for women that they have very little margin for error—and lots of pressure. She found it easier to maintain good relationships as a producer rather than confronting the entrenched patriarchy as a director. Xoliswa Sithole, a filmmaker, actor, and producer, concurs, and states that it is not just race but also gender that constricts black women: "Black women are invisible in the [film industry]." Her film *Orphans of Nkandla* won the best-documentary award at the British Academy for Film and Television (BAFTA) in 2005, making her the first South African to win a prestigious BAFTA award. Yet, the honor received scant coverage in local media. Despite the sexism that even male directors I interviewed acknowledged exist against women, the women filmmakers I met were, for the most part, undaunted. Jyoti Mistry, who is of Indian ancestry, is a rare combination of an academic and a filmmaker. This places her in a privileged position as she does not have to seek the big deals and wide audiences. Her work, she admits, is not necessarily accessible to an audience used to Hollywood fare. Her films seem not to seek a specific South African audience and qualify as experimental or art house in most film catalogs. Mistry's work speaks to the growing diversity of film culture in this multiethnic country. Maganthrie Pillay, also of Indian heritage, is considered "South Africa's first black female feature director" for her debut film *34 South* (2005).

Beathur Baker, whose work crosses both print and television formats, expressed a particular concern for young women and their self-esteem. The business end of production is an area where women are particularly underrepresented. Isabelle Rorke and her male business partner Dumi Gumbi are pioneers in the subgenre of animation production, untested waters for both women and blacks. While entrenched gender inequality adds to the fault lines of the cultural and racial divides in South African cinema, it mirrors the larger society. Such divides appear inevitable, given the history. But like the stuff of good literature, such tensions can feed the emergence of a treasure in the making—a national cinema, fueled not by the politics of forgetting but by the power and promise of what film can offer for human engagement and elevation.

The diversity and talent among young filmmakers, producers, and performers bode well for the future of South African film culture. The increasing opportunities for local film training as evidenced by the spike in new film schools are hopeful developments.[44] Rather than leaving South Africa for film training, as was the case for most blacks in the apartheid era, these facilities will be counted upon to nurture future generations of filmmakers, who include Tongai Furusa, a young, sought-after film editor, and emerging directors Akin Omotoso, Norman Maake, and Sechaba Morelele, as well as critically acclaimed directors Teddy Errol Mattera and Mickey Madoba Dube. They are demonstrating that despite the uneven playing field, infrastructure issues, and the reluctance of significant segments of the population to engage their work, they are, as a group, producing films that attract an international audience. South African cinema seeks the favor of world opinion, partly, perhaps, in response to the expectations of pundits like Gilroy who view the nation as a beacon of light for the continent and the world. Still, South Africa might heed Kenyan writer Ngugi wa Thiong'o's observation that despite its problems and prospects, the real success of African cinema lies in its finding a home in the continent of its birth rather than in first seeking international acceptance.[45] Then, too, Teshome Gabriel's notion of a black independent cinema that occupies liberated spaces outside of the dominant paradigms and generates a still-evolving oppositional aesthetic in a "newly born" cinema" may suggest yet another path for a segment of the South African film community.

While some of the new South African films may confirm such predictions of a not-yet-here-but-no-longer-there cinema, the present situation in the country is not without irony. South African satirist Pieter-Dirk Uys has made the most of it and quips, "We fought for freedom, and all we got was democracy." Still, "all this freedom" (a phrase used by filmmaker Teboho Mahlatsi) is surely not only about the unbridled pursuit of material wealth. The talented artists interviewed here are overcoming a devilish legacy in pursuing their passion for filmmaking and performance. They offer alternative voices that mirror the restless, hungry soul of the new South African nation.

Notes

1. These films received international distribution. *Catch a Fire,* directed by Australian Philip Noyce, starred American actors Derek Luke and Tim Robbins with South African actors playing minor roles. *Tsotsi,* which won the Academy Award for Best Foreign Film of 2005, featured an ensemble of South African actors including Presley Chweneyagae and Terry Pheto and was directed by Gavin Hood, a white South African.

2. Paul Gilroy, "Cosmopolitanism Contested: What South Africa's Recent History Offers to a World in Which Solidarity Has Become Suspect" (keynote lecture, Celebrating Ten Years of Democracy, Wiser Conference, University of Witwatersrand, Johannesburg, South Africa, May 10, 2004).

3. Deborah Posel and Graeme Simpson, eds., *Commissioning the Past: Understanding South Africa's Truth and Reconciliation Commission* (Johannesburg: Witwatersrand University Press, 2002), 2.

4. Mbeki stated his suspicions about HIV and AIDS during a July 9, 2000, address at the Thirteenth International AIDS Conference in Durban, South Africa. He wondered why Africans are disproportionately affected by the virus and whether the types of treatment being used for HIV were adequate.

5. Edwin Hess, "The Birth of a Nation: Contextualizing *De Voortrekkers* (1916)," in *To Change Reels: Film and Film Culture in South Africa,* ed. Isabel Balseiro and Ntongela Masilela (Detroit: Wayne State University Press, 2003), 50.

6. Nwachukwu Frank Ukadike, *Black African Cinema* (Berkeley: University of California Press, 1994), 1.

7. Hess, "Birth of a Nation," 53.

8. Bhekizizwe Peterson, "Politics of Leisure during the Early Days of South African Cinema," in Balseiro and Masilela, *To Change Reels,* 41.

9. Ntongela Masilela, "The New African Movement and the Beginning of Film Culture in South Africa," in Balseiro and Masilela, *To Change Reels,* 18.

10. Masilela, "New African Movement," 19.

11. Peter Davis, *In Darkest Hollywood,* part 1 (Villon Films, 1993); Peter Davis, *In Darkest Hollywood: Exploring the Jungles of Cinema's South Africa* (Athens: Ohio University Press, 1996).

12. Dingi Ntuli and Maganthrie Pillay, "Audience Development Study: Strategies for Growth and Sustainability" (Cape Town, South Africa: Cape Film Commission, June 2004), 7.

13. Bob Nixon, *Homelands, Harlem and Hollywood: South African Culture and the World Beyond* (London: Routledge, 1994), 12.

14. Masilela, "New African Movement," 26.

15. L. Silver, *A Guide to Political Censorship in South Africa* (Johannesburg: Witwatersrand Centre for Applied Legal Studies, 1984).

16. Ntuli and Pillay, "Audience Development Study," 10.

17. Keyan Tomaselli, *The Cinema of Apartheid: Race and Class in South African Film* (New York: Smyrna/Lake View, 1988), 9.

18. Tomaselli, *Cinema of Apartheid,* 10–11.

19. Ntuli and Pillay, "Audience Development Study," 7.

20. Ibid., 8.

21. Ibid., 14.

22. Class discussion, Cinema Studies, Dr. Hassenah Ebrahim, lecturer, School of Arts, University of Witwatersrand, May 12, 2005.

23. Kgafela oa Magogodi, "Sexuality, Power, and the Black Body in *Mapantsula* and *Fools,*" in Balseiro and Masilela, *To Change Reels,* 200.

24. Sarah Nuttall and Cheryl-Ann Michael, eds., "Introduction: Imagining the Present," in *Senses of Culture: South African Culture Studies* (New York: Oxford University Press, 2000), 2.

25. Nuttall and Michaels, "Introduction: Imagining the Present," 3.

26. Zakes Mda quoted in Nuttall and Michaels, "African Renaissance: Interviews," in Nuttall and Michael, *Senses of Culture,* 111.

27. Frederic Jameson, "Third World Literature in the Era of Multinational Capitalism," *Social Text* 15 (Fall 1986): 65–68.

28. Ukadike, *Black African Cinema,* 7.

29. Michael Chanan, "The Changing Geography of Third Cinema," *Screen* 38, no. 4 (1997): 372–88.

30. Douglas Kellner, "Habermas, the Public Sphere, and Democracy: A Critical Intervention," Douglas Kellner's home page, Faculty, University of California Los Angeles, http://www.qseis.ucla.edu/faculty/kellner/kellner.html (accessed April 22, 2007).

31. Fernando Solanos and Octavio Getino, "Towards a Third Cinema Movement," in *Movies and Methods: An Anthology,* ed. Bill Nichols (Berkeley: University of California Press, 1974), 44–64.

32. Haile Gerima, "Afterword: Future Directions in South African Cinema," in Balseiro and Masilela, *To Change Reels,* 207.

33. Gerima, "Afterword," 200.

34. Sylvia Wynter, "Africa, the West and the Analogy of Culture: The Cinematic Text after Man," in *Symbolic Narratives/African Cinema: Audiences, Theory and the Moving Image,* ed. June Givanni (London: BFI, 2000), 40.

35. Gerima, "Afterword," 226.

36. Novelist and playwright Zakes Mda argues that black South Africans feel superior to blacks in other African countries and don't identify with them, due in part to skin color. He says that black South Africans have internalized negative media images about other Africans ("African Renaissance," 111).

37. Kevin Kriedemann, "Controversial Report on South African Film Industry," IAfrica.com, http://writersclub.iafrica.com/kevink/publicity/413186.htm.

38. Eddie Mbalo, "Why South Africans Should Celebrate the Success of the Film Industry," *Culture and Development,* http:/topics.developmentgateway.org/culture/rc/ItemDetail.do~1005507.

39. The interchange of vocabulary among the eleven official languages is an aspect of "creolization" that I observed in Johannesburg. The give-and-take of everyday discourse is often infused with several different languages. This is captured in television soap operas when actors insert unscripted lines in Xhosa or Zulu or Vende.

40. Nuttall and Michaels, introduction, *Senses of Culture,* 8.

41. Ntuli and Pillay, "Audience Development Study," 3.

42. John Walser, "The Film Industry in South Africa," International Market Insight, U.S. Department of State, Foreign and Commercial Service, Travel and Tourism Sector, http://strategis.ic.gc.ca/epic/internet/inimr-ri.nsf/en/gr1260402.html.

43. Ntuli and Pillay, "Audience Development Study," 5.

44. Martin P. Botha, "New Directing Voices in South African Cinema: Graduates from Film Schools," *Kinema,* May 8, 2005, www.kinema.uwaterloo.ca/botha051.html.

45. Ngugi Wa Thiong'o, "Is the Colonialisation of the Mind a Prerequisite for the Independence of Thought and the Creative Practice of African Cinema?" in Givanni, *Symbolic Narratives/African Cinema,* 95.

Interviews

Beathur Baker

Now there is actually an emphasis on empowering women to tell stories about other women, but the problem is the kind of media that has been made for young women has been so boring and so predictable that young women will not watch.

AUDREY THOMAS McCLUSKEY: In the last decade, have film and television been able to tell new stories about Africa that were unknown to most South Africans?

BEATHUR BAKER: That depends. What I have not liked about what has happened recently with film in this country is that a lot of these stories have been colonized or taken over by white filmmakers. In order to attract the majority [black] audiences to television, black writers would be hired, but then the story would be given to a white director and a producer. These guys would insist that actors speak textbook versions of Zulu or Xhosa, which is so different from the colloquial way that people speak on the street. The result was these interesting stories written by black writers, but they'd be in this really antiquated Zulu or Xhosa. Black people would laugh at it. So these became comedies.

ATM: Unintentional comedies?

BB: Yes! [The directors] never caught on. They became an in-joke that people laughed about among themselves, saying things like, "There's another drama on television, and did you hear that fat guy speaking Zulu!"

ATM: What effect did this have?

BB: Well, it was funny but painful also. It limited the pool of stories and the exploration of people's lives—the real stories that people wanted to see on television. [Instead] there were a lot of these nasty game shows—and you could see that it was all staged. These seemed like exercises in puppeteering. It was really controlled expression, especially on television. Radio actually has been the most free medium. Radio was my first introduction to the dynamic possibilities of freedom of expression. Radio talk shows have offered a format where people can express their feelings and concerns about their lives in different parts of the country. Radio is playing a very important role in media culture in this country today.

ATM: I noticed that. It's amazing to turn the radio dial and hear all these different languages, music, and very animated conversations about everything from politics to infidelity. Radio certainly seems most connected to the everyday lives of the people.

BB: Yes, you can find about twelve to fifteen different languages spoken on the radio. Also, radio stations play the music [people] want to hear. It helps them connect with each other across the country. Television hasn't been that accessible. When I began my career in journalism, not many people had access to books and magazines. When television did take off, I knew it would become a very important means for messaging in this country—and it did in the late 1980s.

ATM: How so? What specific changes have you seen?

BB: Well, first of all, there was the language debate about television stations creating channels dedicated to different language and cultural groups such as Sesotho and Zulu and the other official languages. This was the first recognition of the diversity of people's lives and backgrounds in this country. Documentaries became very important because they were a way for our different [cultural] groups to learn about each other. These documentaries were also a way to engage young people with issues they are facing as a vehicle [to develop] a different audience and to influence the mindset of children through the messaging. Those are the reasons why I got involved in *Takalani Sesame,* for example.

ATM: *Takalani Sesame* is the South African equivalent of the American *Sesame Street,* right?

BB: Yes, and it was amazing because we had to make live-action programs for children all over the country—from rural areas in Venda [in northern region of South Africa in the province of Limpopo] to kids who were horseback riding in Sandton [upscale section of Johannesburg] to kids who are part of a fishing village in Cape Town. We had to reflect that diversity. I loved it! It really spoke to me. I wish I had had this kind of program when I was five years old!

ATM: You spoke of "messaging" children. What kind of messages did you want to convey with this program?

BB: The concept, of course, was education based, but we chose to concentrate on accepting and acknowledging diversity. Awareness creation: "This is a boy who lives in a fishing village. This is how he lives." It was portraying his point of view. We are segmenting his life with a little girl in Venda and a little boy in Soweto. We would use counting and singing and the alphabet but from the perspective of different cultures. It was really incredible, and [the results] showed in testing the children. They loved just seeing other kids speaking and singing in their own languages.

ATM: Is that show continuing now?

BB: It is in its third season this year. I had the opportunity to go to New York and do the handover training with the local production company. I was the head of the live-action division. It was interesting to see how Americans dealt with diversity in their program.

ATM: What did you take away from that experience?

BB: What I found was that it was much more difficult to do it there [in the United States]—to create a sense of equality and representation because blacks constitute a community that is really a minority in America. It is difficult to create a sense of belonging as easily. In terms of representation, there were far fewer segments for black and Hispanic children, whereas here we are in the majority. We can do a lot more to instill diversity in a natural way. We do songs and counting and live stories in different languages—English formed a very small segment. It served as a crossover language in the series. It wasn't the key focus of the series, and that was much nicer.

ATM: Moving from that project, which direction did you go?

BB: Well, after I worked for *True Life and Drama* magazine, I worked in current affairs programming for SABC [the state-owned South African Broadcasting Corporation] news. Then I moved into the documentary format. I worked on an arts program called The Works.

ATM: Did you have specific ideas and goals that you wanted to accomplish, or did the organization you were working for set the artistic priorities?

BB: I certainly knew what I wanted to do, what I wanted to achieve. For me, the obstacle of a controlled media is not an insurmountable problem. I know that I can work on this arts program and tell stories about the cultural life [of the people], and I'm going to try to do that. Now I'm going to start making a documentary because I want to change perceptions that people have of a certain segment of society. It's very much based on my values as a journalist and as an individual and what I think is underrepresented in the community's eyes and in the country that we live in. What I find challenging is to do it in a way that engages ordinary people, that really allows them access while making hard-hitting points but not being didactic or boring. This objective has determined my format.

ATM: Do you choose the genre based upon the subject matter?

BB: Well, in documentaries, you are getting people to tell the story from their point of view and in their language. It's powerful because it's an issue that usually affects a lot of people—like unemployment among young people. People connect and recognize those characters as being like themselves. They can see the choices that are being made for better or worse and relate it to their own lives. I feel documentaries can be quite effective. Young people really talk among themselves. They also watch a lot of soaps. They watch a lot of action and drama and comedy. Our challenge is basically to get them to watch [what we produce].

ATM: Yes. I see the proliferation of soap operas. They are on at all times of day on South African television. Most seem like standard escapist melodramas. Is my perception wrong?

BB: No, it's correct. I think what's interesting is that initially the soap operas were almost exactly scripted in English. They sounded exactly like international ones, and then actors would start slipping in their own languages—like Zulu and Xhosa expressions—and now the soaps are multilingual and are able to really capture the nuances of every day life. The soaps have become much more addictive because—unlike *The Bold and the Beautiful* or the Western-style soaps—these are very local, but they are [also] very stereotypical.

ATM: Particularly in how women are represented. From what I've seen, women, as in the U.S., are mostly viewed as sex objects.

BB: That is true all over the media.

ATM: You have now formed your own company with two other women. What propelled you to make this move?

BB: I found that all three of us—our company is called Traffik—had worked in environments where it was always about keeping up and earning respect and being noticed for what you were doing in a very male environment. All the while [we were] contributing to the success of other people in these male-dominated companies. We realized that it's like a treadmill—you just keep going, and the conveyer belt keeps going, and sometimes you fall underneath it and get trampled. We decided to start out small and team up with other companies that are run by women, and that's exactly what we did. I grew quite tired of working for one of the big media conglomerates in South Africa, now black owned. Even though it was great working in a black-owned company, there was also a really ugly part to working there. *Takalani Sesame* was one of their projects. I could see that they were never going to want to make the kind of stories I wanted to do because those stories wouldn't make them money. [I had] too much of an independent point of view, and that wasn't going to work for them from a budget[ary] point of view. The big challenge—I don't know if other documentary filmmakers have told you—is trying to make media that's relevant and interesting but will still make the broadcaster some money. There's a whole corporate-commercial situation above and beyond gender. [Otherwise,] if your stories are good and interesting, they will be made whether you are male or female. Now there is actually an emphasis on empowering women to tell stories about other women, but the problem is the kind of media that has been made for young women has been so boring and so predictable that young women will not watch. We have pitched a series called *True Life,* which is the true-life stories of young women. It showed on SABC-1, which is the youth channel, and we turned [conventional wisdom] on its head. It was like *Girlfriends* meets *Sex in the City.* Now we are waiting to hear if the series is renewed. We decided that we are going to just go out there and get [young women] to explain why they wear so much makeup, why they wear weaves in their hair, where they go dancing, who their role models are—unapologetically from their point of view. *True Life* became the series that young women would watch and say, "That's me! That show doesn't ask me to be a feminist. It's not telling me to be [anything]; it's telling me to believe in myself, look at the lives of other women, and make choices based on what works for me."

We would find a group of friends, spend a few days with them, see their family relationships, their employment dilemmas, their love relationships, their goals, dreams, and disappointments. Young women loved [the program]. They talked about it among themselves and watched it every week. It has been quite interesting for the channel because this [focus on young women] had never been attempted before. We heard that a similar feminist-slanted show had been turned down.

ATM: Do you think it tried to promote a feminist message?

BB: Driving the message but too hard. We realized that when you want to drive a message home, you need to find a young woman who embodies that message.

ATM: An example, not a sermon.

BB: Yes, an example, like [a woman] who when she tells her story gives a positive message of liberation and self-actualization and independence. You are not wagging a finger at your audience. We found a mix of people in professions like nursing or [law enforcement] who were very strong and ambitious. One might say, "I'm a police officer now, but I want to become a sergeant. This is how I'm going to do it."

ATM: I can't imagine them not renewing this series.

BB: It's been a milestone for me and my colleagues because we have always wanted to either start a magazine for young women that spoke very openly and directly to them or do a television program, which we did. It was fun. We spent time with the women's soccer team—our national soccer team—and talked with them about the challenges of being a woman soccer player. This really touched other young women who called in and say, "Can I please have the address?" or e-mail us and say, "I want to become a soccer player but I live in a rural part of Natal Free State." What it meant was that girls wanted to engage with other girls and find out how they lived their lives—which for me was a triumph because I always thought that should be the role of the media. It should help people discover who they are by being critical of or engaged with what they see. It gave me a lot of hope about working here and the future of young women because there was no voice for them. They have a lot of pressure to conform in terms of how they look, the way they talk, and how they conduct themselves in the world. They are expected to conform to this underdressed, overly sexualized, and objectified way of being. We explained to the young women that if that doesn't suit you, then choose something else. That's what our work is about.

BEATHUR BAKER is a documentary filmmaker and content producer for the state-funded South African Broadcasting Corporation. She began her career in media as a print journalist before moving to television documentaries. She produced a weekly talk show *True Life* (2004) and an award-winning documentary, *Very Fast Girls & Very Fast Guys* (2004). In 2001, Baker cofounded Traffik, a collaborative effort of print and wire journalists designed to produce socially relevant content across different media. Her focus has been on providing content directed at the youth market including music shows and the South African adaptation of Sesame Street, *Takalani Sesame.*

PARTIAL FILMOGRAPHY

***Twenty-two Years and Counting* (1998).** The deadly June 16, 1976, youth rebellion against apartheid and its effect on present-day youth are commemorated.

***Love Is Not Blind* (2001).** A young blind woman shares her experience of blindness and how she manages to incorporate it into her love life.

***SEXual MENtality* (2001).** An HIV-prevention project focuses on the complicated dynamics of male sexuality in South Africa.

Pascal Mzwandile Damoyi

We have to create new distribution settings, different distribution outlets that are altogether different from what exists now.

AUDREY THOMAS McCLUSKEY: Pascal, I want to begin by asking you about how you are involved in filmmaking.

PASCAL MZWANDILE DAMOYI: My involvement is in a number of ways. One is the putting together an arts festival in Alexandra Township, which is about twenty kilometers north of Johannesburg. It's an annual event produced by my company, Kopitseng Productions, a film media and entertainment company. This is my second year doing this. The reason for this project at this point in time is not profit making. It is a project that connects me to the social milieu and historical issues of Alex [Alexandra Township]. I'm from Alex, and I have a passion about its history.

ATM: Tell me about Kopitseng Productions.

PMD: That is the second reason for my involvement. My company produces documentaries. I produce corporate videos for my clients. The documentaries are government sponsored—events and projects that are intended to serve as an educational need or to provide information for the larger community. I put content together for government documentaries about fifteen to twenty minutes in length. The third level of the company is the festival—the arts festival—that focuses on the production of feature films. This year we are going to be producing five feature films. It is a hopeful dream and a plan that we are [working on].

ATM: Do you have the films already planned, or are these still on the drawing board?

PMD: They are still on the drawing board at this point in time. My company will be the executive producer, but I would like to engage the young people in the process for scripting, directing, and working along with professionals. Our [main] objective is to tell stories that people see and live with on a day-to-day basis. We say that people are tired of watching Hollywood movies. We think that because of the enthusiasm for an African Renaissance, people are clamoring for new stories that actually connect them to each other, that actually reflect who they are and articulate their aspirations. For us, the production of these movies is an opportunity to celebrate [our] democracy and tap into our heritage. It is also a project that enlightens our community.

ATM: What evidence do you have that there is a market for these local films? All the ads that I see in the newspapers are for Hollywood productions.

PMD: It's a brilliant question. Our approach is that we will have to deconstruct the current [situation] and construct a new one in South Africa, especially in terms of production and consumption. For me, Hollywood has exported the types of films that do not touch the lives of black people. They've never intended to [do so]. They have just been imposed on the community. We are battling a strong presence because of the resources Hollywood is able to expend on the population.

But I think that there is a lot of imagination in our people. With the coming of democracy, people have transformed themselves. You see this on many levels. You look, for example, at television production. The ratings show that local content programs have the largest viewership. This is an indicator that people are ready to watch their own productions. That's the first instance. But I think that you also need intervention in this industry. You must build an audience. You must tap into the market, but the demographics are favorable. We must build it as we go. We are becoming critical consumers. My company is ready to enter that market and grow with it. We're really ambitious. We're looking at the production of alternative films and distributing them. Internal distributions of these movies at arts festivals such as in Alex [Township] offers an opportunity to create a new platform as part of this new paradigm. We're going to be using shebeens, for instance, to show our films.

ATM: *Shebeens* are small taverns?

PMD: Yes. We are going to be using them as outlets where these movies can be shown. Taverns are cultural [entities] and well socialized. I go and enjoy them because I sit with my friends. We consume media together. Television sets are usually on and show SABC news, sports, et cetera. Our tendency is—we don't just consume passively—to interact with what we see. I think we need to incorporate this [interactivity] into a new model, a new paradigm. That is, we have to create new distribution settings, different distribution outlets that are altogether different from what exists now.

ATM: You don't need a multiplex theater to do that. They can have that experience in their own neighborhoods.

PMD: That's it! In their own preferred environment. At the same time interacting with [the media] as a community.

ATM: That's so much like what Oscar Micheaux—I don't know if you know that name, but he was a pioneer in what we call "race" films back in the late 1920s–30s. He produced and directed low-budget films about African Americans and distributed them himself by arranging screenings in black communities and advertising in black newspapers. He created quite a buzz with his films. What you describe reminds me of his approach. What about infrastructure issues that such resources would require?

PMD: The government has made very clear policy interventions. For instance, there's an institution established by our government called "Create South Africa" that trains youth in arts and project management, giving young people skills in managing festivals and the arts in [different] fields. We will be tapping into that resource because it's really unbelievable. We are relying on what exists institutionally and what has been created by the government.

ATM: How do you go about raising money for these productions?

PMD: The reason I was in back-to-back meetings today is that I'm unlocking doors, trying to show people the value of what we are doing in Alex. We are looking to private companies for help also.

ATM: Can you say what type of companies are interested in supporting this initiative?

PMD: We have a mobile-phone company that is quite keen because they support the arts in South Africa. We also have proposals at the Department of Arts and Culture. So, yes, our films are going to be very low-budget at this point in time. We accept that these are new concepts that need to be tested, but we have a vision. We have a five-year plan—looking at collaboration and doing really big operations for the continent and people in the [African] diaspora. Maybe we will have some live transmissions of [festival] events in Alexandra Township—and link up to other [localities] on the continent and in the [African] diaspora.

ATM: So you're interested in film as a pan-African idea?

PMD: Most definitely, because the project is actually intended to empower people. I believe in the African Renaissance. Of course, there are commercial interests as well—but at the end of the day, I don't see myself independent of what is happening in the world. Together, we must find a way of articulating those issues, because they manifest themselves in many ways. The community must really [be involved].

ATM: Why do you think that film is such an important source at this stage of South African history as a new democracy?

PMD: Film is a medium that is very captive. People see their lives or lives to which they aspire. In South Africa, film, television, the media, and the motion-picture medium have been used to indoctrinate people with feelings of inferiority. It has reinforced complexes. However, film can be used as a tool to undo what has been done to black people as well as serve as an entertainment tool. It can be both an educative and an informational vehicle because of its visual quality, [it is] very impactful. People react to it immediately, and people will actually create a subculture out of what they see.

ATM: Do you have specific scripts or ideas that you want to cover in these five films that you are planning?

PMD: For example, my father was a prison warden. We lived in a very protected area. I grew up in an area about thirty kilometers from Alex—but I was schooled in Alex because there were no schools where we were. We lived in a three-bedroom house. We could not leave because my father was the warden and working there as a prison guard. So we had to move and come to Alex. Coming to Alex, it was such a difference. We were confronted with poverty. We all stayed in a one-bedroom house.

ATM: From a three-bedroom to a one-bedroom house?

PMD: A one-bedroom. My mother and my four siblings. My two older brothers were very involved as activists, but their minds changed—it was a dramatic turn of events.

ATM: How did it change them?

PMD: The way they changed was very interesting. I still have those memories vividly in my mind. They turned to drugs.

ATM: How old were they when you moved?

PMD: I was fourteen. My older brother, I think he was about twenty-six, twenty-seven. The second-born was about twenty-four years old.

ATM: They were already adults.

PMD: Yeah, they were already adults, but it impacted them very hard. Given the time, staying there as a youngster of fourteen years, we were in the paths of the local authorities a lot. We had permits, because people were not allowed to come to urban areas. There was a permit system. People who had the permits would [still] be chased by the cops. I was observing everything. Some of them were quite humorous—how they would escape from the cops using imaginative and innovative ways.

ATM: You want to recapture some of that past on film?

PMD: Yes. A lot of people experienced harassment. It's part of the history of Alex. The other thing that I want to look at is gang culture.

ATM: Gangs?

PMD: Yes, gangs. Gangsterism. Because Alex is still known as a haven for bars, dance bars. It was once very cool to some. Some people [involved] are still living—they're old people now, and that history has to be captured. I also want to [tackle] contemporary issues, but I want to leave it up to the youth as well to see what comes from their workshops and the subjects they are interested in.

ATM: What traits do you want these students who you will train to have?

PMD: They must have a passion for film. Their work must show a sense of belonging for all of us.

ATM: You are establishing a certain kind of symmetry. You have the production. You have the distribution and the venue. Do you need all of these coming together in order to make the statement that you want to make?

PMD: Yes. That's going to be a lot of hard work, I must say.

ATM: That brings me to this issue of multiculturalism, which I think has become so much a part of the official rhetoric of the government in promoting the idea that people are not to be viewed as racial beings, to try to have a nonracial society. What role do you foresee for film in the discourse of multiculturalism?

PMD: It's a very tricky question I must say, but for me it is very clear. I think it is our people who are putting effort into the concept of multiculturalism. What has been termed the first economy and the second economy manifests itself here. There's a trickle-down economy that misses a lot of people. You have a film industry supported by the advertising agencies in this country that asks, "Why must we tell all apartheid stories when we must move on?" There is pressure on that point.

ATM: That point of view, "we must move on," seems to be prominent in some quarters, to leave the stories of the past behind.

PMD: I don't know whether it is a question of guilt or whether it is a question of disinterest. They can't tell stories because they don't know those stories.

ATM: Overall, then, Pascal, how optimistic are you about the future of South Africa's film culture?

PMD: I'm optimistic because of the vision I have. It's a vision that is intrinsically linked to the vision of this country. It's a vision of the African Renaissance as espoused and articulated by President [Thabo] Mbeki. It's a vision of committedness to people, not just one's own locality. We South Africans must be part of this vision, using technology to connect to people. It's not going to be easy, though, because we are competing against established norms, mindsets, and paradigms. To crack those, you must have success stories; you must build on success stories. That is why our projects must capture the imagination of people.

PASCAL MZWANDILE DAMOYI is a film producer and media specialist. He is a founder of the media company Kopitseng and organizer of the Alexandra Film Festival, an annual event in the Township of Alexandra, near Johannesburg.

Mike Dearham

We were in the formative stages of making films without any sense of audience, patterns, or trends. That's a problem.

AUDREY THOMAS McCLUSKEY: Mike, you do a lot to promote and support black filmmakers on the continent at FRU (Film Resource Unit). Why are there so few women filmmakers included in that group?

MIKE DEARHAM: On one level, access to information on finance and economic benefits for women is just not in place. Secondly, policies in African countries don't favor women. Thirdly, the whole culture is crazy thinking that men are the head of the community and the home. This is still present in the thinking of people of influence on this continent both in government and the private sector. Women struggle to find a place within the economic sector, and because film is such a cost-intensive business, this is an added challenge for them.

ATM: Of the films that you are distributing right now, are there any women filmmakers?

MD: There are women filmmakers like Jenny Hunter, Palesa Letlaka-Nkosi, and Xoliswa Sithole, and Andi Spitz. These are some examples of the women that have braved tremendous odds to produce their stories.

ATM: As a distributor, you are at the end of the process of filmmaking. How do South Africans get in the pipeline to become filmmakers, and what structures are in place to help them at the outset?

MD: The main source of information about film as a career is from the National Film and Video Foundation (NFVF). They have regular news and updates to dissect the film industry. They provide bursaries [scholarships] for new, emerging talent to be trained. Of course, these bursaries and scholarships are about 20 percent of our annual budget, where eight million or so rand [over US$1.1 million] each goes to supporting emerging filmmakers. Of course, they've got a very particular [historical] bias to black filmmakers. That's the one source. The Department of Arts and Culture also prioritizes this kind of information—it's primarily led by NFVF. Of course, when we, as a distributor, go out to townships and rural areas and show these films, there is a lot of interest from the audience—some wish to get involved. We then refer them to the NFVF and even provide on-site advice as to how they can go about getting information.

ATM: Are the films that you are distributing competing in the mainstream—whatever that means—South African film industry?

MD: The document I will give you shows a breakdown listing of films released in our cinemas for the past ten years. In that, you will see that film content that is slapstick, comedic, and trivial was the most successful. You also see that the more serious films dealing with social issues and issues of national identity were not successful. Why? Many reasons: (1) The access to the places where these cinemas is mainly urban. They are not accessible to the twenty million or so people living in townships and rural areas—mainly black people. Access is an issue. (2) When these filmmakers take these films on, they do not provide the necessary publicity or marketing to ensure that they are successful. So that's a problem. The number of prints that they choose to release is also restrictive—two to five, two to eight if you are lucky. Eight prints if you are really lucky. (3) I think that our independent filmmakers still need to perfect their scriptwriting abilities. They still need to ensure that their competencies in production and so forth are sharpened. That's a challenge. But, of course, it's a challenge given our history. Filmmakers didn't have the opportunity to make their product and to learn from their mistakes. So, it is kind of chicken-and-egg—but I think that outside of that, there is still a lack of state support to provide marketing and distribution that compete with the *Spiderman* blockbusters when that person walks to the cinema and has to make a buying decision. Finally, our filmmakers are still very much production led. They are not distribution led. Hollywood success and India's success, to some extent, is that they are distribution led. Film is made based on box office and feedback. That's why you have *Rambo 4*, *Rambo Whatever*, and *Spiderman 3*—because it is genre driven. We don't have that around here. We were in the formative stages of making films without any sense of audience, patterns, or trends. That's a problem. These are the things that obstruct the blossoming of filmmaking and distribution in this country.

ATM: But perhaps there are different ways of defining success, beyond a Hollywood-driven formula. Can success here mean something different?

MD: That is true. The question is: Is a film successful as a result of the number of tickets you sell or a paying audience? Is a film successful as a result of the number of people that *see* it? Be it paying or nonpaying? Our definition is a [combination] of both. On one hand, filmmakers must get paid a royalty. The paralysis on this continent is that there is no credible royalty-payback system for filmmakers. Copyright law has been abused. There is no monitoring of this. Filmmakers don't get returns to make the next project. They have to constantly rely on the state.

ATM: You mean there is knockoff immediately?

MD: Yes. I am saying that if a filmmaker or a production house seeks to be viable, then it needs to have returns on intellectual property that they produce. That is not effective and fluent in this country. It's not happening. So I think that, yes, we ensure that people see it widely, but we also make a point to try to solicit payment from people who view these works. In the townships, we charge 10 rand [less than US$2], which is a tolerable fee. In cinemas, people are charged 30 to 40 rand [US$5–7], and there is, of course, pricing for videos and television license fees. So we pay back on an annual basis, approximately three to four million rand [up to a half million dollars] per annum to filmmakers on this continent. It is a very unique thing. I'm not aware of any other agency that generates this kind of fiscal flow back to filmmakers.

ATM: Is there a standard contract that you use for all of the filmmakers?

MD: Yes, there are two financial formulas that we follow giving the international, legal parameters of distribution. One is that if I take on a film, I will sell it to all media markets and retain a percentage. If the cost is in my account, I absorb every cost—marketing, publicity, government, et cetera—then I retain a higher percentage. If the cost is from the producer's account, then I retain a smaller percentage. These two financial formulas are what we follow in engaging filmmakers.

ATM: In talking about your work to an outside audience, what can you tell me about the films that you have distributed so far?

MD: Well, depending on which audience you refer to, I think for an institutional audience in the U.S., the kind of documentaries that are produced presently deal with democracy's success, gender, the environment, and labor—those would be of interest. For a more mass market, we need to clearly have films that are entertaining, that are sensitive to what audiences in the States are used to. They [must] have a high production value. Those are few and far between. I think for the television market, especially the niche television stations, both these institutional kinds of products and feature films will be of interest. There are nine film productions right now in this country that are in postproduction or released. Films like *Wooden Camera, Zulu Love Letter,* and *Drum*—Zola Maseko's story of Sophiatown—and *Tsotsi* [2005]—also a township gangster type of film. These are the films that are in the pipeline—despite being rejected by the Cannes competition board—are quite well shot. I think they could work for your U.S. audience.

ATM: Yes, the Black Film Center/Archive screened Raoul Peck's *Lumumba* [2001] in our last film series and designed a discussion around it with a moderator. Patrice Lumumba's story is internationally known, and there was no real gap between the audience and the drama. It was very well constructed and had no problem in communicating although American audiences are considered kind of parochial in their taste. What are the kinds of things that you can do to help an audience relate to a film with a certain message?

MD: Well, it's a major challenge because my sense of the American audience—and I say this with due respect to clusters and niches and communities that are politicized in your country—is generally [an] apoliticized citizenry. I am making a big general sweeping comment, I know, but on this continent—to some extent the developing South—South America and India—are very politicized citizens—citizens that have been [at] the forefront of these abuses and political incursions over the years. In other words, you have an audience that is ready for this kind of social-political genre. Even still, when we released *Lumumba* in this country, we had to embark on a series of actions to prepare the audience. Many people didn't know that Lumumba was the elected prime minister of the Congo when he was assassinated, despite more political awareness. We found this to be especially true amongst our youth—[there is] a certain historical amnesia. What we'd done is to embark on a long trailering period before the release date. We then took three to four months showing the film trailer and the documentary to universities and schools. We don't show the feature film. We build up a certain sensitivity to the man. The result was that *Lumumba* broke box-office records in this country. It was the most successful market feature film spearheaded by FRU.

ATM: That was good marketing—building up audience anticipation, building the audience, and creating buzz.

MD: Yeah. It's a sophisticated marketing approach really that we are forced to do given the juggernaut of the studio that faced us and given the historical amnesia.

ATM: It seems like a very good strategy.

MD: It's essential. Otherwise you would leave it to a random marketing approach done by some insensitive cinema owner and, voilà, it fails. And the paper I was referring to shows you here the kind of listing of films where you see just how poorly the more sociopolitical-content film done—from *Mama Africa, Fools, God Is African, The Regional Man,* and *Lumumba. Lumumba,* despite just going on two prints, made more money than any one of these down here, and that was just halfway through the campaign. The gross box office was double that, ultimately. But there you have your slapstick comedy that is really designed to be your candid-camera kind of a film. That is what topped the box office for the past ten years. That is part of what we face.

MIKE DEARHAM is CEO of the South African video distribution company Film Resource Unit (FRU). He forsook medical studies at the University of Witwatersrand to join the anti-apartheid movement. While in exile, he gained extensive knowledge of communication strategies and became interested in African film. FRU is dedicated to promoting and distributing African films throughout the African diaspora and increasing its global market share.

Mickey Madoba Dube, Sechaba Morojele, and Akin Omotoso

Mickey Madoba Dube

Sechaba Morojele

Akin Omotoso

I think as filmmakers, particularly black filmmakers, we need to change the discourse. We need to find a way of not continuing the safest course.

—Mickey Madoba Dube

[South Africa] is the best place to be as a black filmmaker at this present time.

—Sechaba Morojele

We are in a very terrible moment where our stories are being stolen.

—Akin Omotoso

AUDREY THOMAS McCLUSKEY: Today I am sitting in on a roundtable discussion with filmmakers Mickey Madoba Dube, Sechaba Morojele, and Akin Omotoso. Akin graciously allowed us to meet at T.O.M., his film production company's office here in Johannesburg. I would like to continue this conversation by asking each of you to comment on the health of the film culture in South Africa at the present time.

MICKEY MADOBA DUBE: I think that what's happening now is the beginnings of the rebirth of cinema. Until a few years ago, most of the films made in South Africa were Canadian or European productions. Sometimes films have been serviced here by South African companies, but that's not South African film. In terms of what we would describe as a South African film—written by a South African, directed by a South African—it has increased in the last few years. I don't know if you are aware, but the first South African film was made around 1903. The industry is quite old; it's really as old as the industries throughout Europe and in the U.S. There were a lot of films made in South Africa that were similar to your blaxploitation period, around late 1960s, early 1970s. These films were made for the black market but by white companies. White directors, white producers, and writers, with black actors. That's why we call it the blaxploitation period.

ATM: When did you make your first film?

MMD: I made my first film while in [film] school in Los Angeles. The story and language was South African. We tried to create a South African setting except that the main actor was American, and the rest of the other guys were South Africans who were just there; they were not actors. I tried to make it as South African as possible, but obviously there were limitations.

ATM: What is the name of the film?

MMD: *Imbazo.* It means "the Axe." I made my first feature film in 1999, *A Walk in the Night*. Have you seen it?

ATM: No, but I wrote my master's thesis on South African writers, including Alex La Guma [the author of the novella inspired by Shakespeare's *Hamlet*]. I will definitely take a copy of the film back with me.

SECHABA MOROJELE: My first film was during school in Los Angeles as well.

ATM: Really, were you guys the South African wing of the L.A. Rebellion? (All laugh.) [The L.A. Rebellion was a group of politically conscious black filmmakers in Los Angeles in the late 1970s.]

SM: Yeah, but we came a bit later. I just got back two years ago, so I'm still in the process of putting my first film together in South Africa.

ATM: What brought you back home?

SM: Because everyone tries to get into the Hollywood framework, but it is five hundred thousand people trying to get in. So coming back here, the climate was very good, and there are a lot of distributors—like the National Film Foundation—pushing filmmakers, especially black filmmakers. It is the best place to be as a black filmmaker at this present time. There is a huge drive to get our films out there. There is a drive to do one's own stories. The health of this industry is very good. There are a lot of films to be made, but it boils down to the bigger picture of having to compromise something. For example, the film that I made is a political film, and I can't get it on the air here in this country. HBO bought it, and it was played well on that side.

ATM: Your film is *Ubuntu's Wounds* [2002].

SM: Yes. The bigger picture is if you talk politics, race, or racism, people go, "Sh-shh." White people still have a strong hold over our society. I remember this one initiative for documentaries, and all the panelists were foreign. Of all the films submitted, about 90 percent were about personal tragedies and stories about the past. The panel said, "Ehhh, we don't want this!" But at the same time, we haven't even started making those kind of films because the people who made them before were either foreign or white. You [have] never really seen a black South African make a true black political film about the past.

AKIN OMOTOSO: Well, [there is] Ramadan Suleman's *Zulu Love Letter* [2004]. But I agree that political films are not encouraged. I was reading the *Sunday Times* and saw where this white actor said, "Why are we making these highly political films that nobody wants to see?" So I started writing this article—"Who says? You might not want to see it, but don't let that become gospel truth." I think that's the unhealthy thing. People also say there are no black directors, or there are no black writers, and nobody wants to see political films. This creates an unhealthy climate. But then when you have a film like *Red Dust* [2004] with foreign stars, everyone is going to want to see it, because it's got that appeal.

MMD: The truth of the matter is that—and we must say this—it is really that white people can do what they want. When they want to make a film—political or not—they go out there, and they make it. That is not true for black filmmakers.

AO AND SM: Yeah, yeah.

ATM: Whites are usually seen as having more objectivity, especially about race, and thus more validity.

MMD: I've never seen what I would consider a quintessential film about slavery. I've seen films about slavery—you have a [Steven] Spielberg film [*Amistad,* 1997], Haile Gerima's film [*Sankofa,* 1994]. I think it pulled something out which was not there, not there at all. It is almost like that story [of slavery] will never be told.

AO: And why won't it be told?

ATM: It is such a conflictual discourse. I compare it to what some say is happening in your country in regards to apartheid. People would rather not deal with it, but at least you had the TRC [Truth and Reconciliation Commission]. Remember *Beloved* [1998]—I don't know if you saw it—adapted from Toni Morrison's novel?

AO, SM, AND MMD: Yeah.

ATM: The film did not do well at all. People stayed away in droves, including black people, even though it had big stars like Danny Glover and Oprah Winfrey. Do you find a similar avoidance of the painful past among black people in South Africa?

AO: It's like the memory is too painful. I've watched *Zulu Love Letter,* which I thought was brilliant. I was watching it with a white guy, and he kept going on, "This film is bad, this film is bad."

ATM: What did he mean?

AO: Oh, well, because it is telling the truth. It is not trying to candy-coat the truth. Compare it to *Forgiveness* [2004] for example. *Forgiveness* [by South African director Ian Gabriel] has won several international awards, including the Cape Town World Cinema Festival's Best Film of the Year and is a much more tepid title. It's very forgiving, following the white guy who seeks forgiveness, and he is forgiven so quickly.

SM: At the end of the film, there is a statement by Archbishop [Desmond] Tutu about forgiveness.

ATM: Sounds like the official discourse of the state.

AO: *Zulu Love Letter* has none of that. I don't know if black people will go to see the film. You can't predict the audience, but at least, for me, the beauty of that film is the truth. It is telling the truth.

MMD: The truth of the matter is that we as black people have been convinced that white people make the best films. That is what we grew up with—Hollywood films. They are violent and predictable, but that is what people have learned to want and expect. The truth of the matter is that action films, thrillers, romantic comedies, and so on is what people go to watch. In fact, when you look at the distribution to the cinemas where most black people go, most of those films are very violent. Those are the films that get distributed to us. We are so used to them from when we were kids, so used to them that that's what appeals to us [now]. Suddenly, you bring a film like *Zulu Love Letter,* which doesn't have the same the structure and is not your typical [blockbuster]. It challenges you as a viewer. You're not supposed to think, you're not supposed to engage in what's in front of you.

ATM: That's a real interesting point. Do audiences have to be "educated" to appreciate certain films? Chris Rock [a comedian] and Tom Joyner [a radio host] have both joked about how Spike Lee's very important film *Bamboozled* [2000] flopped with black audiences. Joyner joked that if a bank robber were trying to get away from the cops, the best hiding place would be in a theater where *Bamboozled* was playing—because nobody would look there.

[Dube, Morojele, and Omotoso all laugh.]

SM: I think like Mickey was saying we have been conditioned. We now need to uncondition ourselves. Yes, we love our mainstream, we love American films. But what are we doing to change that? What ten-year plan, what processes, do we have to [that will] increase our love for our own?

ATM: You think the government should have a more specific role in it?

MMD: I think as filmmakers, particularly black filmmakers, we need to change the discourse. We need to find a way of not continuing the safest course. We have been fighting against a system that is oppressive, that was looking at us as nonhuman. We fought for the freedom cause. Now that we have these tools in front of us, how do we use them to effect how we want to be seen? This will involve challenging the notion of telling entertaining films. What do we mean by that, really? All these films are entertaining; they can draw you in. But we can do more than repeat what others have done. I think we need to find new ways to engage with our audience.

ATM: Perhaps there is the idea that film is a finished product. It has already been invented, the conventions are already in place, so you just have to deal with what's already on the plate. But what you're saying is that we should probably break that plate and bring in another model.

SM: For instance, you can take a plate and use it. One of the things that black people do very well is take something, change it, and make it mean something different. Look at what we do with the language, for example, "Where you at?" Seriously. We make our words mean something totally different.

[All laugh. Morojele excuses himself for another appointment.]

AO: Look at the explosion of our music. It has gotten to a point now where you go to a party, and people insist on their local music. They switch off R and B, but in films it hasn't happened. We haven't had the chance to come up with a new kind of film.

ATM: So film is actually behind the curve in local South African culture?

AO: It is because of white dominance of the industry.

MMD: Also, because it's expensive.

SM: I remember somebody saying that as a new country, we have to be careful that our stories aren't stolen. It takes us a while to get the money together, prepare the script, and make the kind of films we make. If someone from Hollywood comes with money and wants to make a certain film, it will get made because they have the money. It's like you almost need cultural police at our borders. They will come and make a film, but when it's time for us to make our own film, they will say, "Well, it's enough. We've seen that."

ATM: It's already been done.

AO: That's a whole other argument. When we step up to the plate and say, "I want to do the true AIDS story," they'll say, "Look, it's been done." We are in a very terrible moment where our stories are being stolen.

ATM: What can you do to defend yourself against that?

AO: We can't. What can you do?

MMD: The U.S. film industry differs from the industry in Europe in [that] in the U.S., you find people who are willing to work for free. Because there are so many actors who don't want to just sit around and be idle so they are willing to work for free, for maybe a cut in the film or whatever. Often when you really want to tell the story the way you want to tell it, you need a little more money down to say to people come help you. I know when I made my film with 600,000 rand [approximately US$82,000], which, when you see the film, you see so many locations and different actors. I am still paying some people in postproduction even today. [I did this] in order to get it to look like a decent film. You don't want people to look at it and say, "Oh, no."

ATM: Returning to the idea that film can also be a tool, do you think that film can be an agent for empowerment in a broader sense?

MMD: Film for me is like music, it's like poetry, it's like dance, it's an expression, really. Your thoughts, your principles, your philosophy can be expressed in film. Film can be a tool for confirmation, a tool for empowerment. It's really finding the right script that has power in it. It can move people. The beauty of a film is how it can reach you emotionally. Music [can move people], obviously. Because of film's visual power, you are able to get to people much quicker and intimately. In a sense, you manipulate people. Remember how *Dead Man Walking* [1995] inspired so much talk about the death penalty all over the world?

ATM: Film, like money, can be a tool for good or bad. Hitler used film brilliantly.

AO: Mobutu [former dictator of Congo Mobutu Sese Seko], too. He had this image of him coming down out of the clouds. I agree with Mickey, because, for me, the thing about film is the beauty of it. It is permanent and enduring. I also like the way film can provoke discussion. I hate it when people watch a film, and then nobody wants to talk about it afterwards.

MMD: I'm sure you are aware of what is happening now with special effects. It started with *The Matrix* [1999] and its use of special effects that had never been seen before. Now, a challenge for filmmakers—even films that don't need special effects—is to do something that is visually different as an enhancement of reality. The latest thing that is happening now is 3-D, which is very powerful. [It's] amazing what you can do with it. Of course, you wear the glasses but you forget about them. After watching that, I went to an African film festival, and it was difficult for me to feel it. The experience of [3–D films] had been so powerful. The notion of film being a tool of expression has never been stronger for me. I'm sure there will be something bigger, newer, but the technology is always changing and manipulating reality.

ATM: But I wonder whether the maze of technology can get in the way of the story, and I wonder if that is especially true for emerging cinemas like here in South Africa.

MMD: Often they do, but I must confess when I saw *The Matrix,* number 1, I thought that it was the first film to take special effects and change them to tell the story. It was not for the sake of the effects, it was for the [story]. Without the special effects, that film would never have been that successful. That is what I appreciate.

ATM: Can we talk specifically about South African films? Are such special effects part of the future? A few years from now, what will people identify that defines South African films? Will it have a language all its own?

MMD: I think you can get there once you start making the films. If you make three films a year, there is no way you can do that; if you make even ten films a year, it's still difficult. When you look at Australian film, it took them fifteen or twenty years before people could say there is an Australian film language.

ATM: Having said that, how do you define yourself as a filmmaker?

MMD: I believe in film in its total form. I've made commercials, I make documentaries, I make fiction as well as corporate [films]. I also do theater. I believe in the total form and in looking for new ways of telling a story. It is a process. I like for people to look at my work and say, "That's interesting, but I could take it further." That is how you build a film community, a language.

ATM: Is there a spirit of cooperation among filmmakers here, or does competition for resources diminish esprit de corps?

AO: I don't see it as a competition, I believe in the [film] community. I'm a film groupie. I think that if I were not a filmmaker, I would hang out with filmmakers because I just enjoy talking about film. I think that what we've been trying to do is find ways to cooperate.

MMD: This is really a new initiative among a group of black filmmakers who get together and talk about the issues related to film. It begins and then dies off, and then a new one comes through, and then it dies off. But it will always be there because of the nature of where we have been and what [the country] has experienced.

ATM: One final question. Should there be more of a relationship between the film communities of South Africa and the larger African diaspora? What should such a relationship be about?

AO: I'm very much interested in the wider African film [market]. I think other filmmakers are starting to think more broadly, too. The more we study or travel to other places, we better understand this need. In Nigeria, where I was born, the film market is exploding.

ATM: Mickey?

MMD: In the long run, I have no doubt that there will be a very important relationship between our film industry here and other [film] industries. In fact, there's going to be a conference of African filmmakers here soon. There are already initiatives in the works. The truth of the matter is that East Africa and Central Africa seldom release films. I don't know why, but when we talk about African film, we usually mean French West African films—and it's really the French who have the power. These are French films. Even today, they are the only people who are fighting Hollywood [in terms of a different definition of film]. It is their recognition that film is an integral part of a society's cultural expression. Maybe that is one thing that we could learn from those foreign films is how important it is to have your own culturally based films. I have confidence in the notion that as time goes on, it will happen here. If Nigerians are making films here, others will know about it. We will have a new OAU [Organization of African Unity], which is trying to redefine relationships from one African country to another and remove colonial influences. It is about how we move forward and become participants in the twenty-first century. Film, sooner or later, is going to participate in that. It lags behind now because film is so expensive. A lot of Africa has come to see South Africa as being in the forefront of a lot of things, rightly or wrongly, but it's something that we can use. The truth of the matter is that South Africa is [torn] between past, present, and future. I think that if we allow ourselves, we can be an important player in bridging the gap in a positive way for the whole of Africa. For me, I want to believe that the future is bright.

ATM: A final word about your current projects?

MMD: Well, I am working on two documentaries right now. One is about three former prisoners of Robben Island who become singers. It is about these three friends who have fought and killed, [who have been] tortured, arrested, and thrown into Robben Island for many years. They came out and formed this recording group. Within their relationships, we explore so many issues related to struggle, human nature, et cetera. The other film is about HIV/AIDS and how people are living with it, how people are staying alive. The film is looking at alternative initiatives, and it is incredible what is happening, including people who keep others alive by talking to them. I am also working on a fiction film.

ATM: You are, indeed, a busy man, Mickey!

AO: I just finished a short film, the one I told you I was going to do last year, *Rifle Road.* I just finished that. I also finished a documentary on Monday. I'm in a just-finished mode. I am researching a project about farm killings, murders. It's a detective story called *The Hound.* I have been working on this for three years. My other project that I am also obsessed with is deejays. Not just that but how this culture works. How this guy can provide you with everything you need for an evening. I am interested in how the nightclub scene has evolved in the ten years since the end of apartheid. The architecture of nightclubs, that whole scene. I am not sure if it will be fiction or not. The story is still developing. Clubs used to be all white, then moved to colored [racially mixed] people, and then to blacks. And, you know, even though apartheid is supposed to have crumbled, that architecture still stands.

ATM: We will certainly stay tuned! It sounds intriguing. It is important to understand what the first postapartheid generation is carrying in their heads.

MMD: It's the subject [nightclubs] he likes. [*All laugh.*]

AO: Yes, so I'm trying. . . . I'm doing a lot of research, hanging out at clubs. All my friends laugh at me.

ATM: Hey, and you can write that off as business expenses! [*All laugh again.*]

AO: Exactly! They'll be, like, "What are you doing?" I'll say, "It's research." But it's amazing in a way, because I have been interviewing a lot of club owners and deejays and just get the sense and talking about apartheid and clubs and how in this particular club before clubs in Cape Town, Jo'burg, the clubs in Durban. I thought it was going to be a documentary, but I don't think documentary is the form.

MMD: I think it will be a great document. I'm not sure. But if you want to do it as fiction, you need to find a story.

AO: Well, that's the problem. That's the struggle. It might be a documentary with fiction. You document stuff, then you [infuse] it with a fictional storyline. I don't know what it is yet. I'll just say I'm on a journey.

ATM: It'll come, I'm sure. Thank you, Akin, for sharing your office, and, Mickey, thanks for this tasty breakfast.

AO: My pleasure.

MMD: Thank you.

MICKEY MADOBA DUBE was born in Soweto. He returned to South Africa after graduating from film school at the University of Southern California in Los Angeles. His first film *Imbazo* (*The Axe*) won prizes at several international festivals. He directed projects at the South African Broadcast Company before founding Waapiti Productions, which has produced many of his projects including films, videos, and commercials.

FILMOGRAPHY

***Imbazo* (*The Axe*) (1995).** This short fictional film was shown at the FESPACO Film Festival in Burkina Faso in 1995.

***A Walk in the Night* (1997).** A frustrated mixed-race man kills a white neighbor in this adaptation from the Alex La Guma short story of same name.

***Saints, Sinners, and Settlers* (1998).** Testimony before South Africa's Truth and Reconciliation Committee is dramatized.

***Takalani Sesame* (2000).** This series is a South African version of the well-known U.S. PBS children's educational program *Sesame Street.*

SECHABA MOROJELE received a Master of Fine Arts degree from the American Film Institute in Los Angeles. Since returning to South Africa, he has worked on several film projects. The award-winning *Ubuntu's Wounds* is his first feature.

FILMOGRAPHY

***Ubuntu's Wounds* (2005).** A black South African lives in exile in Los Angeles and encounters a member of the apartheid hit squad who murdered Ubuntu's wife years before.

AKIN OMOTOSO is a native Nigerian who now lives in Johannesburg. He received a performer's diploma in speech and drama in 1996 from the University of Cape Town. He has extensive acting experience on stage and television, the latter of which includes stints in popular programs such as *Double Shift*, *Generations*, and *Big Okes*. He won M-Net's Best New Director award for *God Is African* in 2003. He had an acting role in the Hollywood film *Blood Diamond* (2006).

FILMOGRAPHY

***God Is African* (2003).** The mistrust and hostility that many South Africans express toward immigrants from other parts of the African continent are examined.

***Rifle Road* (2005).** The lives of young South Africans are caught up in the world of risk taking and gun violence.

Ingrid Gavshon

Ingrid Gavshon

> If you didn't have a history of being in the struggle, it was, "Well, who are you?" You had to explain yourself in order to get people to talk or to trust you or open doors for you.

AUDREY THOMAS McCLUSKEY: You returned to South Africa, your home, after living and working in Europe. What were the circumstances that got you started in film, and what are your impressions of the changes since you returned?

INGRID GAVSHON: Actually, it goes way back. In the 1970s, I worked for a photographer and for a lawyer. In 1988, a friend of mine—a South African living and working in television in Britain—knew that I wanted to get into television as a researcher and gave me a break. I worked there for two years, two and a half years. In 1989, I came back and worked on a film for Dutch television. In 1990, I decided to come back to South Africa again. Things were changing. The climate was changing. So I came back, and very fortuitously or very luckily, the same friend told me that some Dutch filmmakers had come to South Africa and wanted someone to help do research on independent black churches, and would I be interested? I said, "Of course, I'd be interested." I came back to South Africa after living abroad for fifteen years. This opened other opportunities to work with other Dutch filmmakers who hadn't been allowed into South Africa for about twelve years because they used to make these really strong anti-apartheid films, and [the apartheid government] was really angry about that.

ATM: How much of the past has to be involved in the construction of the new South Africa, and what role does film play?

IG: I think there's a whole generation of young people today who don't really know about apartheid and the Pass Laws [the laws requiring nonwhites to carry identifying permits, effectively controlling their movement]. They don't know what really happened, and I think that while we have to move forward, we have to look back as well to find new and interesting ways of telling stories of the past in order to move forward. I think we have to learn the past. It's the role of the filmmaker to do this. Filmmaking is about communication. For me, it's about using images, words, and people with interesting stories to tell. Stories are universal, and I think the stories in South Africa are really important because we have had a smooth transition. One cannot deny it wasn't very good [before]. I was at the Union Building just before the first election—five days before the first election—when it was touch and go whether Mangosuthu Buthelezi [leader of the Inkatha Freedom Party that opposed Nelson Mandela's African National Congress] would come on board or not with the new government. All these really well-known international journalists, reporters, and filmmakers were here to monitor the election. That was a huge moment in time. It was a huge turning point. Although we have had a smooth transition, I don't think as a country we'll be free of the past until people actually understand what they have gone through. There are a lot of white South Africans who were in complete denial all of those years of apartheid—who didn't know what was going on or didn't try to find out what was going on. They didn't read newspapers like *Mail and Guardian*. They didn't really talk to people who worked for them. They wouldn't actually engage with them about where they came from or what their living conditions were. They didn't have interest in what was happening to their children while they were working in their homes, shops, whatever. If I, in some way, could contribute to [their awareness], that [would be] very attractive.

ATM: Now the second part of the question?

IG: When I came back to South Africa, it was a very closed society. People were very, very nervous.

ATM: This was in 1990?

IG: I came back in 1990 and moved back in 1993. South African media had been pushing at the boundaries for years—not so much SABC [the state-owned South African Broadcast Corporation] but newspapers—there'd been some independent newspapers and journalists who had really been pushing, also. When I came [back] to South Africa, it was quite strange for me, because everybody spoke in codes.

ATM: What do you mean?

IG: Everybody was very suspicious of outsiders. If you didn't have a history of being in the struggle, it was, "Well, who are you?" You had to explain yourself in order to get people to talk or to trust you or open doors for you.

Now, the media is much more free. It's much more open. There's a transparency in the media. We hear what's happening in government, whereas with the previous government, it was really difficult to expose what was really happening. It was a very tight and a closed group. Now there's a sense of aliveness. There's a sense of debate. There's a sense of freedom in the media today that wasn't there in 1990. People are more interested in South African stories than they were before. They are looking for interesting ways to tell South Africa's history, which was not being done before. There's been some groundbreaking programs and groundbreaking dramas that really are widening the media's role in South Africa in film and television. There's much more space, not only to tell the past history but also to tell new stories, human stories about love, anger, pain, crime, or thrills. People felt more responsibility.

ATM: Did you feel a particular responsibility yourself after coming back?

IG: Yes, because I wasn't here for the struggle years. I was living in England and watching television obsessively about what was going on here.

ATM: Did you purposefully leave because of the political situation?

IG: No. I left to study design, and then when, in 1976, the Soweto uprising started, I sat and watched television every night, and I thought, "How can I go back to this country where they butcher children?" I thought about coming back after two years. Then I thought, "No. I can't. I can't come back to this country." When I came back, it was like a wall. Living in Britain, I felt a freedom that there wasn't in South Africa. You felt that everyone was operating against a system that would never collapse. It was only in the mid-eighties that one began to feel that change would come.

INGRID GAVSHON is an independent director and producer who founded Angel Films in 1990. Since returning to South Africa, she has made several award-winning films and current-affairs documentaries about social and political issues, including abortion, AIDS, land rights, Holocaust survivors, and the role of women in the Anglo-Boer War. She has also worked with Free Film Makers, an independent production company that trains young filmmakers from disadvantaged backgrounds.

FILMOGRAPHY (RECENT)

Facing Life . . . Facing Death (2002). Duma Kumalo, an innocent man, faced death by hanging by the apartheid regime but was granted a stay of execution at the last minute that led him to a search for life's meaning.

Nelson Mandela **(2002).** This is a portrait of the internationally esteemed leader, considered the father of postapartheid South Africa and its first democratically elected president.

Being Pavarotti **(2004).** In this South African television documentary, a fourteen-year-old boy from Zwelihle has inherent musical talent and the ability to imitate the great tenor Luciano Pavarotti.

Nikiwe **(2004).** In a life-affirming story, fifteen-year-old Nikiwe struggles to take care of her siblings after both parents die of AIDS.

Angus Gibson

Angus Gibson

> The thing that has particularly distressed us as a group of filmmakers [in South Africa] recently has been the relationship between South Africa and the rest of Africa. [There is] extraordinary xenophobia against other Africans.

AUDREY THOMAS McCLUSKEY: Angus, how long have you been directing films?

ANGUS GIBSON: I've worked in film for about twenty years. I entered the film industry with the intention of making narrative fiction, partly because of the way that the industry was in South Africa and finding myself unable to engage with the local industry. The space I found to make films was in documentaries—with funding from abroad.

ATM: What was the subject of these documentaries?

AG: In the eighties, I decided I wanted to do an epic kind of verité documentary about the comrades in Soweto. I, in fact, secured the money from Channel 4 in Britain. It was the first time they'd ever given a full commission. And just then, the second state of emergency was declared with all these press restrictions. Basically, if I were to stay in this country and not go to jail, I could not actually make the film that I wanted to make. It was clear I would endanger the people that I was filming. Suddenly, I had all the money and couldn't make the film. I had been working with a Dutch theater company on a play that we had been workshopping about the suburb of Johannesburg called Sophiatown, which was [where] the first big removal [of blacks took place] when the National Party came to power. In doing the research, I realized that having grown up as a white South African in perfect apartheid isolation, I had not seen images of the removal. I began to dig them up in the archives, and I said, "Well, if I can't make the films that I want to make about the contemporary [issues], let me use the past to say what I want to say about South Africa now." For a period of my life, I did a huge amount of archival research and started making films that used archive [material] and history in order to comment on the present. So the film that I made using a portion of the budget that was supposed to go towards the verité film was used for the play about Sophiatown. It has subsequently become a huge hit, both in this country and abroad. This was the first time images that had been lost in the archives were up on the screen.

ATM: This was in 1986?

AG: This was about 1986 or '87. It was a very stylized documentary that took the style of the play. All the interviews were lit in the same way, and the interviews had backdrops. The reason that we used these backdrops was because I wanted to show that the South African community at that point was fragmented. There were people in exile who could not return home, and I wanted to create the illusion of all these people coming back together. I traveled around the world with these backdrops. They are fantastic interviews, and, in that moment, it felt [like] they were telling it fresh.

ATM: Who was the audience for this film?

AG: Of course, it couldn't be shown in this country. Subsequently, after the unbanning of the ANC [African National Congress], it's been shown in this country quite often. It was very frustrating because I made these films in this country, and then they'd be shown in communities that I was not part of. It felt as if I didn't do anything. I could never have a dialogue with the people who were seeing the films out there.

ATM: Do you think that film contributed to the world's condemnation and revulsion about what was happening in South Africa? Did it have an impact?

AG: I assume it did. It certainly took a strong line against what was happening in South Africa.

ATM: I ask that question in order to gauge your feeling about the future, particularly how film fits into the construction of the new South Africa.

AG: I think film always has a role. Culture always has a role. I think culture found itself in a bit of a quandary post 1994, but the projects that I've engaged with since '94 [have been successful]. In the early nineties, I did a big documentary on Nelson Mandela, also with a substantial budget.

ATM: Yes, that film received lots of international attention. What was the full title?

AG: It was called *Mandela: Son of Africa, Father of a Nation* [1996], and it was nominated for an Oscar that year. It was knocked out by *When We Were Kings,* which is the better film, I think.

ATM: You are modest. When you came to the U.S. for the Academy Award ceremony, how did representing your country at this huge event resonate back home?

AG: I can't explain it. I returned to South Africa, I found that I had a profile as this leftie, sociopolitical documentary filmmaker. In fact, at the time, everyone said I was crazy to leave the States. If you are nominated for an Oscar, you must stay there and have a career. First, I felt the Mandela film didn't represent where I wanted to go at that point in my career, and, secondly, the work that I do is so connected to the site I live in that I can't imagine leaving. At that point, I simply didn't want to leave South Africa. I wanted to be part of what was happening here. When I came back, I wanted to make a space for people to write features. I tried to raise money for that [purpose], which was incredibly hard. I teamed up with two people. One was a friend of mine named Isaac Shoengwe, who was an entrepreneur and was confident that he could raise money for the project. The other one was a guy named Teboho Mahlatsi.

ATM: Teboho is getting deserved attention right now as an up-and-coming filmmaker.

AG: Teboho and I wrote a narrative film together called *Street Bash.* In its first moment, it reminded me a bit of punk rock in London in the seventies, and I was very excited by that. Our script, first, was not in English. Secondly, the script we were working with was quite a bleak tale and funny, too. But it was certainly bleak. Everybody was very kind of saying, "There's not space for this kind of narrative in South Africa right now." They thought it doesn't represent the kind of rainbow nation that is painted.

ATM: Why? Does it go against a party line?

AG: It's about four young friends who steal money from a club in the early hours of the morning, kill somebody in the process, and return back to the township. You begin to realize the person they stole the money from is the person that they work for. There was a phenomenon at the time—at that moment—of street bashers. The streets would be closed off for a street party which was happening that day. And these guys party through the day—knowing that they aren't going to [last] the day out, and most of them don't. So it's an extraordinarily bleak, but it's a very funny story. I think it's a very good script, actually. It hasn't been made. And now, of course, several years later, you look at *City of God* [2002], and it feels like we were there four years before. What happened was that Teboho and I were looking for money for *Street Bash* and got this contract to make a television series. Neither of us had any intention of doing television, but we did. A lot of the spirit that was in *Street Bash* found its way into the television series, which was partly funded by the Department of Education. The intention was to draw attention to the crisis in the township school. It was a series called *Yizo Yizo,* which I'm completing the third season of.

ATM: I hear that's hugely popular throughout the country.

AG: Yeah, it received the biggest viewing figures ever in the country.

ATM: Are you still partnering with Teboho?

AG: Yes, we remain partners. Some projects we do together, and others we don't. There's always a project we both do. He does a lot of commercial work, which I don't do, that keeps our company on track. Hopefully, he will make a feature film this year. I don't know if you know the series *7 Up,* which Grenada Television did in Britain in 1964. They took a group of kids that represented a cross section of seven-year-olds in Britain and spoke to them about the world, about sex, religion, their futures. Then every seven years, they have returned to that same group. Next, they're doing *49 Up.*

ATM: I am aware of it, yes.

AG: OK. In '92, they decided to do one in the States, one in Russia, and one in South Africa. They asked directors from the different countries to do it. They asked me if I would do the South African one. So in '92, I did *7 Up South Africa.* In 1999, I did *14 Up,* and in 2006, *21 Up.*

ATM: That will be a fascinating way to document social change in South Africa. What changes have you seen you already?

AG: Well, in a way, at the risk of sounding completely crazy, I think *Yizo Yizo* has changed film culture in this country.

ATM: How so?

AG: In terms of local television, there has been a kind of apartheid thing about purity of language. So everybody spoke "pure" Zulu or Xhosa or Sotho. It was this weird thing on television of this antiquated language being spoken. Obviously, it was part of the divide-and-rule notion. In a sense, people began to accept that's what television was. With *Yizo Yizo,* the crew that had worked on the television in the past was constantly saying, "You can't do that! You can't do that! You can't say that!" All these things that we couldn't go to—you can't say "shit." I said, "Well, why can't you say 'shit'? It's on television all the time." They said, "Well, it's OK if it's in English, but don't say it in Zulu." This is a legacy of our past. What it meant was for the first time, people mixed languages in the way that people mix in this country. We were very careful to cast families in ways that were realistic. Language is spoken like you hear it on the streets here.

ATM: Who were the writers?

AG: There were five writers—two were black, and three were white. In fact, the scripts were written in English.

ATM: What kind of instructions were the writers given, and how did everyone work together to create this new experience?

AG: It was a huge partnership with the actors. We were very careful to cast people who had a life experience which was similar to the role that they were playing. We were careful about accents. If you are a black South African, and you have been to a school in the suburbs, you will speak quite a different Zulu than somebody who has been to a school in the township. Those things were very important to us—the differentiation between Zulu speakers, so we would cast very specifically for that. In this last series, for example, there are three different Zulus in the series. We have the Zulu of a group of taxi drivers who are from a particular part of Zululand. People would come to us and say, "It's the first time there's an image of somebody on television that I can say, 'That's me! That's my life.'" It was, in a sense, a revolution.

ATM: Has the series had the same kind of effect behind the camera? Is there a similar revolution, a kind of verticality among the crew and staff?

AG: The majority of the crew is black; the cameraperson has always been white. On this third series, there are three directors. I directed five [episodes]. Teboho directed five. The middle three, in fact, are directed by a Nigerian director, a guy named Andrew Dosunmu, who is a truly fabulous director. There have been core issues that each series has addressed, and the thing that has particularly distressed us as a group of filmmakers [in South Africa] recently has been the relationship between South Africa and the rest of Africa. [There is] extraordinary xenophobia against other Africans. We decided we would tackle it. In fact, the final episode is a marriage between a Nigerian character who becomes one of the heroes of the series and one of the old characters of the series.

ATM: So the series will potentially transform people's attitudes—

AG: It has already. One thing that I know of is that it has split the ANC.

ATM: How? What do you mean?

AG: Because the Women's League in the second series called for the show to be banned, and the Youth League came out very militantly in its defense.

ATM: Why did the Women's League want *Yizo Yizo* banned?

AG: Because there had been a representation of sodomy in the series. In the first series, there are two thugs that became antiheroes called Chester and Papa Action. You could literally walk into any township and see their names on the walls, which was something we hadn't anticipated. We hadn't intended that they become this kind of cult figure. So in the second series, we took them to jail, and it was the first time—there has been a theme in South Africa of "jail is the university of life." [In this country], there is a very complicated relationship with jail because of the legacy of apartheid. It was a fact that perfectly respectable people did their time in jail.

ATM: Yes, so how did you maneuver around this difference between jail for activists and for criminals?

AG: There was a kind of emotion, a certain cool around jail which was affecting certain attitudes towards criminality. We wanted to really take a stab at that in the second series, and we shot the second series in the jail with real prisoners. As for the sodomy, it was very discreet, and I remember it was just fourteen seconds. It caused the most unbelievable furor. There had been a call for the first series to be banned mainly from the Christian right, and the second series, there was a huge call for the banning, and it was debated for two days in parliament. It was a very interesting moment. Curiously, within six months, the camera was smuggled into the prisons, and everything that we had exposed in the series was shot verité. As a result, there was a commission investigation of the living conditions in prisons.

ATM: You can't make much more of an impact than that! As a result of this extraordinary experience with *Yizo Yizo,* has your orientation changed from primarily being a filmmaker of narrative film and documentaries to doing television?

AG: People on the pavement have an opinion about the work that I was doing. It wasn't going to America or Europe into some kind of vacuum that I had nothing to do with. People here were watching it, and people on the street were watching [the show], and they either loved it, or they hated it. For me, that was so fantastic to have a dialogue with the people that I live with and so hard for me to give that up! I won't do another series like *Yizo* for the moment because each time it has bankrupted our company because the economics of it don't work. But I'm probably going to now develop a new soap.

ATM: A soap?

AG: Yeah. You know, all the soaps in this country have always been in the tradition of *Dynasty* or *The Bold and the Beautiful.*

ATM: What is your attraction to soaps, especially since they are not held in high esteem in many quarters?

AG: Well, I don't watch soaps.

ATM: Why do you want to produce that genre if you don't watch them?

AG: There are a number of reasons. One is because everybody watches soaps in this country, so there's a power there. They have huge power. The economics of soaps work in this country. You can make a living making soaps. As actors, you can make a living. It's the one place that an actor can find a home and actually send their children to school. You know, it's a poor life being an actor in this country. A real dilemma that we have found is with *Yizo Yizo,* we cast a huge number of unknown people, and they became these stars, [but] they have no money and no job to go to. They didn't speak English in the way that we found [in] advertising or the English that soaps [demand]. Despite the fact that they were geniuses at what they do, actually, there was no home for them. I want to do what *East Enders* does for British television—a working-class soap. I think it's very important to represent a working-class position. I still plan to return to feature films, though.

ATM: If you had to state your philosophy as a filmmaker, have you consciously thought of what your mission is as a filmmaker?

AG: I haven't consciously thought of it. But I think I realized quite recently, it was curious, I suppose, that I'd take a position which is critical of the powers that be. I've always been an ANC supporter. [But] recently with this election, I [feel that] the ANC needs an opposition. I still went and [cast my vote] for the ANC, but, in fact, I have no relationship with the ANC.

ATM: Or any political party?

AG: Or any political party.

ATM: Do you think it a good thing for filmmakers to be close to the power structure?

AG: I don't know whether it's good or bad. I suppose I do want to question our society. For example, our country has a huge problem with xenophobia. We also have a huge problem around sexuality. Homophobia in this country is a real problem. We have a constitution that is incredible. It supports gay rights. But, in fact, we have a population that is deeply homophobic. In the series, one of our main heroic characters that South Africa has very close to its heart has a relationship with another man. We are on episode 6 at the moment, and it will become clear in episode 9. I know it will just cause complete shit. But, for me, those things are very important. I think in terms of moving a society along. I suppose that's the way that I want to engage with the society.

ATM: On the issue of xenophobia, how do you approach that topic as a filmmaker?

AG: I don't know. I think South Africans are very boorish, in a way. I think that there is something curiously like Americans. I mean, Americans have such an extraordinarily high opinion of themselves. I suppose all empires do. I don't understand what it is about South Africa, but there is a sense that we are better.

ATM: Better than the rest of Africa? The world?

AG: It's not specifically the rest of Africa. I think that as an African American, on the whole, your experience in South Africa [will be] a much easier one than someone from Ivory Coast or wherever. I think that you'll be embraced. It's quite a comfortable space for African Americans. I don't know what it is. If you are from another part of Africa, there still is an attraction to be in South Africa because it is an economic powerhouse, but it's a tough time. The police make their living off of Africans [from other countries] by taking bribes. It's tough.

ATM: I have one final question. Most of your work has a multicultural focus, which is representative of this diverse country, but there is a sense that this is still a nation divided. That may show up in what movies or television shows people choose to watch. What is your impression of what the "typical" white South African viewer thinks of what he or she sees on television today? If they don't watch *Yizo Yizo,* what do they watch?

AG: At the moment, they have a choice. *Yizo Yizo* is on at the same time as *Angels in America* [the HBO series].

ATM: Well, that's a *real* choice. I doubt if very many black Americans or even working-class or middle-class whites watched that original HBO production. It is a great production but was not designed for mass appeal. Do white South Africans prefer the foreign import *Angels in America*?

AG: I'm making an assumption, but I assume that's what they watch.

ATM: Is there any overlap between the kinds of shows blacks and whites watch here? In America, it is usually sports—NFL football—that link television viewing across different races.

AG: God, I don't want to generalize, but I think that if you are black, you have to be born more diverse because everything presented to you is made from a white perspective. Obviously, black South Africans will watch Americans movies that aren't mostly white, but black South Africans will watch good and bad local television. If there is something that is in Zulu, you have a relatively captive Zulu audience. White South Africans, however, pretty much watch American and European/British fare. I think they watch very little that's local.

ATM: So there is no South African cinema, there's no South African film or media culture that white South Africans identify with?

AG: Absolutely not. No.

ATM: Is there anything that can be done to change this? Or are these simply divergent interests that won't be ever the same?

AG: I think it will change. My son watches *Yizo Yizo.* My son has a different experience of the world than my experience of the world. I think, literally, that's what it's going to take. Also, I think it's about us making better films. I think we make pretty damn deplorable films. I mean, we don't make films that stand up. I think *Yizo Yizo* stands up a whole lot taller than any of the films that are made.

ATM: When and how will this change?

AG: I think it's about to happen. I think that very soon films will be made that stand up. It's partly to do with the legacy of apartheid beginning to recede. My contemporaries among black South Africans—I'm generalizing—didn't have a film culture because they had been moved into townships with very little access to cinemas. I lived in a suburb where, probably like you, there was a place down the road where I could watch cheap movies every week. Whereas the generation before me of black South Africans that lived in urban ghettos were completely cinema literate. When you speak to somebody like Don Mattera, his knowledge of movies of the forties and fifties is incredible, but that was all destroyed, literally, with the destruction of places like Sophiatown and people being moved into places where culture didn't exist. It's the generation after me—of the youngest South Africans, who once again have the access and are cinema literate and have a passion about cinema. I think they will make different demands. The natural fruit of that is going to be good films.

ANGUS GIBSON is a native South African and pioneering filmmaker whose documentaries have earned him an international reputation. He is codirector (with Jo Menell) of *Mandela: Son of Africa,* which earned an Academy Award nomination. He also directs and produces for television.

PARTIAL FILMOGRAPHY

7 Up in South Africa **(1993).** Nineteen South African children through several phases of their lives are shown in this hopeful journey.

Mandela: Son of Africa, Father of a Nation **(1996).** The extraordinary life of Nelson Mandela is traced from his tribal beginnings and young adulthood through his activism and imprisonment and to eventual freedom and his election to the presidency of South Africa.

Yizo Yizo **(2002–4).** An acclaimed television series shatters many cultural taboos.

Kevin Harris

I was very young in those days, but I wanted to make films because my burning outrage was that I didn't want people to be able to say, "We didn't know."

AUDREY THOMAS McCLUSKEY: Kevin, tell me about your involvement in documentary filmmaking in this country.

KEVIN HARRIS: It goes back to 1974. I was studying electrical engineering, and halfway through college, I realized I really did not want to do it. I was interested in popular music and playing in a band, and I thought I would become a music producer, using my technical background. SABC [South African Broadcasting Corporation], which is the [national] broadcaster—there was only one back in those days—was controlled by the apartheid government. I joined the SABC as an engineer, but I immediately asked for something creative. I got wind of television training programs that were starting up in 1974. I said, "Well, what about television?" And they said, "Well, yes."

ATM: This was all in the apartheid state?

KH: Yes—under the apartheid system. Absolutely. In those days, television was white. There was no black television. It was a service for the white viewer. Their whole thrust was to make one-dimensional films about life in South Africa. Soap operas, that kind of thing, which reflected a white society as whites saw it. You had black townships like Soweto, which was over the hill. Basically, black people came into your homes to work for you during the day, and at night they went back to their homes. Television very much endorsed and propagated that [ideology]. It was broken down into an English department and African department [separate programming by race]. I got to know and respect a number of filmmakers who were good and serious about film and who—although this may sound like a contradiction—they were absolutely aware of who they were working for, but they were trying to be socially relevant. One by one, out of sheer frustration, I saw them resign because they just reached the limit of what they could do. The big watershed around this occurred in 1976, when the Soweto uprising happened. There was a lot of debate within the documentary department [about whether] we should be doing something. We should be covering this. We should be reflecting this. We should be—but, of course, we did not. News was carefully controlled. I realized that one has an enormous responsibility working for the only broadcaster which is [doing] propaganda, but you are a part of that machine. Films were made that just ended up on the shelf because the person in charge would insist on changes. Eventually, the program that you set out to make would just be a whitewash of the issue.

ATM: What was the moment of decision for you?

KH: I put forward a lot of proposals. One of the films I put forth was a film about Baragwanath Hospital. It is still the major hospital that serves Soweto. I believed that a film about the hospital would be a way to show the social environment, and that's how I proposed it. It was received with great enthusiasm because they saw it as a wonderful way of showing what whites were doing through this community hospital for the black community. They thought that they could use this. Anyway, I rushed off and made the film. I had a courtesy viewing for the hospital staff because they'd contributed, and they loved the film. There was one man sitting there shaking his head—and he was the superintendent of the hospital. Afterwards, he said, "I'm sorry, this film cannot go out." It was the first time a film was being made [about the township], and all you see is poverty and degradation.

ATM: What did your supervisors say?

KH: When I saw that first frame go up, I realized that they hadn't [seen the content], so the film went out. It didn't start the revolution. I was fired within twenty-four hours. That was the start of my career as an independent filmmaker. I discovered it was very difficult thereafter to get work. The SABC, one way or another, influenced the outside industry. I also realized that the BBC would come into South Africa and cover issues but take the story out with them [to be] shown overseas. White South Africans were not confronted with what was happening in their name. I was very young in those days, but I wanted to make films because my burning outrage was that I didn't want people to be able to say, "We didn't know." I felt indignant that as a South African, I had every right to make films about what was happening in my country and to project my point of view.

ATM: What was your first independent film?

KH: *This We Can Do for Justice and for Peace,* which was a film about the Council of Churches and their stand against the apartheid. Bishop Desmond Tutu was the general secretary, and a white man was the president. I took these profiles and examined what the churches were doing against apartheid.

ATM: Did you consider what you were doing radical?

KH: I didn't consider it radical in the sense that I was first and foremost a filmmaker. I was not a political activist. I didn't have an axe to grind. I wanted to make films, and I wanted to make films that were relevant and had something to say. I guess in that way I was slowly being pushed across the line into the anti-apartheid camp. My beginning point was that I wanted to make films to show what was going on in this country. Local people could not say, "Oh, he's some overseas communist-inspired troublemaker." I'm a South African, and this is a concerned South African's perspective.

ATM: Where was this film shown? Was it banned?

KH: I wanted to confront the censorship system. I had the backing of the Council of Churches, but the film was banned. We launched an appeal that resulted in thirteen cuts being made in the film and severe restrictions as to where it could be shown and under certain conditions, such as only twenty people at a time and an age limit of eighteen or something like that. But that was a partial victory.

ATM: How many films did you make under that kind of structure?

KH: Well, that was 1982 to 1994. I must have made probably twelve films under those kinds of restrictions.

ATM: How did you finance your films?

KH: I met a lot of people in audiovisual sectors, and some helped me. I managed to raise a bit of money here and there, because there was no money inside the country, obviously. The problem was that nobody actually has a funding line for filmmaking. So, people who became interested in my work had to twist it out of education or development. It was always an extremely difficult fundraising process.

ATM: How has your life changed as a filmmaker since 1994?

KH: Before 1994, I could *never* work for the local broadcaster, [but] in 1994, that happened. First of all, 1990 was a critical period. Apartheid was [waning]. All the structures that I set up [inside and outside the country] just fell away. Suddenly, all kind of lifelines I had established—they all just disappeared. So 1990 to '94 was extremely difficult. Nothing had changed locally, but everything had closed off internationally. During that period, if there was any association with the ANC [African National Congress] in anyway whatsoever, you would be detained and locked up. I was an independent filmmaker, and I didn't cross that line because I knew that would put me in jeopardy.

ATM: With the ANC coming to power, how did that affect your work?

KH: I came to be marginalized. But in the late 1980s, we started an organization in South Africa called FAWO—Film and Allied Workers Organization—which started looking at and anticipating the restructuring of the film industry. Something that needed to be done. The whole move in culture and the arts was about anticipating the new South Africa. I was very much involved in that process. I was on the executive [board] and the production committee. We identified things like training [in filmmaking] and [targeting] previously disadvantaged groups by going into townships and actually holding film festivals. We wanted to start to getting people involved in acting and running training programs for youngsters who were excited [about] the prospect of [working] with film companies again. There was quite a lot of movement within the country.

ATM: Is that still going on now?

KH: No. What I wanted to say to you is that there were two results from that, which, if you want to ask me how to still make a change or what is good about now, there are two things. One is the National Film and Video Foundation—the NFVF, that wants to set up a legitimate structure to handle government financing that is coming into filmmaking. [This includes] grants to first-time filmmakers and funding local filmmaking. It took a long time to set up the National Film and Video Foundation, but, for me, that is one of the most exciting things that has happened. It's up and running, it's been through all the formative stages, and it is now quite solidly established. I think they are doing very good stuff. The other thing is a distribution company called FRU—the Film Resource Unit. That is one of the most exciting and legitimate things that has happened. They take themselves very seriously and run it like a business.

ATM: How has your own life as a filmmaker changed? Has the content of your films or audience changed?

KH: Yes. In 1994 after the elections, I could go to SABC and put in proposals with anybody else. So, yes, I've done work for the SABC. The past ten years, I've probably made about eighteen documentaries that have been aired. I also include M-Net [a South African subscription television network], which had its own very particular agenda and was very much aligned with the apartheid regime. So, yes, I have been able to compete with everybody else.

ATM: What about content?

KH: I've continued to focus on social and political issues. In fact, the story I told you about the SABC and my experiences with them, I made into a film called *SABC: Twenty Years, the Untold Story.* I looked at the way SABC was politically controlled and some of the things that were going on behind the scenes. I've made films about street kids, homelessness, child abuse, woman abuse, behind the scenes in South African prisons, the transformation and about the medical sector, focusing on the Johannesburg hospital, for example. That hospital used to just serve the privileged white community. Now it has to actually readjust and cope with a much bigger constituency. I've made films about AIDS. One of my films is called *Unfinished Business,* which looks at a young man who did not return from exile but was executed at an ANC detention center in exile.

ATM: So you are not a friend of the ANC?

KH: Um . . . no. Let me go back a bit. In that period in 1990 to 1994, I was saying how difficult it was because the ANC came back. I did strike up a relationship with one John Samuel, who is now the gatekeeper to Mr. Mandela's foundation. He was heading the education desk, and I made three films for him on education—early childhood education; the transformation of education, and adult education. I made a short, twenty-minute documentary for them which was used in their election campaign. I was really pleased to do it because obviously it was all about Nelson Mandela, and I was totally in synch with that. But, no, no, I remain independent. I'm not anti-ANC at all. Should it come to a difference of opinion, I would not be scared to state that opinion and to state it in the film and defend it. In fact, nobody here has ever come to me [to question what I do].

ATM: That sounds like a democracy at work. What is the environment in general for filmmakers in South Africa now?

KH: I'm not quite sure where to start on this, but I think there is a sense in some quarters that you've got to be careful what you say. I just think it's nonsense. I understand where the feeling comes from, but I certainly have not experienced it. I do have a major problem with the way the press works in this country. I think some of the reporting is atrocious. I think that stipulation easily becomes fact. At the same time, I have a problem with Thabo Mbeki's piousness, saying, "We are the good guys. Why are you attacking us?" So I think it's a little bit of both, but there are definitely situations where I can understand [why the ANC objects] because of things that have been said and wrongly reported. What exacerbates this is the sudden vocalness of the conservative white community. Before 1994, it was absolutely silent.

Now, all of a sudden, they are new activists. [As for me], I've always operated as an independent. I've tried to preserve my journalistic integrity, which I value very much. I have never been a party member—my films haven't reflected being a party member, but [in the new government] nobody has ever challenged me. They didn't come back and say, "Excuse me, if you do this, you won't work again."

KEVIN HARRIS is one of the most prolific documentary filmmakers in South Africa. Embarking upon a filmmaking career in 1978, his work has earned international recognition and several nominations for film awards. He is an independent filmmaker whose subjects cover mostly social and political themes.

Partial Filmography

***This We Can Do for Justice and for Peace* (1981).** South African Council of Churches oppose apartheid.

***Struggle from Within* (1985).** Made with the South African Council of Churches, this film shows efforts to oppose specific apartheid policies.

***Namibia, No Easy Road to Freedom* (1989).** Made during the Namibian War, *Namibia* examines the harsh conditions experienced by the civilian population.

***Namibia, Rebirth of a Nation* (1990).** In the follow-up to the 1989 film *Namibia, No Easy Road to Freedom (1989),* the Namibians engage in rebuilding their country after war and colonial domination.

***No Middle Road to Freedom* (1991).** A memorial service held in a Soweto church commemorates those who died at the hands of the South African Defense Force attack on an ANC refugee camp.

***Education: A Basic Human Right* (1992).** Maintaining two separate educational systems, one white and one black, costs in terms of loss of human potential.

***Of Courage and Consequence* (1995).** The great changes that have occurred are the subject of interviews with young South Africans who opposed each other during the apartheid era.

***Somebody's Child* (1996).** The tragic lives of street children in South Africa are examined.

***Judgment Day* (2001).**The Israeli-Palestinian conflict is compared with the South African conflict in making a universalistic claim about the effects of war.

Letebele Masemola Jones

> I think that film is critical to this [new] environment—a transforming environment needs images of itself that it can pass on to future generations that show African life, where our children and our grandchildren can feel proud of being who they are—South African and black.

AUDREY THOMAS McCLUSKEY: Letebele, thank you for meeting with me. Tell me, what kind of projects have you been working on in recent years, and are they influenced by the political conditions in the country?

LETEBELE MASEMOLA JONES: I've been working in film now for about eight years in South Africa and involved in the development of film through two projects, a drama project called New Directions, which deals not only with filmmakers in South Africa but emerging filmmakers in a couple of other countries on the African continent. I think that film is critical to this [new] environment—a transforming environment needs images of itself that it can pass on to future generations that show African life, where our children and our grandchildren can feel proud of being who they are—South African and black.

ATM: Would you expand that response a bit more?

LMJ: A lot of new images have come about in the last eight to ten years. We are beginning to see ourselves more on the screen—not so much in film but definitely on television, and it's a very strange little thing that while we do have stars, they are mostly television stars. They are not film stars. Big stars of television film don't necessarily translate to the big screen for one reason or another.

ATM: Do you think that television, as a more accessible and popular medium than film for black people in this country, will always be the most popular? Is this a unique development, or is it something that will change over time?

LMJ: I'm hoping that it's something that will change over time. I think most filmmakers are hoping that. Certainly, television is the medium that's more accessible for people across the country. Even here [in Johannesburg], cinema isn't an area that is traditionally available to blacks; you will hardly find any cinemas [in the townships]. Cinemas are in the white areas—there's certainly more in the white areas. And while people do move—do go to the cities—it's a very small number of black folk that actually migrate to the cinema. I couldn't even put it in the simplest terms, the number is so miniscule.

ATM: Is this true even for the Hollywood blockbusters?

LMJ: Absolutely. I think they do go and see those films more, anyway. Most of those films get good distribution. The big distribution companies control those films, whereas they don't necessarily [control] local films. They put very little into the film advertising or the previews, so distribution is really difficult with local films for local filmmakers.

ATM: Does that mean that you may find the most innovative and high-quality work being done on television ?

LMJ: Not necessarily. I think there's some great film work that's happening, and some great filmmakers who have been working the last ten years—black filmmakers who normally never had a chance to be involved before 1994 in the making of a film, either as director or producer. There are lots of people on the filmmaking landscape now.

ATM: Can you name some of the notable ones?

LMJ: Yes, among the key directors I would say Zola Maseko, Dumisani Phakathi, Teboho Mahlatsi. He's amazing. I think he's one of the most powerful film directors in this country. Very young. Very talented. Xoliswa Sithole, a female filmmaker—a black woman. She did *Screaming Silent.* It got a lot of attention. It's certainly a good pool of talent out there. I'm sure that there are even younger ones that are beginning to come up now. I just recently finished working on a television documentary series under the banner *Stories of Freedom.* Some were directed by new filmmakers, and some were directed by experienced filmmakers. Each director created very personal documentaries on their lives in the last ten years.

ATM: Very interesting. Probably many parallels to the changes taking place in South Africa. How will these be broadcast?

LMJ: They'll be broadcast on SABC-1 [South African Broadcasting Corporation], which is our public broadcaster—one of the three in public broadcasting channels. A lot of the filmmakers have been invited to film festivals around the world since we launched the project. We actually launched at the Berlin Film Festival earlier this year.

ATM: So the individual filmmakers were invited to submit proposals for their own town narratives?

LMJ: Exactly.

ATM: Was this a very diverse group?

LMJ: Very diverse. Well, mostly black and white, actually. [*Both laugh.*]

ATM: That used to constitute a diverse group in America but not anymore! [*Both laugh.*]

LMJ: In South Africa as well! These films were very, very personal stories in some cases. While they were not exactly political stories, the personal was actually quite political, so you've got stories that give you a background and an idea of what even the political landscape has been like—that the people seem to react in a way they haven't been over the last ten years. They were really interesting stories, great stories from around the country.

ATM: Yes, your name keeps coming up as I talk with other filmmakers.

LMJ: Well, yes. I have mentored quite a lot of the younger filmmakers, even in some other African countries, and I have produced several films and about twenty-five shorts in the last few years, including two features, and served as executive producer. I just finished working as a producer on a documentary project about the creation of Freedom Park, which was formed to remember and recognize those in the struggle for freedom in South Africa.

ATM: Please tell me more about Freedom Park.

LMJ: Dr. Wally Serote has been putting on this ceremony to promote the cleansing and healing process. What happens is that [participants] go out to different provinces where South Africans fell during the struggle. They have ceremonies in recognition of those who died [for freedom]. It includes the slaughtering of the beast—spilling its blood, and that's supposed to be a cleansing effect—and they actually do it in places that were really contentious—where people actually fought for freedom.

ATM: Is this a government initiative?

LMJ: Yes, it is a presidential project located in Pretoria [the capital]. It was set up by the president of this country. The Freedom Park Trust was set up to implement the whole idea.

ATM: Are these cleansing ceremonies based on cultural practices?

LMJ: Yes. On African cultural [practices], but they invite different faiths to participate.

ATM: Who is being cleansed, and who is being healed?

LMJ: Everybody. The nation.

ATM: Do you invite people who may have been on opposite sides of the struggle?

LMJ: Absolutely. Everybody. Everybody needs to be cleansed and healed.

ATM: But does everybody come?

LMJ: Not many have, particularly whites. Very few! [*Both laugh.*]

ATM: Why do you suppose whites don't generally participate?

LMJ: One gets the feeling that we as black people are doing more reconciling than white people, and that's just across the board in this country. Why that is, I don't know. Whether they are not interested or because this country didn't blow up in flames like they thought it would before the '94 election. I don't know what it is or if they just couldn't care less. That [reconciliation] was Mandela's big thing throughout his five-year [presidency]. It has been mostly from our side.

ATM: That's what I've heard most about since I've been here—that reconciliation has been a one-way street. I wonder about film and its role in this reconciliation process. What about the concept of restorative justice?

LMJ: I can't think of anything offhand that addresses it directly. I mean, one of the things that Freedom Park has been doing is consulting with different groups within society—religious leaders, the youth, handicapped organizations, trade unions, people in different areas of society—about how they want to be represented at Freedom Park. They've been archiving these responses on tape and film, asking, "What does Freedom Park mean to you?" They're trying to get people to come together. I can't honestly think of any films offhand that really have addressed the topic in that way.

ATM: Is it okay that films have a certain historical amnesia, no acknowledgment of the past?

LMJ: I find that very disturbing. [Film is] still very white male dominated. Often there'll be people saying, "Oh, we shouldn't be making films about the past. Let's make films that will be purely for the international [market]," and I'd think to myself, "What exactly does that mean?" For me, a lot of those stories haven't been told, and they need to be told, because we must never go back there again, for starters. If we don't have the films that represent some of that, we can easily go back there at any point in the future, and we don't want that. I remember less than a year ago I went to a film festival, and a white woman filmmaker said to me, "You should forget about films like that. People should just get over apartheid."

ATM: How did you respond?

LMJ: I was with several other filmmakers. Every single one of us at that table came down on her like a ton of bricks, and by the time she left that table, her eyes were red with tears because she said the wrong thing to the wrong people.

ATM: It was just an offhand remark, showing her true feelings.

LMJ: Yeah. There is also a cultural-identity crisis going on. White people in Africa are not European, but some *feel* like Europeans in Africa. When they talk about making films that appeal to the international market, they are talking about films that you find in Hollywood. We are not Hollywood. This isn't Hollywood, this is South Africa. We have our own stories that are very different from the stories of people in Hollywood. If people pick them up around the world, that's nice, but we should appeal to ourselves first and create our own images of ourselves.

ATM: You don't go looking for universal appeal. You invoke it through rendering your own human experience.

LMJ: Exactly.

ATM: Is there a difference in taste for film among black and white audiences?

LMJ: I think even the black audience is directed toward [America] because of the films that they get to see in the theaters. There's nothing else, really. They don't put South African films in South African cinemas. It is very rare that they do.

ATM: But even having said that, my experience in America is that oftentimes films that you expect will do well or *should* do well among black audiences don't necessarily. Black audiences in America have not always embraced well-intended black films.

LMJ: That's true. I'm not sure what the answer is, but I guess that if people are exposed to it, they will develop a taste for it. There are a lot of Indian films in South Africa at the moment that are actually very popular. That's something that is a recent development. These so-called Bollywood films are getting on the big screen, and they are staying there because there's obviously an audience for it.

ATM: Is this a mostly Indian audience? When it comes to Hollywood, those tastes have been cultivated over time, and Hollywood is good at reproducing and referencing itself. Having said that, isn't it possible to have a more diverse selection of films available? Is that what people want?

LMJ: I wouldn't say so. I think that our stories are quite unique. They are very different from a lot of stories that are being told. Even the action drama series that I worked on was made by another black filmmaker, I can't remember who it was. There were about three of them, and they were different. The films here are not like a lot of African films that you see in the northern part of Africa where everything is very rural. A South African doesn't necessarily relate to a village. He [or she] might relate to Soweto, but that's not a rural area. Yet, people, including a well-known film distributor [whom I will not name], act like they expect to see some cows coming down from the valley in all African films. I am actually very irritated by that.

ATM: Why do you think that is? Are these built-in assumptions the same ones that limit women filmmakers?

LMJ: I think there are structures that have been established to deal with that, such as the [National] Film and Video Foundation of South Africa. It was started by the Ministry of Arts and Culture to try to coax change, open up the film industry, and demystify it so that [more] people—women and younger blacks—get into the industry and change these assumptions. This money gives them support to make their films. Yet, in some cases, you can't even walk through the door, literally, because you know that you don't have what it is that they are looking for.

ATM: Well, tell me this: despite these handicaps, what has made the difference for you? How have you been able to walk through the door and accomplish the many things that you have done? There are very few women, black or white, who have done this.

LMJ: I'm still struggling to walk through the door! [*Letebele laughs.*] I'm taking things to another level now. I was in a very fortunate position. When I first started in film in South Africa with the television network—it's a private production network in South Africa—and it was at a point where they were interested in expanding into black Africa. They never had black people as employees really. They had employees who we called colored or mixed race and Indian women who were secretaries. That was about it. It got to the point where they could no longer afford to be doing things like that and had to look for people who had some kind of track record or knowledge and experience.

ATM: So it was partly timing?

LMJ: I think I was in the right time at the right place. Even with the opportunity, I didn't think they necessarily did this out of the goodness of their hearts. There was an expansionist strategy into the rest of Africa eventually. I worked really well for them. I remember that a lot of people would say, "I'm the only colored person here," because a lot of the white people thought it was for black people only. Some of the black people thought it was for white people only, so it was ridiculous. I remember trying to rally black filmmakers and get them involved. I said, "Whatever you think of these people, here's an opportunity to get into film. There is nobody who is going to give you this opportunity—a half million rand (US$66,573) to go and make a short film. So take it! It doesn't matter where [the money] comes from. Take it, and run with that opportunity. Take your film at the end, and move along from there! At least it will give you something." Some took advantage, some didn't.

ATM: What have the obstacles been for you?

LMJ: There have been obstacles. It would have been great to be more involved in feature-film production. The biggest obstacle there is finance obviously.

ATM: Is that still a goal for you?

LMJ: Oh, absolutely. Definitely. I would like to get into it, but I'm moving my business into a different level where I'm coming together with two other women, and we are setting up a strictly film company. We want to do film development because there are a lot of film [companies] that are coming into this country and making films. We'd like to be of service to some of those companies.

ATM: In terms of locations, infrastructure—

LMJ: Exactly that. Setting up the whole production crew for them, those sorts of things. While that doesn't give much satisfaction on a personal level, it, hopefully, will build up some capital and pay the bills and, hopefully, will enable us to eventually do our own thing. We all have our own ideas that we are quite passionate about.

ATM: Are these other two women also filmmakers?

LMJ: Yeah. One is South African, and the other is an African American married to a South African. Together, we have lots of different experience. We plan to work in other countries on the continent—the African continent—as well. I think it's clear with the resources that three of us have that we will make quite a strong team.

ATM: What's the name of your company?

LMJ: It's called Ayate Films, which means abundant.

ATM: You're enacting a pan-African dream—working together with Africans from different places to form your company. I was really surprised by some of the stereotypes that people in South Africa have about African Americans—and certainly African Americans have them as well. Your company, I think, has transformative possibilities.

LMJ: Absolutely. We are grateful.

ATM: I'll conclude by asking you about the future of South African filmmaking. How would you assess the prospects at this particular time?

LMJ: I'm an optimist. I would like to think that it's very positive prospects, because I think there are incredible stories to tell in this country, within our borders that will interest people everywhere. In fact, this Project 10 series that I've just completed, the interest it has gathered around the world, actually proves that. A lot of those stories are very personal South African stories, but they translated across the world and have had really great comments coming back from the festivals. I'm very positive about the South African [film] industry. I think more needs to be done on the financial side—we need more financial support because black filmmakers are so much more behind than their white counterparts are. It is very difficult as a black filmmaker to be making films and not do anything else. Yet, there's also an abundance of talent here as well.

If you just think of theater during the apartheid years and what theater did and translate that same talent to the screen, it gives you an idea of what film can do. We have incredible stories, amazing stories to tell. We need to be in a position where we can tell those stories ourselves. Nobody else is going to do it. One of the myths, even among some filmmakers, is that the only stories that will travel are the stories that you see on CNN and the BBC—[about] babies on their mothers' back with flies around them. While that does exist—I don't deny that it exists on this continent of ours—there is so much more that people haven't even begun to tap into that people don't know about. If they just scratched a little bit beneath that, they would see the abundance of talent and stories that we have to offer.

LETEBELE MASEMOLA JONES is a pioneering film and television producer with a long list of innovative television and film projects to her credit. She completed a Bachelor of Arts, cum laude, in film and video and a Master of Arts degree in international relations at Boston University. Since returning to South Africa, she has produced several film and television projects and has served as a prime agent for advancing film production in South Africa and other parts of the African continent, especially as mentor to a new generation of black filmmakers. She also serves as director of program production for the African Broadcasting Network (ABN), the fastest-growing TV network in Africa. Its objective is to fund, produce, and broadcast locally produced content.

PARTIAL FILMOGRAPHY AND TELEVISION PRODUCTIONS

Project 10. The television series focuses on contemporary issues in South Africa.

***Flying over Purgatory* (2002).** This stage production starred Ruby Dee and was directed by Ayoka Chenzira.

***Mama Africa* (2002).** The anthology of short films showcases emerging African filmmakers in several different countries.

Freedom Wasn't Free (2004). Human elements of the struggle to end apartheid is depicted.

***A South African Love Story: Walter and Albertina Sisulu* (2004).** The long-married freedom fighters are documented.

Ntshaveni wa Luruli

> I decided to come to South Africa and be part of laying down the foundation of the film industry. That was my romantic dream after apartheid. I would come back here, and there would be all this creative energy in film, music, and everything.

AUDREY THOMAS McCLUSKEY: Ntshaveni, in addition to your writing and directing, you also teach here at the University of Witwatersrand?

NTSHAVENI WA LURULI: Yes, I am a senior tutor in the School of Arts. I teach and tutor screenwriting for film and television. I tutor the third- and fourth-year students.

ATM: What current projects are you working on?

NWL: I have finished my film *The Wooden Camera* [2003]. While I was on sabbatical, I went to Cape Town to make this film, which is a coproduction with French companies and the British Film Council. The National Film and Television Foundation [NFTV] here in South Africa also contributed money. Now I'm working on my third feature film. I'm going to shoot it on DV. It is my first experience working with DV. The film will be called *Selina's People.*

ATM: *Selina's People?* What is it about?

NWL: Selina is a maid. In South Africa we say domestic workers. It's about her relationship with her white employer, Marta. They have grown up together on a farm and been raised like sisters. But at the moment the film opens, Selina has decided that she wants to retire. She doesn't want to grow old with Marta. She wants to go away, raise her own children, and try to catch up because she has given up so much [of her life] in this situation. Basically, the story is about the desire of these two characters to return to the paradise where they grew up. [They learn that] paradise can only be reached through memories, but it cannot be re-created.

ATM: Is this the time period of apartheid that they want to return to?

NWL: Yes, but that's the whole thing, because Marta's family, who employed Selina's parents, lived in such a way that they were oblivious to what was happening around them. Their situation was like a paradise to them. The farm is surrounded by mountains and very isolated. Their only contact with the outside world was through radio and television.

ATM: They created their own culture.

NWL: Yes, but as they grew up, Marta went away to boarding school and to the university. She was exposed to the real world. This real world told her to view her relationship with Selina not as a sister but as a master-servant relationship. Selina also had to adjust when she got married and was exposed to the real world.

ATM: Is it based on a true story?

NWL: No. It is fiction. I wrote it and plan to direct it.

ATM: Do you think about the audience as you are writing and directing?

NWL: Yeah, yeah, I always do. For this film, the theme is more philosophical, but anybody who sees it can relate to it. I mean we all want to live in the past—especially the good part of our past—and in some ways we think that we can return to it.

ATM: How is this theme different from *The Wooden Camera*?

NWL: *The Wooden Camera* is a postapartheid story. It's about two kids who grew up together as friends—black kids in a township. One is homeless, and the other one has parents. One day as they are playing together next to the railroad, they come up across a dead body, and next to that dead body is a briefcase. They open the briefcase and find drugs, cocaine, and other things. There is also a gun and a video camera. One of the boys chooses the gun; the other one takes the video camera. This act seals their destiny.

ATM: Ah!

NWL: The story follows how their lives unfold. One becomes an artist, the other one, a gangster.

ATM: You're making a philosophical statement here as well.

NWL: Exactly. What I am saying applies to youth today in postapartheid South Africa. The main characters are fourteen-year-olds. They were babies when [Nelson] Mandela was released from jail. They don't have a sense of apartheid like we do. I belong to the generation of what we call the strugglers. These are our kids, and their struggle is to keep the democracy going, to make it work. Yet, because of the sociopolitical situation, there is so much violence in South Africa. I'm saying to the youth of today that they have a choice. They can either take this democracy further—hence the life of an artist or take the fatalistic view that has destroyed so much of the continent.

ATM: What has been the response so far?

NWL: It has been traveling around in film festivals in Europe, mainly. So far it has picked up four awards—in Berlin, Montreal, Paris, and Stockholm.

ATM: Did you also write and direct it?

NWL: It's from an idea that the French producer had, and I adapted it to a South African situation.

ATM: What was your first feature film?

NWL: My first feature was *Chikin Biznis* [1999]. It's a comedy. It's about this middle-aged man who's been working as a messenger for the Johannesburg stock exchange for years. Because of the release of Mandela and the new democracy, one day he goes to his job as a messenger boy and says to himself, "I'm tired of being messenger boy here!" Because it is a new democracy where everything is supposed to be possible, he decides to become an entrepreneur by selling chickens. He wants to come back to the Johannesburg stock exchange as an investor—not just as a messenger boy. That's the story.

ATM: You have made three films in four years. That's quite an output!

NWL: Yes, it is. It is very unusual in South Africa. At the moment, we don't have a film. The South African film industry is basically a service industry, but things are beginning to pick up.

ATM: Yes, I have seen some of the statistics about South Africa being one of the leading destination for filmmakers from abroad. Why is this?

NWL: As a service industry, we have desirable locations and well-trained technicians for foreign film companies. The currency exchange [rate] means it's cheaper for foreign companies to make films here. Cape Town is like Europe to some [foreign] filmmakers.

ATM: Does that inhibit your own development of an indigenous filmmaker?

NWL: It does. The irony is that South Africa's film industry historically is one of the oldest in the world. It started in the late 1800s, long before apartheid became law, which was in 1948. Still, there was colonialism, and blacks were viewed as inferior. Apartheid just made it official. Films that were made up to 1990 were mainly films that were from white people's points of view in which the natives were part of this beautiful location. They see the sunrises and sunsets and gazelle and lions and, of course, natives who just sing all day long.

ATM: I've seen a few of those!

NWL: Yes, it's a Tarzan [mentality]. That kind of film was a way for the settlers to entertain themselves. After 1948, the documentary films that were made espoused apartheid as a good thing. There were also films made by certain individuals in and outside the country that expressed a dissenting voice, such as films by Anant Singh, a South African of Asian descent who is now a really big South African film producer. When he started back in the 1970s, his films dealt with what happened to people during apartheid. His films were censored, and some were banned.

ATM: Were there any black filmmakers during this period?

NWL: None. For a black person to be trained as filmmaker that person had to leave the country. In the 1960s, the late Lionel Ngakane went to Britain in exile and made his films. He made very few films precisely because it was very difficult. He is highly regarded and considered the father of South African filmmaking. But resistance like that happened more in the theater than in film. You know why? Because it was cheaper. We could [perform] plays in the garage, in the bedroom, while film is very expensive.

ATM: I am glad you took time to retell that history. It is very important to understand that this did not begin in 1994. Tell me about your education.

NWL: I studied at this university [Witwatersrand] during the apartheid era. That was in the 1980s. The law of the land at the time was that no black was allowed to study at a white university. You see, there was black education, colored education, Indian education, and white education. Indian and black education were the most inferior, but the best, of course, the best was the white. When I decided to study film, this was the only place where it was taught.

ATM: How did you get in?

NWL: Every black person who wanted to study something that was not offered by the black universities had to apply for a special permission from the minister of education. I was given a hard time, because this profession was not viewed as a one suitable for blacks. They asked me why I wanted to study film. I was refused admission three times. I stacked appeal upon appeal until I finally got through. I was the only black student in the class.

ATM: Were you given a hard time?

NWL: No. Not by my colleagues, because this was a liberal university. To them I was like a newfound teddy bear. They could say, "Hey, I've got a black friend!"

ATM: When you graduated, could you get a job?

NWL: When I graduated, I got a Fulbright Scholarship—an American Fulbright Scholarship—to study in America. I studied at Columbia University.

Then I went to film school in 1985. My intention was to just finish there and work there. I wasn't going to come back to South Africa.

ATM: You weren't coming back?

NWL: That's the whole point. Until the miracle happened in 1992, nobody knew that Mandela would be released; that black organizations would be unbanned.

ATM: You were able to work in film in the U.S. for a while but decided to come home after Mandela was elected?

NWL: Yes. I decided that I was going home! I would rather make films about the things that I understand at home than live in America. In the States, there were the John Singletons, the Spike Lees, and many other directors, but the only person who was making films almost every year was Spike. With everyone else, it was hard to be black in the United States as well. Those were lessons that I learned. I couldn't go to these producers and ask them to make an African film. I would never [film] African American stories. People there are doing it, and that is their strong point. I decided to come to South Africa and be part of laying down the foundation of the film industry. That was my romantic dream after apartheid. I would come back here, and there would be all this creative energy in film, music, and everything.

ATM: It sounds like this feeling did not last long.

[BOTH LAUGH.]

NWL: After six months, I realized I'd been viewing my country through a rose-colored glass fog.

ATM: What did you find?

NWL: Well, I found it was very hard. There were no jobs. There is no film industry literally, and everybody is depending on the South African Broadcasting Corporation. I didn't know anybody to approach and say, "Hey! I have experience. I went to film school." I found myself again a stranger in my own country. White people were nervous about the fact that I'm here with this knowledge and training from abroad.

ATM: They felt threatened?

NWL: Yeah. Certainly, and black brothers looked at me and thought, "He's coming to take our jobs. He's been away for too long. We've been struggling here." Before I did *Chikin Biznis,* I was on the brink of going back to the United States to work.

ATM: What was the breakthrough for you?

NWL: I was invited to do a writing workshop school by M-Net, which is an independent cable TV. It's like HBO in the States. It was a training program for young filmmakers. *Chikin Biznis* was their project of choice. It was like everything else in the arts—being at the right place at the right time. I think it was a political move. They needed to make a feature film directed by a black person.

ATM: Do you still find that although you've made these three films in the short period of time, it's still difficult to bring together funding and resources?

NWL: Extremely! Yet, several black filmmakers have emerged in the postapartheid era. Some of them—I can count about four who went abroad to film school—have come back home to make films. Now we talk about who is qualified—I shouldn't say qualified, because qualified is almost like they went to film school, and they have experience. What I'm saying is, discounting all the affirmative action, we've been well trained. Some of us went to film school, and some stayed here. Some came back from exile. Obviously, there are those who didn't go to film school but grew up right from the grassroots in South Africa. They all have contributed to the body of work that has been produced since 1994. I mean not just quantity but quality. We have brought more international awards than all the white filmmakers combined.

ATM: Are there any women filmmakers who are on the horizon?

NWL: There are women who have made short films and who work in television. I just forget their names. You can imagine that it's even worse for black women. Here in South Africa, we're still living in a chauvinistic society, and that is part of the problem.

ATM: Some of their names will hopefully soon be remembered and be added to the list of award winners you just described. In the meantime, does the international recognition that you have achieved mean the same thing at home?

NWL: Now you just said it! The funny part of it is that in South Africa, we don't have an audience for South African–made films. That's the biggest problem. Now, other people are going to give you a whole lot of reasons why. The thing that we all agree on is that during apartheid, there were no cinemas. We've got about six million people right now, and you'd be hard pressed to find one single theater—movie theater. Do you understand? That's a problem here. In the suburbs, there are cinemas everywhere. In fact, they are closing down some because they can't fill them. I need someone to explain that to me.

ATM: What is your explanation?

NWL: Well, black people don't have enough money to go to the theater. We are facing about 30 percent unemployment in South Africa. It's even worse in rural areas, even for white people there's one or two cinemas [where they live]. Rural people don't have [public] art, just a recreational hall. Take a township like Soweto. Since Johannesburg is the economic engine of South Africa, you would expect that a black person living in [the nearby township of] Soweto would be financially and economically better off than anywhere else in South Africa. Not so. In order for Sowetans to watch films, they've got to [catch] trains or taxis to come to the city theater, and the tickets are very expensive. They've got to pay just like rich people in the city. You have to go there at specific hours because you can only go there between two and five, taking into consideration the violence here in South Africa. It is only now that we are able to even know—ah, there are actually black writers and black African filmmakers like Ousmane Sembene.

ATM: The self-designated father of African cinema. Is he well known here?

NWL: Not yet because his films are not shown. Where would they show them? African films don't make money. White people don't watch them. Even in America, white people don't watch Spike's movies. There's only a handful of educated liberals who do. In South Africa, 80 percent of the people have no access to cinema. An intelligent businessman would say, "Well, let me invest in that because that's where I can make money."

ATM: There's a disconnect between the arts and business communities.

NWL: There's a disconnect. We have not changed no matter what people say. It has been ten years, and white people are still complaining about things. [Yet,] they are the ones who have work. They are the ones in top management in this economy. They are still holding the economy. They have their houses, their maids, but they are still complaining. It's not good.

ATM: Some blacks have become quite wealthy, too.

NWL: Well, there are one or two people. Even the States is like that. There are tokens all over. Still, they complain about affirmative action!

ATM: Ntshaveni, isn't there something that you can do about this simply because black people are the majority, unlike blacks in America?

NWL: That's what we say. We have to take our films to the people—

ATM: Cultivate an audience? Distribute your own films? Think about new paradigms?

NWL: Yeah. Exactly. The challenge is to shift the paradigm. What you are talking about is happening in Nigeria. Nigeria produces made-for-TV films on video. You take a video camera and shoot it. The quality is terrible, but people are buying it like they can't get enough. That kind of market is not yet here, and it would not work in South Africa.

ATM: It would not work here? Why not?

NWL: Because of the mentality of the South African consumer—black people. They want quality, like African Americans. They want Spike [Lee]—the real thing—not this kind of stuff. The [people] in the township want to see Hollywood [quality], which [my friend] calls Hollyweird. [*Both laugh.*]

ATM: What do you see happening in the next ten years in South African film?

NWL: The government [must] get involved directly. I'd really like to keep the government away from film as much as possible, but there are certain places where the government has to intervene. The government will say we need to use the money to build clinics and schools. [Most people will] agree. But what are we talking about? Two million rand? That is about two hundred thousand U.S. dollars to make a movie. Sure, there are certain social needs that the country has, but the truth of the matter is the amount of money that the government pumps in sports development is unbelievable, much more than a mere two million rand.

ATM: Speaking of sports, I witnessed the celebration following South Africa's successful 2010 World Cup bid. They pulled out all the stops to win that premier sporting event. But that event is viewed as an economic engine for the country.

NWL: Yes! "It's the World Cup, man!" The government actually has made it a priority to force white people to let black kids to play rugby and to integrate the sport. Now, from my point of view as an artist, I remember that during apartheid when the press was silent, it was the artists who kept the world aware of what the political situation was in South Africa. It was the poets, the artists. It was theater, film, music. Now that we have succeeded in [ridding ourselves of apartheid], we are getting a kick in our butts. The cabinet minister for the arts was the last one that the president thought about.

ATM: An afterthought?

NWL: You know that! An afterthought! Do you know that we have nine provinces in South Africa, and each province has a minister of arts and culture? Here in our province in Johannesburg, I do not even know who the minister of arts and culture is. What does he or she do? The only time I see these people is when they come and bury us. . . . When an artist dies.

ATM: Well, there a National Film and Television Commission that supports artists.

NWL: Yes, but it is not well funded. In the States, I could go to Chemical Bank and ask for a loan. In South Africa, the business mindset when it comes to entertainment is that it's not something to invest in. But sport—if I was a cricket player, I would be getting offers.

ATM: Maybe you should do a film about sports.

[Both laugh.]

NWL: Oh, yeah. The arts are really treated like a stepchild. The government has to intervene. All these Hollywood films that come here and all these videos that we buy, there has to be a tax on it. Why not? For every rental, there could be a five-cents tax added. That money could be put in the national endowment for the arts. They tax other imported stuff, but when it comes to entertainment, they don't tax anything.

ATM: That sounds like a good idea.

NWL: The government has to be forced to [support the arts]. The arts are the soul of any society. The funny thing is if Queen Elizabeth comes to South Africa to visit, suddenly everybody thinks of the arts. The World Cup is coming. Who is going to open the [ceremony]? I was called to go to London to open my film for the commonwealth festival. I went there with my heart heavy because I said, "Well, yeah, I'm holding my country's flag. It's a South African film, and here I am [in London showing it]." When it matters, the country wants to send me there. I nearly said, "Why don't you send rugby or soccer [players]." [*Both laugh.*] Mandela stood in front of sixty thousand rugby fans, and everybody white and black came together. We have this false sense [of ourselves because people] are joining hands and singing, "We Are the World." The struggle is not over.

NTSHAVENI WA LURULI was born in Soweto in 1955. He was one of the first blacks admitted to the University of Witwatersrand School of Arts. He received a Master of Fine Arts degree in screenwriting and directing from Columbia University as a student of Milos Forman. He worked with Spike Lee on several films in the early 1990s. Since returning to Johannesburg, he directed two films while teaching scriptwriting at the University of Witwatersrand. He has since left the university.

FILMOGRAPHY

***Chicken Biznis* (1999).** A man, feeling empowered by the new democracy, leaves a menial job at the stock exchange to become a seller of chickens.

***The Wooden Camera* (2003).** Two young boys find a dead man's attaché case containing a camera and a gun.

Norman Maake and Tongai Furusa

Norman Maake

Tongai Furusa

> It was just two [black] kids in the classroom. The certainty of your voice being heard was diminished. I think a lot of my desire to make films was about that—about finding a voice.
>
> —Norman Maake

> The future lies in people who have decided to continue despite the fact that they have no money or not enough resources.
>
> —Tongai Furusa

AUDREY THOMAS McCLUSKEY: I am chatting with Norman Maake, filmmaker, and Tongai Furusa, film editor—two enterprising and up-and-coming young members of the film community here in Jo'burg [Johannesburg]. I want to begin by having each of you talk about your own work and the project you're currently working on. Norman, would you begin?

NORMAN MAAKE: I started at film school [the South African School of Motion Picture Medium and Live Performance (AFDA)], where we made my first film. It was a student project called *Home Sweet Home.* I also made a film called *FiFi,* which screened locally. But more important, *Home Sweet Home* went into festivals, which is what gave me a chance to expand and do more films. I got to make another feature film called *Soldiers of the Rock,* which was recently released.

ATM: Is it a full-length feature?

NM: Yes. We did it through the film school, using the school's cameras and students as support. We didn't need much money. It is about mine workers in South Africa and was shot underground. It was very low budget, and M-Net [a South African subscription television network] gave us the money. It took us four years to complete.

ATM: Who else was involved in the project?

NM: It was the whole school.

ATM: How were you chosen to direct this production?

NM: Because of *Home Sweet Home.*

ATM: OK, *Home Sweet Home* opened up the opportunity for you to direct. What is it about?

NM: It is about a young woman who had been studying in the States. When South Africa is liberated, she comes back home. She's thinking that people are free, and she wants to be part of the new society. But when she returns, she finds a different reality. She discovers new things that happened during the struggle. She discovered that her father was a gang lord, her brother was in a gang, and lots of people were just trying to get rich. She ends up questioning the meaning of freedom. What do you do? What is true freedom? Is it something that someone says that makes you free? So she has to adjust her views and start all over again—to find freedom.

It was fortunate that the time we made it was 1999, five years into the liberation period, and the society was still divided. White people didn't know about life in the townships. Nobody understood the problem of the township. So, for us as young filmmakers, it was great to expose that world, and at that time, it was a fresh world. I think that was why the film was a success. It is thirty-three minutes long.

ATM: Did you write the film as well?

NM: Yes, and because of that, people got excited and said to me, "OK, make *Soldiers of the Rock* an official project of the film school."

ATM: Norman, what inspired you to go to film school in the first place?

NM: That's a hard question. I could never answer that question.

ATM: Why not? Did you just wake up one morning and say, "I'm going to be a filmmaker"?

NM: Yeah, it sort of ended up that way. We grew up in a transitional time, my generation in the township.

ATM: Soweto?

NM: No, Alex [Alexandra]. We were the guinea-pig babies for transformation. I had Bantu education my first seven years, then I changed to multiracial education after 1994.

ATM: So you experienced both sides?

NM: Yeah. It was a big mess-up, because I had attended a school where everyone was black, and I was switched to a school where almost everyone was white. It was just two [black] kids in the classroom. The certainty of your voice being heard was diminished. I think a lot of my desire to make films was about that—about finding a voice. I grew up with those politics, with being in a school where people say, "You're not clever because you can't speak English," although you have your own first language that you can speak perfectly, and no one else can.

ATM: How did the last phase of your schooling—the multicultural schooling—affect your outlook?

NM: I suffered in that system. I suffered to a point where I didn't want be [a] good [student]. To me, I'd be failing.

ATM: You didn't want to be a good student? What do you mean?

NM: I didn't want to get an A in English or Afrikaans because it would be backwards. Why would I want to excel if these guys think they're clever? So I did enough just to get by.

ATM: You were resisting, being subversive. That often happens when school is seen as part of an oppressive and dehumanizing system. In the U.S., some educators call it "disidentification." But this, of course, has its own consequences.

NM: Yeah. It meant pretty much that at the end of high school, there were no options for me. I could not be a doctor. [*Both laugh.*]

ATM: You still had ambition, of course.

NM: Exactly. I didn't think about that when I was in school. All I thought about was fighting for my rights and saying, "This is wrong!" I was fighting with the teachers all the time. I became a hassle.

ATM: Did you feel prepared for film school?

NM: It was good, because when I went to film, I was used to nagging [people] and standing up for my views. I would protest if something wasn't right. So in a way, it was natural. In film school, [my resistance and questioning] were recognized as talent. I was someone who everybody else found irritating. I did not conform with everybody.

ATM: You were fortunate to find a channel for your talent. I can imagine that many young men and women with talent have given up on the system, or the system gave up on them.

NM: I guess it works both ways. I think a lot of [what I felt about being oppressed] is in *Soldiers of the Rock.*

ATM: The film is about miners? Black miners?

NM: Yes. It's actually about a couple of black miners who, when their mine is closed down, one of them hears that there's a black-empowerment initiative that will help them organize so they can own their own mine and get the money to start. Because they've been working for someone else all this time, how are they now going to change their mindset, do their own thing? It's very hard. It's about dreaming, staying the same, and how much pain change causes. We get to deal with a lot of this hidden darkness within these individual characters, what they have to overcome in order to be able to change, to want to chase their dreams. It was an amazing film for me to make because I put all of my anxieties into it.

ATM: With a good result. Tongai, I want to ask you basically the same question about your inspiration to pursue a career in filmmaking. Why did you specifically choose editing as your specialty?

TONGAI FURUSA: I could start with reasons for going to film school. I used to do drama at school, so I don't know if it's the same thing 'cause [Norman] purposefully didn't get good grades. I didn't get good grades at all. Drama was what I was strongest in. I was going to go into drama, but I figured I would probably make more money in the film industry than I would trying to be an actor. The most exciting thing was when you get to film school, you do everything first. Nobody tells you you're this or you're that, you're the director, or you are the producer. You just go into film school the first year. You are working with every single aspect of filmmaking; you see which aspect you like the most and which one you are better at than the other. Editing seemed to be it for me.

ATM: What projects have you worked on thus far?

TF: I've worked on quite a few. Most of the directors I think you have interviewed—Norman [Maake], Khalo [Matabane], Dumisani [Phakathi].

ATM: So you're the man they all call?

[Both laugh.]

TF: I don't know if I'm *the* man.

ATM: Tell me, both of you trained at the same institution. When you came out, did you feel that your training was on par with everyone else? Did you feel ready for the world and on par with students who had attended film school in New York or Los Angeles or elsewhere?

NM: That was the funny thing about AFDA. As soon as you entered those gates, that was the world [you knew]. They made you believe that you were the best of the best. That's how it's always been for all of us, which is the strangest thing because we studied the same works that you study at your New York University. I remember one of the things we learned was to copy a scene—it was an American film—we copied a scene from *True Romance* [1993]. Everyone would choose which scene they wanted to shoot. Everything—lighting, performance, everything. We would watch the original scene, then the one we made, and the question would be asked—what's the difference between them? What did that movie have that the movie you tried to copy didn't have? What you learn from this is to discover your own originality. The fact that you have copied something, you don't know where it really came from. Therefore, you begin to decide for yourself. This is the creation of the director. At the end of the year, we made our own films. Some of them were great, some of them were not, but you had already started to see something which was very exciting: the world of film and what was possible. Even outside of the school where the industry was operating, we were making films for something else. It wasn't for money—it was to express yourself. It was to express the voice that you have inside. This was true whether we were from a township, the suburbs, or a farm. Our school was multiracial in that way. You could never feel inferior watching someone else's work. Because then, it would mean that you undermine yourself. Film for us came from a true place.

ATM [TO TF]: Was your experience similar, Tongai?

TF: Yeah. I can definitely agree with that. When I graduated, I did feel like I could compete. The more films you do, the more confident you become. You've got these films under your belt, but you are never really there. You begin to believe in yourself more on the competitive level. Even now, it's about my next project. I have to just keep working. I'll be able to realize whether or not I'm as good as somebody else or if our films are on the same level.

ATM: Do you get the same opportunities to work that any other South African with your talent would get, or is it still a segregated market?

TF: That's a hard question.

ATM: No easy questions!

TF: No easy questions. OK. It depends on what you're talking about. There is still the question of what part of the film industry. The opportunities that I've had range from documentaries and music videos to commercials. I can say that I have done more documentaries than a commercial guy has done, but we both still say that we are in the film industry. I could say that certain [segments] of the industry are a bit harder to break into.

ATM: Norman, you want to answer that same question?

NM: I agree with Tongai. [*All laugh.*]

ATM: You brothers are in synch! You totally agree?

NM: Yes, I totally agree.

ATM: I will put it this way: Is it a level playing field? Do you feel that you get all the same opportunities, or are you restricted in any way other than by your talent and work ethic?

NM: I think you have to look at it from where we come from to really know the answer to that question. South Africa endured apartheid where the black people were never expected to be the best at anything. Our society is still full of that, and we're trying to change that. It's hard, because there are some who have been making money from that system for years. For us, we are trying to break through this, but some people don't want to hear that. You can feel it. But the problem can be solved.

ATM: How?

NM: I don't know. I'm just saying I'm fighting to be one of those people who solves problems. The first problem is how do you bring people into the cinema? How do you shoot with more black people in the cast and crew? There are so many elements to the problem. How do I write stories about black people, for black people, and get the translation right? We're still struggling. We're struggling with the little things and with the big things, too. Of course, at this level, you need some kind of support. I mean, the support for us is not that great.

ATM: From whom are you seeking support? Do you feel that the society is not supporting you? Is it the film community or the government?

NM: That's where I can't answer you. This problem can be solved, but it's, somehow, not being solved. I know in some industries it's a lot easier. When I went to America, [I saw filmmakers receiving] support. If you make a good film, there's a general understanding that it is your talent—

ATM: Your talent is nurtured.

NM: That's the thing. You will get somewhere. Here, talent is not enough. You can be as talented as possible, but people will recognize you overseas more than here. But if you look at it, it's the system. It's not that people don't want to appreciate you, [but] what *do* people appreciate? That is the question.

ATM: It seems that you are asking the right questions.

NM: That's what we have to remember all the time so that [we] don't run out of steam and just lose it. We're still very young.

ATM: Yes, you are. Do you plan to stay in South Africa to make your films, or do you see yourself in the international film arena, located someplace else? Clearly, you wouldn't turn down international offers, but do you see yourself primarily located here?

NM: I do—in terms of my stories, but in terms of who I make those stories with and who they reach, I would like to be more international. There's this thing in South Africa—you have to make it overseas before people here believe that you are truly a star. You have to win an Oscar, then people will say, "Let's go watch him. You know what, he's good."

ATM: Does that have to do with the fact that the center of gravity for filmmaking is elsewhere right now? You have to prove yourself elsewhere before you are accepted at home?

NM: You know you haven't even gotten anywhere just in a meeting with your distributors, who are more interested in American films. Ten of the films in the multiplex cinemas [right now] are American films. So the priority is not with the local product. Who is this film made for? The distributor is asking, how are we going to distribute this film? Do I have to worry about *me* selling it, or is it about me finishing the next film that I'm working on? You've got to choose one film or the other.

ATM: You can't do both?

NM: You can't do both. That means that for the next three years, I'm out of making films. I'm into distribution, fighting, just like I fought to make the film. Fighting to get this film where it can be watched.

ATM: It's like you're a one-person team, selling out of the back of your car with your trunk open.

NM: Exactly. Somebody has to do that, though. But what does that mean? How many black people are in this country? What does it mean if we could find a market in that black audience for black filmmakers? We still don't know the power of this [market].

ATM: Well, Tongai, can you talk about your intentions and style [as a film editor]?

TF: When everything comes together, you're basically trying to put a light on each scene and make it clear. I don't know if I've got a style. I don't know if I've done enough movies for someone to say, "That's his style." It's a very funny art. It is something that you have to keep doing, keep working at. After I've done about eight movies, maybe I'll know. That's the whole thing about editing. It's about understanding people and their reactions. I don't know if anyone has a signature edit. It is something that you only know at the end.

ATM: Black characters have often been edited in demeaning ways. Are you conscious of this in your approach?

TF: I hear what you are saying. There was a point where I always wanted to show black people in a good way. In a way, that was all the emotion, but it has to come from somewhere. For example, this kissing thing. When [films] show white people kissing, it's all romantic and good. When they show black people, it is the whole jungle thing where they are ravishing each other. As an editor, you've got these visuals of black people kissing. I try to tell their story, not to laugh at them. Editing is about connection. You always try to portray everything in its truest sense. That, for me, is when the editing works at its best. You've got to show people to tell their story, because [a character's motivation] is coming from somewhere, you can't just have a neutral scene.

ATM: As the [film] editor, you can establish a context; a sensitivity, and a history to a film.

TF: You know what it could have been. Editing is about making those connections. You have to let your heart connect with the visual. So maybe a lot of [white] editors could not connect or relate [to] the fact that these black people could actually be in love and kissing. By the same token, I can't edit a corporate [film]. I don't relate. I think it's the same thing.

ATM: Why can't you edit a corporate film?

TF: It's something that I'm not connected to. As an editor, you distance yourself—you're over there, it's over here, you link this story together, and let it go. I think that once you've got that connection, there's no way you're going to portray people [stereotypically]. It's like you represent yourself. You're just shining the light back on yourself.

ATM: What about the two of you working together? Clearly, you're friends. Does that help your friendship? Does it help your collaboration? Norman, do you have to know him well [enough] to trust him with your film and vice versa?

NM: No. [*All laugh.*] I think the two have no connection whatsoever except for our love of film. When we do film, we handle difficult emotions, and even I don't know if he's been through it or not. It's a thing we never talk about. We both understand what it is about and give each other a few things from the start. We relate to the vision and where it comes from. We don't walk around every day thinking about it. People are like that.

ATM: What have you learned from your last project that you will use in your upcoming films?

TF: It's funny, because when we worked on this last project together, beginning with *Home Sweet Home* that he was talking about—to do the film that he's just finished now, *Homecoming.* It's leaps and leaps ahead.

ATM: In what ways?

TF: Like what you're talking about. . . . It's not just [filming] people. It's in finding that emotion in true reflections of the human spirit. [Norman] has gotten very good at that. So good that you're sitting in the edit suite, and you have this shot, and it's coming to another shot, and it's all in there. In that person's expression, you don't have to cut, you don't have to do anything, it's all in there. It's all the stuff that you need and you want that's going to make the film better. So I think it's just [for me to] recognize those things and for him to find and [shoot] those things. I just have to recognize it and say, "OK, there it is!"

ATM: This is my last question to you. I want to get a sense of where you think South African film is headed, say, in the next five years.

NM: I think there has been a lot of interesting things in South Africa, and I think that it may be because of the way the country has moved so quickly. The pace of filmmaking will [also] speed up. I think there's a certain originality, certain stories that South Africa still has to tell. The only enemy that South Africans have is themselves. You often hear people say, "Don't tell the story about apartheid. Nobody wants to watch that." If it's something that happened to people for fifty years, you cannot, as a filmmaker, say, "You know what? I'm going to distance myself from apartheid, and I'm going to make entertaining movies because the people are not watching." I think that if you want to make movies about fast cars, that's the kind of movies you want to make. Every form of film should be accepted as legitimate. Let's watch these films, too. This country is going to make its greatest films about the liberation of the spirit and what this country stands for. America has always made films about what it stands for. If you look at every movie, it is always about the American dream, and you can trace it back to the 1920s stock-market crash. Every single film is about believing in oneself. We can say we were in oppression, we've found peace, we've found some kind of inner peace which we couldn't understand ourselves. I think it's a South African thing to adopt cultures across the world and think of them as our own. If you look at 1950s Sophiatown, we thought we were Americans wearing [zoot] suits and looking at gangster films. After awhile, it became our own culture. We tossed out the guns, which was the oppressor's language, and made it [our culture] beautiful! I know we have yet to tell those stories. We're still just beginning, and I think twenty years from now, there will be a space for our type of films. I think the future looks good.

TF: I can say that the future of South African film lies in people that I call the "sons of the soil." It's people who love South Africa and the people of South Africa and want to let the whole world know about them. The future lies in people who have decided to continue despite the fact that they have no money or not enough resources. They do it because they love the people, love filmmaking, and want to make films. They write scripts, they go out there and look for distribution, for producers, shoot those movies, and maybe they distribute them on video. It doesn't matter. I think the real future of the South African film industry is in these dedicated people who believe in cinema.

NORMAN MAAKE is a twenty-nine-year-old who began his promising career while still a student at the South African School of Motion Picture Medium and Live Performance. He directed several notable student productions and began his award-winning film, the international hit *Soldiers of the Rock,* as a student project.

FILMOGRAPHY

***Home Sweet Home* (1998).** Corruption in South Africa in the postapartheid era brings disappointment to a woman returning from abroad.

***Soldiers of the Rock* (2003).** In a gutsy view, the hardships of men who work in the mines are examined, raising questions of reparations, landownership, and labor issues.

TONGAI FURUSA is a graduate of the South African School of Motion Picture Medium and Live Performance, whose skills and previous successes have made him a much sought-after film editor. He worked with Norman Maake on his films *Home Sweet Home* (1998) and *Soldiers of the Rock* (2003). He has also edited films by Dumisani Phakathi among others.

Kgafela oa Magogodi

Kgafela oa Magogodi

I think the time to scream is now—the time to holler is now when things seem OK—so that we don't fall into patterns that we really hated before or fall into traps that we had before. The problem with these orgies of celebration—nobody hears the scream.

AUDREY THOMAS McCLUSKEY: Kgafela, you have such a broad portfolio as an artist. You are a filmmaker, a poet, and I just saw the wonderful spoken-word theater production you directed with your students. You teach and direct. How do you describe yourself?

KGAFELA OA MAGOGODI: I can say I'm an attempted filmmaker, but I must carry on as a poet. I have performed my poetry with music. I direct spoken-word theater. I am so interested in these questions that you are raising from the point of view of a scholar. That's the long and short of it.

ATM: You also teach poetry, spoken word.

KOM: Oh, yes. I teach here at Wits [University of Witwatersrand] in the School of Arts. I teach spoken word and film studies.

ATM: Your latest theater production *Soil* opened here to good reviews. How was this project born?

KOM: That production was born out of a course I teach here called "Poetry in Performance." Annually, I take students through poetry writing and performance-skills workshops. What I intend to do is to give them a theme out of which they build poetry as in the case of *Soil.* Last year the theme was war. Our production was called *Peace War.* We've been working on *Soil* for the past few months up until its recent opening. It is a production that was born out of those workshops. Thematically, the idea of *Soil* addresses issues of land dispossession whether in South Africa or elsewhere in the world. The symbolic meaning of *Soil* is its life-giving qualities, as in the thin line between the womb and tomb and so many other questions that I think I am raising in that production, but I'm not just raising these questions for myself. It's also about other voices. The voices of the students are speaking to these themes, and I encourage them to find their own space and speak their own voices so that what comes out of the production is a dialogue, not a monologue.

ATM: Did you have a pan-African vision in the back of your creative mind as you developed *Soil*? Your production and workshop include exchange students from the U.S. along with South African students.

KOM: Absolutely. The dialogue between the students from the U.S. and South Africa is a great one. In one particular scene, there is an African American woman talking about her experiences in the ghetto and a South African maid talking about her experiences in the ghetto. It begins with some animosity because one thinks she knows better than the other. One thinks she knows the real shit, and the other thinks, "You know, my shit is bigger than yours"—that kind of crap. Anyway, in the end, they realize that in fact they are on the same page. That scene reflected how they worked it out. There is a sense of a common history of bondage, a history of resistance. I like to tap into those questions. As to whether I'm a pan-Africanist or not is another matter. But, yes, I do come from that tradition.

ATM: What kind of fissures do you see in the relationships among African Americans and Africans on the continent?

KOM: Beyond the fissures, there is a sense in which people need to understand each other a lot more. I think what you don't have is proper dialogue. A lot of times, we put up faces, and everything looks nice—"Brother, sister, what's up?" You know. Getting down. Until such a time that we are prepared to even open wounds and face realities, we can never be able to engage in true dialogue. I was walking down the street in Manhattan, and there were these brothers who I think they were black Jews or something like that. And as I was walking down the street—I don't know what is it about me that shows that I'm not American—but I'm sure there was some indication because these guys were preaching in the streets about the black movement, and one says to me: "Hey, brother, where are you coming from?" I say, "I came from South Africa." This guy then says, "You black people from Africa sold the black man to slavery." I say to him, "Why are you accusing me of selling you to slavery now?" He pulled out his Bible. "I'm not accusing you. It is the good Lord who is accusing you," he said. I laughed. I don't think this guy appreciated my sense of humor. There was a near altercation.

ATM: It is interesting that he picked you out because you are African and used the Bible to indict you.

KOM: He also said, "Anyway, we don't care about you people from Africa. That's why that chimpanzee Nelson Mandela was locked up for twenty-seven years."

ATM: Oh, no, that's terrible! African Americans really love Mandela, and most have certainly supported the anti-apartheid movement. That guy was very misinformed, ignorant. Did you read his outburst as an aberration or as reflective of the separation among African people?

KOM: I think it's ignorance because people have not, as I said, had a proper dialogue about what's happening in South Africa and what's happening in the U.S. Even with us here [in South Africa], our assumption about what African Americans seem to represent is based on this consumption culture and the Hollywood picture of blackness and what Paul Gilroy called this morning at the conference, [The Decade of Democracy Conference at Wits], "video blackness."

ATM: "Video blackness"? That's a good term for it. Black people certainly have been marketed to each other in very destructive ways. I'm wondering how you think the arts, particularly film, can be a bridge to a more constructive understanding [of each other].

KOM: I think the arts have played an important role in a number of struggles. We may be building bridges for a number of years. It would be a great thing to bring out material that will, firstly, help to facilitate the dialogue. One way of doing it is, of course, the kind of exchange programs that we have in place. We are able to see each other through reflections of the arts—but the whole thing should be organized towards a specific goal. It shouldn't be left to chance. Like, "OK, let's just meet, and then we'll see what happens." If it's geared towards a specific plan or goal, you can expect to get visible outcomes. It's what in the struggle in the eighties was called "each one, teach one." We need to teach each other things and through our artists. We need to transcend the whole minstrel scene. It's about more than showing each other teeth and smiling broadly. It's also about moving beyond that—plenty of other things that are beyond just smiles.

ATM: How does the double-voiced discourse of reconciliation play into the equation? South Africa seems committed to it on several levels. One level, of course, is the rejection of South Africa's recent history and the striving for a multiracial society. On another level, there seems to be this notion that reconciliation between black people throughout the diaspora is also necessary, as the ignorance of the brother in New York showed. Since I've been here, I've asked black South Africans how they perceive African Americans in the U.S. One of the responses that I got seemed to be shared by some others in a group of women that I was dining with. It was that African Americans have a romantic notion of Africa. They come to Africa and say, "This is the motherland. This is the motherland I want to reclaim." They [the women] seemed uneasy with that and a bit mocking.

KOM: It is complex. I was at NYU [New York University] six weeks for the summer program, and I met this guy who said he was from Holland. Then he said to me, "I have a friend in Holland who is more African than you." "How's that"? I asked him. He [responded], "Well, this guy wears these robes. He's not like you [wearing Western] jeans and t-shirts. I don't know what he eats" [but it's not what he'd see me eating]. He continued, "But he's also never been sick in his whole life." I was really shocked by his words because I didn't know that if you are African, you are not supposed to be sick. This is part of consuming this "video blackness." There is also another side to which ordinary African Americans consume an Africanness that is based on ideas espoused by European colonialists. This is a Tarzanic understanding of the African continent [derived] from Tarzan movies. These are anecdotes, of course.

ATM: Anecdotes are stories that travel well. Among Africans and African Americans, there are a lot of these anecdotes. I think they sometimes mask a desire for some kind of linkage or connection. The trick is, how can you do that in a way that is not trivial and reductive?

KOM: Yeah. Weren't the discussions that led to the adoption of the euro based on some romantic notion? But we are constantly reminded that we are being romantic [in talking about linking African people]. My attitude is that we should not be afraid to be romantic. Why should we apologize for being romantic? Being romantic is fine as long as it helps us find each other. We don't celebrate ourselves enough, and that's another problem. Half of the time, we are apologetic about celebrating our Africanness, and we need to find those connections. When you look at the history of resistance, there was a connectedness born out of struggles on the continent and in the [African] diaspora—the writings of C. L. R. James, Walter Rodney, and Frantz Fanon have, in many ways, connected us. Much of the time when we talk about reconciling, we think it's about embracing white people. We don't see the need to connect as Africans in a very serious way. I think that if we are serious, we need to build bridges through the arts. Music and film are important because they help you to understand the rhythm and feel of a people. Out of that, you begin to have dialogue.

ATM: The notion of a racialized identity has been problematic, causing some people to wonder whether it puts us at a disadvantage to name ourselves

African. Europe is an idea. But it's an idea primarily conceived in terms of whiteness. The current hostility to immigration shows that they want to keep it that way. Africa, by the same token, is perceived as a black continent, sometimes called the dark continent. Yet, you cannot overlook the fact that it is home to many whites. Do these convolutions dilute the power of race associated with place? Marcus Garvey used to say "Africa for the Africans," but that can mean Caucasians, too.

KOM: Yeah. Look, things are really complicated, and we need to work our minds through those complications. Our ideas should not be ahead of the realities that are on the ground, because we try to imagine a future where people are beginning to talk beyond blackness and whiteness. I don't know if you can just change things by weighing them differently. It is certainly a very complex wiring, and the diverse population that is here would want to claim their Africanity. The word *Africana* itself is an indication of that claim. But someone says that within that Africana, it's excluding the African, which is a very interesting thing that requires a lot of discussion. Sometimes people become African when it's convenient. You have institutions like Wits University where much of the curriculum still has Europe as the center of cultural inspiration. How do you respond to that? People have a sense of wanting to be African, but when and how do people *claim* their Africanity?

ATM: The conference that you referenced is taking place here on campus. "Ten Years of Democracy: Freedom and Its Practice" is sponsored by the European Union. I find the politics of it quite interesting. For one, I see an absence of black women scholars and a lot of abstractions floating about that seem so detached from events outside the closely guarded iron gates of the campus. This is the view of an interloper, I admit. I am a visitor here.

KOM: Yeah, I mean there is definitely a missing voice. I also don't know what it means. It's about who's got the sort of power to organize things, whose friends are in high places. It's not even deep.

ATM: Academic cronyism. But the disconnect [from the lives of everyday people] was troubling to me, even as an outsider. I want to get back to your views about what this decade-plus of democracy has meant particularly from your point of view as an artist.

KOM: Look, we are told that this is a county of miracles—the miracle of the birth of a rainbow nation. I wonder. Perhaps the greatest miracle in this country is how we have made silence an industry.

ATM: Explain that, please.

KOM: What I mean is that people see things, they don't talk about them, and they get rewarded for their silence. When you look in the arts, the voices that are promoted are those that buy into this paradigm of a rainbow nation, which is really incarcerating because you cannot go in there with everything. You have to leave some things behind and be nice. That's what the rainbow thing is about. It's about making pleasant gestures. If your art has rough edges to it or recalls things that people want to drop off the national agenda, if your art operates outside of special containers, there is a problem. On the surface, it looks all bright and beautiful, but you need to read the signs. When you look at what was happening on the twenty-seventh of April—the Celebration of Freedom—[you see] a lot of minstrelsy going on. A lot of these guys have been respected over the years, but if you are going to tell me about this country, then start from pre-1994, don't start with the day of the celebration of ten years [of democracy]. There is something wrong there.

ATM: Do you think that historical amnesia subverts notions of justice?

KOM: Yes. There are social movements in this country. Each has its own politics. Whether you agree with them or not is another matter. You have the Landless People's movement. You have the antiprivatization forum. They are raising issues around access to grain, access to land, access to water—those kinds of things. You also have this new dispensation where people are really forced to move from their homes where there were formal settlements. [This happens] without proper negotiations just because big business wants to step into the city center. There is silence about this from a whole lot of artists who should know better—who used to know better.

ATM: Are you saying that these issues are not being addressed by artists today?

KOM: There are very few people who are addressing these things. Look at what people are saying. If you don't understand this country, look at what they bring to their poetry or what they don't bring. I think most important are the silences. It is a struggle [for time and public space] for people who have an alternative reading of events in the last ten years—it is a struggle for them to be heard and understood. Some of us have to incur a lot of laptop lynching—

ATM: Laptop lynching? What is that?

KOM: I mean people writing crap about you in the newspapers and not using their names.

ATM: Has that personally happened to you? Were you attacked for your work or for any particular reasons?

KOM: No, but I was [attacked]. These things are masked. A journalist using a false name writes that I am imitating American writers, not drawing heavily from tradition. If I were to stand on stage with a spear and loincloth, that would make a difference. I guess he would like it. Then talking about me using lights—that's theater. I'm not supposed to use lights.

ATM: So, again, someone is looking for the primitive African?

KOM: Yes, and I failed him. [*Both laugh.*]

ATM: What has the reaction been to your other work?

KOM: My last play is called *i MIKE What i LIKE,* which I must say, I wasn't playing games. There were strong reactions.

ATM: You were invoking Steve Biko's legacy?

KOM: Yes, there is definitely a tradition playing itself out here, although I don't state that. I move towards a different direction because Biko was a man of his time. I'm not interested in turning him into part of this political aristocracy. I am just interested in his spirit, and then I move on. A Biko of his time would appreciate it if you engaged people about issues in the present, not simply making it a mosaic piece and misquoting, without saying anything about the present. Much of my work is about looking at contemporaries in South Africa and what I think doesn't work. [My work] also celebrates myself and the people around me. Somebody asked me why I can't balance out things. I seem to be too harsh on the government. If I have five minutes to say something, why should I waste that five minutes on defending the government? I'm not crazy. I had a very interesting conversation with a writer who said, "I like your spirit. You shouldn't let these guys sleep." I asked him what he meant. He said based on his experience, dictatorship starts in a very seductive way. It starts out with small things, and once it gets comfortable, you wake up, and you find yourself in serious trouble. My sense is that, based on his advice, I think the time to scream is now—the time to holler is now when things seem OK—so that we don't fall into patterns that we hated before or fall into traps that we had before. The problem with these orgies of celebration—nobody hears the scream.

ATM: That's a potent observation. Tell me, what connection do you see between your political ideas and your performance as a poet, and how does this relate to the market for image making in this country, the film industry?

KOM: With film in this country, I think there's a lot of exciting talent out there—the likes of Dumisani Phakathi, Teddy Mattera, and Zola Maseko, Teboho Mahlatsi, Ramadan Suleman, and so on. Having said that, when I have watched their films over the last few years, I see a lot of growth with the way they handle stories, the way they understand narrative. That is well and good. Moving to content, there is a sense of dealing with the present but to what avail? There is a sense of dealing with history but what to what avail? In my view, our filmmakers are not engaging enough. In the manner of Haile Gerima, and I'm not saying that everyone should be a Haile Gerima. But it's all cute stories—not about how the past speaks to the present in dynamic ways. But that's too hard. So you get a lot of dancing and flowery [stuff].

ATM: Are you saying their stories are not ambitious enough? Could it be a matter of resources?

KOM: Yeah. But it's all flowery, light, simple, and people are dancing and crap like that. You get a sense that there's a lot of playfulness here, which I think has to do with a similar thing in poetry, which I call the poetry of proposals. You propose to make a film about [a certain topic] to certain people, who agree or not based on what it is that you are proposing. When we are not proposing, we can never have our voices—because much of the time what comes out [reflects] whoever is financing it. It's a problem, but people still have to make films.

ATM: It sounds like you are proposing a guerrilla type of filmmaking. A filmmaking that comes from the grassroots, from the ground rather than from the suites.

KOM: There is a man, Jeffrey Mphakati, who lives in Pretoria. After seeing what was happening with the twenty-seventh of April, I had a discussion with him, because I could feel something tearing inside me. I needed an elder to show me the way. I remember him saying that an artist doesn't say "our government," he says "the government." And there's a lot of "our government" in our artists, filmmakers, and musicians. There's no sense of distance so that you can actually be able to tap into the social struggles of the marginalized; so that we can actually be able to offer a competing version of reality. "*Our* government will do this for us." You go to government offices, and much of the stuff is also patronized by the government. I'm just saying that one should enter thinking in terms of national goals. That's important because you shouldn't come out sounding like the DA [Democratic Alliance—a right-leaning, oppositional political party], which is another matter. How do you engage in government without sounding like the Democratic Alliance?

The thing is to just strike a balance. What I'm talking about is an art that honors memories of what our people fought for, whether that has been achieved or not. When you talk about the land question in this country—has it been answered? For me, there is a serious gap in knowledge—a serious gap in memory, and the arts are supposed to help fill that gap. As far as our filmmaking is concerned, I'm not convinced that there is a very clear sense of that. I'm still waiting for such a movie.

ATM: I hope you're not waiting for Godot!

KOM: Yeah! I hope I'm not waiting for Godot, because sometimes you wait forever.

ATM: To conclude, tell me about the projects that you are envisioning right now, that you are beyond the proposal stage.

KOM: Well, I'm still running in this *i MIKE What i LIKE,* a theater piece that I want to move around with for a while. It's myself, a painter, and a musician on stage at the same time just flowing from one home to another in a seamless kind of way—moving forward, coming back and forth again. Part of the movement is always forward. While I'm doing that, the musician comes occasionally to weave in melodies, and the painter captures the spirit and images that's in *i MIKE what i LIKE,* which is a project about the here and the now, and imagining the future.

ATM: Do you plan to film it?

KOM: I shot it [in collaboration with filmmaker Jyoti Mistry]. Also I plan to do a road show. Perhaps we will produce a DVD. At the moment, I'm speaking to a publisher. My book *The Second Coming,* which is a book of poetry and short stories, will soon be published. Those are two of the key projects within my artistic life that I'm sitting on at the moment. I think they will lead to other things, hopefully, more interesting things in the future.

KGAFELA OA MAGOGODI, a well-known poet and spoken-word theatre director, is a film scholar and screenwriter who teaches at the University of Witwatersrand. His work in these multiple venues, his scholarly endeavors, and his fierce social and political engagement have burnished his international reputation. He is currently completing a PhD dissertation as well as a new volume of poems and essays.

FILMOGRAPHY/SCREENPLAYS

Yeoville Blues and Valentines (1997).
Shoot First, Laugh Last (1998). (co-wrote)
i MIKE what i LIKE (2007). The work of poet Kgafela oa Magogodi is the basis of this spoken-word film, in collaboration with Jyoti Mistry.

POETRY COLLECTIONS

Love Thighs Lies (1997)
Book Revelashinz (1998)
Thy Condom Come (2002)

Teboho Mahlatsi

Teboho Mahlatsi

For me, that's been the difference, and my work is trying to capture the complexity of independence—all this freedom.

AUDREY THOMAS McCLUSKEY: Teboho, what you have been doing recently in the arenas of scriptwriting and filmmaking?

TEBOHO MAHLATSI: For the last six years, I've mainly been doing television. One of the biggest projects I've been involved with is a drama series called *Yizo Yizo,* which is slang for "This is the real thing." It's a series on SABC [the state-owned South African Broadcast Corporation] about high school kids dealing with drugs, guns in schools, and teachers who are not motivated; teachers having relationships with female students, and so forth. This is based on our research and is supported by the Department of Education. It's been a hugely popular series because the focus is on young people. In South Africa, television has largely focused on adults with lots of soap operas. To suddenly have a very gritty show focused on young people—using their own music and styles—introduced a new landscape for television programming. It is loaded with messages that show the problems while posing some solutions at the same time. It broke viewership records. Of the eleven million people who have televisions in South Africa, about four million people watched every week.

ATM: That kind of success creates a lot of pressure to keep it up. How long do you plan to stay with it?

TM: We are in the fifth and final year of the series, which is showing now. I'm moving on, trying to do a feature film. Also, I did a short film in '99 called *Portrait of a Young Man Drowning,* which has done very well at international film festivals, winning some prizes. I've also been working on music videos and commercials in South Africa, but *Yizo Yizo* has been my main focus so far.

ATM: How did you get your start as a filmmaker?

TM: I started as a documentary filmmaker. After film school, I trained with different film companies and started developing a documentary series called *Ghetto Diaries.* The concept was to give ordinary people in a neighborhood called White City small video cameras and have them do a portrait of their neighborhood. They would record themselves over a period of time using the camera as a diary. I gave them input and technical help: "You want this kind of story, this is what you need to do." It was also shown on SABC. That was my first work on television. It was a very popular documentary that landed me a second season. Then, I started to write fiction. I wrote a film script that nothing happened with and went to television. I started developing a future film project that I took to Sundance film lab last year—the filmmakers' lab and the writers' lab. Hopefully, I will film by the end of this year.

ATM: Which project did you take to Sundance?

TM: It's a feature film script called *Scar.*

ATM: What is it about?

TM: It inhabits the same territory as the TV show, capturing young people's lives and how they are defining themselves in the postapartheid environment. Young people today are quite different than the young people during the time when I was growing up under apartheid. When I was in school, we were dealing with a set of different issues. Today, music is a big thing that young people use to define themselves. So, it is like a music [video] movie. The film is about young people and music and how they celebrate their lives today.

ATM: What is the main difference that you see in the generational change that you have witnessed?

TM: During my youth, there was a lot of focus on politics because that was the everyday reality. When I was in school, there were riots all the time . . . confrontation with the police all the time, political meetings—right in the middle of the class. A teacher would be checked out to make sure she wasn't an informer, and suddenly there would be a meeting where political issues were discussed. Obviously, the democratic transition was about addressing all of that. It was about having a new government in place. The physical manifestation of politics was no longer a pressing matter. Now, the issues are much more intellectual. It's much more personal. Young people now express themselves in a different way politically. They use poetry, for instance, rather than throw a stone. Spoken word and music are how many young people communicate. [Most young people] are not interested in politics per se. They say, "I just want to be with my girlfriend and wear these pants." One can say maybe that's what's having democracy is about—that young people can be whatever they want to be, choose what they want to be. For me, that's been the difference, and my work is trying to capture the complexity of independence—all this freedom. We can do what we want to, but, then, what is that? Young people are asking themselves those questions. That is what I deal with.

ATM: What does it mean for you to be in this environment? You focus on young people, but you also are defining yourself through your work. You grew up in the eighties under apartheid.

TM: As a filmmaker, it means that I can develop a personal voice. South African cinema has always been very physical. It's all been big comedies, with mobs of young people in the street, for example. Everything is so big. In my work, I'm trying to get to the personal—a story about a father and son, a mother searching for her kid. I started that with *Portrait*, and I'm hoping with this feature film to also continue doing that. Just in terms of experimentation, there seems to be lot of magical realism in Africa, and there's a lot of literature, especially African literature, that has captured that. It hasn't really been tried in movies yet. I also want to define a new language by using some of these elements—some magical realism—because so much of African culture has that in it already, African religion and the ceremonies and rituals around that. That hasn't been done a lot. A lot of movies that I've seen in Africa focus on the rural story, and it's just a man walking. . . . I guess there are definitely ideas floating around, but I want to acknowledge two things about myself: one, I live in Africa, I was raised in Africa, but, two, I also grew up watching Western cinema. I grew up watching westerns—Clint Eastwood movies in a crowded hall somewhere in the township. I have this—I don't know whether it's conflicting or not—actually, I don't even care if it's conflicting, but I have these two things working all the time. There's so little on urban Africa. I'm much more into urban Africanism.

ATM: Why do you think there is a focus on rural Africa in films?

TM: I want to clarify this before I say it because I think some people will be offended. On one hand, I love those movies. I love [Ousmane] Sembene. He has made some great films. On the other hand, people who are giving money want to see a certain type of film. In France, they have a certain way they want to see Africa. When they give the money to a filmmaker in Africa, [it is usually] in a country that was a former colony of France. For them, it is the idyllic rural landscape [in colonial Africa] that they [reminisce about].

They don't want to see complexity. They don't want to see urban life. They want to see a perfectly imagined setting, not the damage that was inflicted. I mean in Africa, there's so much madness and manifestation of the damage that was done—that's what I like. I like that craziness in Africa. My films are not slow. My films are very fast—the way they are cut, the way they are shot. I experiment with style quite a lot, and I've been accused of being too much about form and very little about content. I'm a filmmaker growing up with these experiences. Even though I had relatives in the rural areas, I was never taken there. I was never familiar with that.

ATM: Where did you grow up?

TM: I grew up in a township in the Free State, about two hours' drive from here [Johannesburg].

ATM: What was that like in the 1980s?

TM: In the eighties, it was about young people being very angry, very confrontational—taking out their anger, burning cars, confrontations with police—that was my experience. After that, I had to leave the Free State to come to Johannesburg. I experienced a much crazier urban experience here. It was faster and crazier than at home.

ATM: How old were you when you came to Johannesburg?

TM: I was about eighteen. It was after high school. I stayed in Johannesburg at film school, and then I went to live in Soweto. That's where I developed *Ghetto Diaries.*

ATM: Which filmmakers inspired you? Whose work do you admire?

TM: It has varied from time to time [as] I started getting access to films. I began discovering films and directors, but there was a big problem of access, just in terms of cinema out there. We don't get as many films here. My film education has mostly been theoretical—just reading about movies. I will read about a movie, and it will be like two or three years before I get to see it. I've worked through different phases. I went through an Italian new-realism phase, then it was Japanese cinema [Akira] Kurosawa, those masters. Then in Africa, obviously, there is Ousmane Sembene. Luckily, I went to a film school called the African Cultural Center, which exposed me to all these filmmakers.

ATM: Is that located here in Johannesburg?

TM: Yes. I came here to go to that school. The emphasis was mostly on African and African diaspora cinema. We got to see a lot of films from Africa that otherwise I would not have seen. Films from Cuba, Haiti, et cetera, not Hollywood. It was great! That was my introduction to [filmmaking]. When I started analyzing film, it was those films. When I was nineteen or twenty years old, that's all I watched. That's what I liked. I liked Sembene and Djibril [Diop Mambéty] because he was, even then in the seventies, already doing what I am trying to do now, which is to engage with urban Africa. You look at Djibril Diop Mambéty's film [*Touki-Bouki* (1973)]—it's just a couple on a motorbike. It's a road movie, and they are trying to [get to Paris]. They're petty thieves. It's their profession. Their story is very beautiful and engaging. [Mambéty] was taking another perspective that was not just rural. He included other things that were rural like his film *Hyenas* [1992] but was his own vision of what that space is. First of all, it's a European text. It's a German play that he imported to Africa. He was really messing around with [a definition of] African cinema. He was pushing the boundaries. That's what I guess—I'm step-by-step—trying to also question, to [ask], "What is African cinema? Is it this realistic, or is it this modern? Am I still an African filmmaker if I'm working with just an urban landscape, and the people are dressing in certain ways and speaking slang?" These are the questions that have been raised in African literature. Is it African literature when you're writing in English?

ATM: Film is following literature with the same questions. Is there an answer?

TM: I would hate for there to be an answer. I would love to say it's a thing of discovery, and you should do whatever you want to do. If a young [filmmaker] wants to represent his community in a science-fiction film—cool! An African thriller is still a thriller. It shouldn't be that because you're using a Western structure or narrative it can't be African. Obviously, the main goal, the ultimate goal, is to engage with Africa.

ATM: It is that engagement that makes it African.

TM: Exactly.

ATM: There may also be a difference between how you see Africa and, say, a European filmmaker who uses an African setting. They are both African films in the sense of locale. So how would you explain the difference?

TM: I hate the idea of voyeurism, and we get that a lot. You can literally feel some filmmakers standing outside and viewing this community from a distance. It's very idealistic but not complex, this lingering on bodies and how beautiful these Africans are—it's exploitation. Not everything is beautiful and idealistic. But from the few films that I've seen made by Europeans, some are really engaging. One was made by a French filmmaker Claire Denis called *Chocolat* [1988], set in French colonial Africa.

ATM: Yes, that film has lots of subtlety and understatement.

TM: This Frenchman is a colonial official who has brought his wife and daughter to this African country. They have this servant, a houseboy. The man spends long periods of time away so the African man starts running the household when the wife begins to fall apart—drinking and not wanting to eat. The African and the young daughter develop a beautiful relationship, but the sole conflict is between the African and the wife, two people who are kind of trapped. The woman is trapped in her own world and her bedroom. She doesn't regard Africans as people. Suddenly, she starts seeing him as a person, and that complexity causes problems for both of them—that relationship would have been very dangerous. I like the way it was contained. In another movie, there would have been, like, sex all over the place with a white body and a black body, but in this movie, that was contained and restricted. You can feel the tension building, but I love the filmmaker—she never lets it explode. It exploded in its own way.

ATM: Explosive but not exploitative.

TM: Exactly. There are very few films that I've seen like that done by outsiders that really present Africans that way.

ATM: Tell me about your next projects.

TM: I've got this [screenplay] *Scar* that I will do, possibly before the end of this year, and another film that I'm developing. I'm a very slow worker—frustratingly very slow. I take time developing projects. There's one more that I want to do. I call it an African Western. It's based in the mountains of Lesotho. In winter, the mountains are covered with snow, and I want to show that as a kind of surreal African landscape. When I was a kid, I was told stories by my family who is Sotho. We have roots in Lesotho. I heard stories about these guys who were like gangsters and stole cattle from the border of Lesotho and South Africa. It was a political act for them. They saw it as a way of getting back what was stolen from them. There would be these battles with the cops as they're dragging cattle into the mountains.

ATM: Sounds familiar but different, which is what I think you're aiming at. How far along are you?

TM: I've done the treatment, and now I'm writing the screenplay. I have a lot of photos, and I've done a lot of research. I'm working with this brilliant young writer who was at University of Cape Town last year. He's doing research for me and interviewing people. He came up with a very interesting idea that we should set it during the Depression Era. That was the time when Lesotho was struck by this incredible drought in the late nineteenth century. Obviously, the need to find food drove people to desperation. So, it's a Western in the sense that the landscape has horses and blankets, and it kind of looks like a [Hollywood] Western, but it's an African story.

ATM: So what will you call it?

TM: I guess I will just call it an African Western. [*Both laugh.*]

TM: There is a Nigerian novel that I'm interested in by—God knows who has the rights to it. It's called *The Palm-Wine Drunkard* [1952].

ATM: Oh, yes, by Amos Tutuola. I encountered it first as a graduate student in African studies at Howard University three decades ago.

TM: Amos Tutuola. I like it because of the surreal elements and the magical realism in that book. This man goes onto this journey to find this tree. . . .

ATM: It would make a beautiful film.

TM: That is something that I want to pursue.

ATM: There is so much great African literature that would be great on film, especially South African.

TM: Unfortunately, in South Africa, the rights to these works get snapped up quickly. So, I'm looking in other parts of Africa.

ATM: How do you deal with funding? Is that an issue for you?

TM: I think it's an issue for everybody, especially if you want to make a different type of cinema that's not Hollywood. I mean, I have a Nigerian friend who's based in New York—Andrew Dosunmu—who's been trying to make a film in America and struggling. He's done music videos for rappers while trying to get a project off the ground, but because it's not a typical Hollywood project, he struggles. I think everybody struggles. For me, the attention from the Sundance film lab has helped. I've taken projects to the Sundance film lab in the States and worked with an Italian producer who is raising money in Italy and South America. I'll probably also get some money from the South African government. There has been a coproduction treaty signed between South Africa and Italy. It's not looking so bad. It's not bleak.

I was shooting a commercial for South African tourism, and what was nice about it was they just said, "Go out and shoot images that represent South Africa to you." I knew I didn't want to do typical landscapes and mountains. My focus was people. I wanted to shoot interesting people in different environments in the country. So it was almost like a road movie. I just went with a 35 mm camera, and I shot these beautiful images in different communities. I shot a baptism in the sea. Just finding these beautiful moments reinforced for me the idea that my movie has to be a road movie. I've done township movies in a confined space. I want to do something that opens up. I'm working with a million dollars at the moment, which is nothing. If I have to, I will shoot it in digital instead of film because I like that medium anyway and maybe transfer it into film later.

ATM: Do you find it ironic that even though you are an African filmmaker that so often your audience is outside of Africa?

TM: I'm surprised by that. I never thought that the work would translate. I took [episodes of] the new [television] series to a lot of places outside Africa, including film festivals in New York. I have been to France, Britain, the U.K., but I was particularly amazed by Americans. In Minneapolis at a film festival, I remember thinking that the people are not going to get it. It had subtitles. It's a different culture. But people were into it. They said they like the way it was shot—it was very stylistic. They were interested in the lives of these young people, and they liked the music. They asked, "Where can we buy this music?" I was so surprised by that. It is looking like the world is opening up to movies that are not just like Hollywood. I can watch *City of God* [2002] because it is a movie that can travel. I think African movies can do the same. It's time now. I feel like we can produce exciting movies that capture an audience. With *Yizo Yizo* and with *Portrait of a Young Man Drowning*, I found that people that got it. People that were truly interested. When exchange students from New York University saw *Yizo Yizo* here in Johannesburg, they knew all the characters and even put posters on the wall and acted like a cult-type following. I felt like, wow, [this exchange of ideas] can work both ways!

ATM: You sound very optimistic about the future of South African film.

TM: I've always been. Definitely. There are so many people that are participating. It doesn't feel like an old man's trap or what just used to be a white man's club. There's so many young people, men and women, black, white, that are coming in and bringing in different styles. Because of the TV show, I have been invited to film schools and universities to talk to young people here in South Africa. I see so much talent out there. The hope for me is that there is so much more to come. It's not going to be a passing thing.

AM: And your own development over the next few years?

TM: I hope to have made five or so films. I would like to teach. I have a film company called Bomb. It is a concept—to bring in young people and work with them in film. I love film, but that is not my entire life. Traveling is quite important for me, just seeing the world, seeing Africa. I live in Africa, but I don't know Africa. This is sort of embarrassing for me. You know, I've been to more places overseas than I have here in Africa. If I can make one film a year and then for the rest of the time travel, it would be great. That is what I want to do.

TEBOHO MAHLATSI was born in the Free State in 1974. He graduated from the African Cultural Centre Film and Television Course. Since then Mahlatsi has accumulated prizes and recognition for both his feature films and his pioneering television series, *Yizo Yizo* (with Angus Gibson). His awards include the Silver Lion at the Venice Film Festival, Best Director and Best Drama Series at the 1998 Avanti Awards, and the Rotterdam Festival and Cinema Tout Ecrand Award in Geneva for Best International Series. He was invited to the Sundance Filmmakers Lab in Utah to work on his last film project, *Scar.*

FILMOGRAPHY

***Ghetto Diaries* (1997).** The lives of urban dwellers are depicted.

***White City, Black Lives* (1997).** Five Soweto residents document their lives.

***Yizo Yizo* (1998–2004).** The school milieu of a black township is the setting for this controversial television series.

***Portrait of a Young Man Drowning* (1999).** An award-winning short shows the bleak life of a former freedom fighter, now the local executioner.

***Moegko and the Stickfighter* (2006).** Inspired by Mozart's *The Magic Flute* and traditional African magic, this tale of elemental conflict is set against the backdrop of Africa's majestic Lesotho Mountains.

***Scar* (2006).** A young man turns himself into a gangster in this drama about the price of reinventing a life.

Zola Maseko

Zola Maseko

> My generation of black filmmakers is the first generation of black filmmakers in the history of South Africa, and we are ten years old, so there is no tradition. There is no track record. We are making the rules as we go along.

AUDREY THOMAS McCLUSKEY: Your new film, *Drum,* created quite a buzz at Cannes [Film Festival]. What is the status of the film now?

ZOLA MASEKO: We are waiting for *Drum* to premiere as a North American release. [The premier was September 2004 at the Toronto Film Festival.]

ATM: I can infer a lot about your aesthetic and political concerns from watching your films, but can you talk about your journey into filmmaking?

ZM: Well, I think that my work speaks for itself. I'd like to think that is the best representation of me. I am a product of exile, born into an ANC [African National Congress] family. I spent a large part of my childhood in Swaziland. My parents were active members of the ANC. We then moved to Tanzania to attend an ANC school. I did my O level—high school—and left school and went to join the ANC army when I was nineteen. I trained in Angola for a year and was stationed in the frontline states for two years of the operative as a ground guerrilla. I left that in 1990 when I was twenty-three, had a son, applied to film school in England, and got accepted to a really good film school called the National Film and Television School in the U.K. I've always wanted to be a filmmaker. Always.

ATM: What inclined you towards film rather than writing—simply writing—or some other field?

ZM: Writing is too difficult. [*Both laugh.*]

ATM: Although you are certainly a writer.

ZM: Well, not really. I have to because I have some things to say, but I think the best platform for me is film—the audiovisual. That's the one that comes very naturally. I don't know where my love of film came from. [It began] very early in my childhood. I think it was an escape, really. It was this dream world that looked more exciting and colorful and more beautiful, compared to my life or my inner feelings, which were very negative. I had low self-esteem and was a very lonely, quiet child. I think it was escapism at first into this magical world [of film].

ATM: What kinds of films did you view growing up in Swaziland?

ZM: It was the [regular] American stuff—Westerns, Chinese—lots of Kung Fu movies and westerns. I was watching *The Deer Hunter* [1978] the other day, and I remember very vividly at age thirteen going to watch *The Deer Hunter* in Swaziland. This was mainstream Hollywood, and it's interesting that my first attraction to it was escapism. As I grew older and became more conscious and politicized, I began to realize the way black people had been portrayed in Western popular culture and are still portrayed in Hollywood is very, very negative and stereotypical. I started to watch the blaxploitation movies of the seventies. When I was in Tanzania, I used to watch a lot of movies and videos from all over the world. It was a very small collection, but I used to watch everything. In film school, I was exposed to European cinema, Japanese cinema, world cinema, and my influences grew. At that time, my political consciousness had also developed, and it became about defining—about telling our own stories from our own perspective. That's what [filmmaking] became for me, and that's what it still is today. A big, big inspiration for me was Spike Lee. I hadn't heard of Spike Lee because I was sort of away from the world for three years and came out in 1990. A friend of mine told me there was this black filmmaker in America who was telling black stories from black people's point of view. I thought if he could do it, I can do it. *She's Gotta Have It* [1986], *Do the Right Thing* [1989] were great inspirations for me—[I like] telling our stories from our perspectives and celebrating blackness, our heroes, our history. I like the idea of putting up our values, our stories, our legends instead of having our kids adopt Hollywood-inspired heroes and values. I wouldn't define myself as an angry black man, but it has to be done. These stories have to be told. That's where I am right now.

ATM: That being true, have you determined the kinds of films you want to make in the future? I know you have a list waiting but what are your priorities in filmmaking?

ZM: Well, there's not enough time in one's lifetime to tell all the stories that I would like to tell. I've been working on *Drum* for fourteen years.

ATM: That's almost half of your life!

ZM: Yeah. I worked on *Sarah Baartman* [1998] for seven years.

ATM: You were doing other things as well?

ZM: Oh yeah. As a filmmaker, you [often] have five projects simmering at the same time. Sometimes the universe is aligned so that this [particular] project must go, but there are projects that I've been wanting to do for a long time, and I'm slowly developing them. Still, I'm open. I'm open to any good stories. It's very difficult being a black South African filmmaker.

ATM: Why is that?

ZM: Oh, there's no support! Like many fields in our country, we black South Africans are the first generation of *anything*. The Thabo Mbekis and Nelson Mandelas were the first generation of black politicians. People in big business now were the first generation of black people in business, in *anything*. We were denied *all* of these opportunities in the past. My generation of black filmmakers is the first generation of black filmmakers in the history of South Africa, and we are ten years old, so there is no tradition. There is no track record. We are making the rules as we go along. It's both exciting but also frustrating. Film is not very high on the government's priority list because there are other pressing needs in the country. Over the past ten years, we have had to beg, scrounge, and live off of measly pickings. We've had to go abroad where there are more developed cinema cultures and beg and plead there, but they say, "If you guys say your stories are so fantastic, how come no one in your [own] country is interested in funding them?" It's like, how do you explain that? It's like, "OK, you've got me there." But slowly government support is growing. Big business is looking in, taking a peek. . . . As the filmmakers, it is on us now to make something decent and make money. Filmmaking is a very high-risk venture business, and all the investors are interested in is the return on their money. We have to make films that have commercial value that sell while trying to be authentic. It's a really tight rope to walk because you are using other people's money to tell your stories.

ATM: Is that always in your mind—the responsibility to investors as you make the film?

ZM: There's a very big responsibility there. If it was South Africans' money, black South Africans' money, there wouldn't [be] the cultural divide. It comes with having foreign funding. They say, "OK, here's money to tell your stories, but this is how you are going to tell it." You respond and say, "But, hey, that's not how we walk, that's not how we talk, that's now how we make love, that's not how we are. That's not who we are." To that they say, "That's how we want to see you, though." That's the only way you are going to sell it, and it's just—

ATM: —feeding a preexisting view of African people?

ZM: Absolutely. I mean, with *Drum,* the responses from one festival—I won't mention any names—is that it's not African enough, and that's because when they think about films that have come from Africa, they think jungle. They think women with naked breasts, dancing, and people coming out of caves—that's the Africa that appeals to them. Now, when you show 1950s Johannesburg, and you show them black journalists and gangsters and politicians and sophisticated, industrialized people, you see a room full of black journalists and a journalist that takes on the system—they can't fathom that. That's like, "Hang on, what is this?" That's what's happening with *Drum* right now. It's not African enough.

ATM: On the other hand, what do you expect of the South African government? You left the state-owned SABC television [South African Broadcasting Corporation] because of the same issues. South Africa is also a capitalistic society. Why do you expect the government to support filmmaking, a huge profit-making industry?

ZM: Precisely because we are very small—we are a very new country. We are a country where even though black people have political power, the economic power still lies with the white people. If you look over the past ten years, more white South Africans have been able to make films than black South Africans. You ask yourself why, and it's simply because white filmmakers have access to the means of production. They can go to uncle whoever, and he can sign them a check. Through their uncles' businesses, they can easily raise money. Black people don't have that kind of economic-support base. It is essential for governments to support black filmmakers. Otherwise, there will be no black filmmakers. There will be no black cultural industry.

ATM: What is the function of the South African film board?

ZM: Well, they get money from the government, and they distribute the money. They get something like thirty million rand [US$5 million], which they have to distribute among all South African filmmakers. So everyone gets ten bucks, ten bucks, ten bucks, because they have to spread it out evenly. You can't make a film with ten bucks, you know. It's just seed money. You can then go out and try to raise money elsewhere.

ATM: What is your take on the issue of audience development in South Africa? As you said, even in Swaziland, you were fed a steady diet of Western cinema and certainly in my experience in South Africa, all I saw on South

African television and cinema other than indigenous soap operas is what I see back in Indiana.

ZM: I don't know how you deal with the problem of audience development. There is a hunger in black people to see black stories, and my job as a filmmaker is to tell those stories. That is all consuming. Once we have a large volume of films, only then can we start to feed these people who are longing for these stories. Right now, there is a demand but no supply. You have to understand that we are only ten years old. Hollywood is one hundred years old. It took them a long time to get where they are. We are a small country with a population of forty million people, 80 percent of which is rural. The country and most people don't have access to movies. When you talk about the filmgoing audience in South Africa, you talk about 5 percent of the population, which is middle-class whites. All the cinemas are in white suburbs, and their cultural values and cultural inspirations are much closer to Hollywood and Europe than they are to black people in this country. When you talk about South African film audience, you are talking about the 5 percent of the population that is middle class and white.

ATM: Isn't that why the issue of developing an audience or at least delivering films to a more representative audience is important?

ZM: Yeah, well, you are absolutely right. I think the model of India is a great example, how India has the rural population, and the government in the fifties and sixties used audiovisuals and film to get its messages to the illiterate peasants. They would go up into the mountains and rural areas with mobile vans and show films about agriculture, hygiene, water irrigation, soil erosion, that kind of stuff. Over the years, the Indian population became cinema conscious and cinema literate. When Bollywood came about in the sixties and seventies, they had a cinema-literate populace of one billion people, and that's why India has the biggest film industry in the world. To apply this model to South Africa, we have [forty] million people—it's impossible to generate those numbers. It's a very tight balance—we want to make stories about ourselves, but we cannot afford to be in those films. So, who is the audience? My audience is black South Africa, regardless of the fact that they cannot see [my films] at this present moment. That is my audience. That's who I'm telling the story for. I think that's the only way we are going to make a genuine influence on the world, and that's why I think that's going to be the only challenge to Hollywood. We cannot beat Hollywood at its game—which is multimillion-dollar films—so we should just tell genuine stories like *Once Were Warriors* [1994] and a brilliant Brazilian film that came out a few years back—

ATM: —*City of God* [2002]—

ZM: —*City of God. Whale Rider* [2002], an Australian film, and a lot of Iranian films have cracked the international market—genuine films about other ways of life, other cultures—and they just touch the whole world. I think that's how we are going to go.

ATM: What do you see as being a defining aspect of South African cinema? I mean, India has a particular model that you just talked about, and there has to be other kinds of models because, as you said, Hollywood is not a realistic one to think about. When will you know that there is a truly South African cinema? Will there be any guideposts or any particular things that one could identify as South African in cinema?

ZM: I don't know. I really don't know. Is there a German cinema? Is there an English cinema? Is there a Brazilian cinema? Is there an Argentinean cinema? There's French cinema. There's Italian cinema—why do we say Italian cinema is good? Italy has had some great directors, and Italy has managed, through its own population, to tell its own stories and distribute them to its own population. I think there are very few countries in the world that can claim that. I don't know when we will get to [have] a South African cinema. I don't know whether it's going to be the volume of films produced. If we can make twenty films a year, will we say that's South African cinema even though 80 percent of the population won't see them? I don't know. When you are in a race or a game of football or basketball, it's only afterwards that we look back at the tape and say, "Hey, we should have done this like that." History will tell and will say that these guys made a mess here. That's only hindsight. Right now, as filmmakers we have to use whatever means possible to tell our stories. That's it. It's so time-consuming and so difficult.

ATM: That's enough for now, isn't it?

ZM: That's enough for now. Later, we will do intellectual jogging. We'll tell the story and let the critics take it from there. African cinema—what are the destinations? We know what Bollywood is, because it's there, and it has been there for forty-six years. We know what a Hollywood film is because there's a tradition. We are in the process of making a tradition.

ATM: What makes you—in spite of all the obstacles that are clearly there like funding issues and audience development—optimistic about the future of filmmaking in South Africa?

ZM: I'm optimistic about South Africa in general. I think it's just a fantastic country with limitless opportunities. Right now, I'm feeling very, very low and very indifferent about my country, but that has to do with the death of my best friend and producer.

ATM: Oh, no. I'm so sorry to hear that.

ZM: Yeah, he was shot and killed about two months ago.

ATM: Oh boy.

ZM: There's lots of obstacles and lots of stuff we have to deal with, but on the whole, it's an opportunity to define ourselves politically, socially, culturally, in any way we choose. Apartheid has dictated where we sleep and work, when we work, how we work, whom we sleep with, everything. It has determined our history. For the first time, we have the means to tell it, not just tell it but to retell [our history]—to tell the truth because so much of it was evil and distorted.

ATM: I guess that's why the world, at least a large part of it, is so interested in South Africa. I feel a personal connection myself. Many of us have been drawn to South Africa despite all the issues it presents. America is the only country that I've lived in and truly know, but many African Americans feel a connection to your history because of our own in America. We know that most of us know we will never *own* our country, not in the way that black South Africans feel they own their country, even with all its problems.

ZM: I know exactly what you are saying. I hear you, because it's a blessing to be South African and black at this time. There's a sense of obligation. We have to do this for our children. We have to say, "We were there, and this is who we were." That's what the struggle has all been about, and now a different struggle begins. I think black South Africans in all fields feel this obligation—this sense of history and sense of readdressing the injustices. I certainly feel that as a filmmaker, and I know a lot of my friends who are natives also feel this way. There is passion and drive, and that's why it has been an exciting and privileged time to be living. Today, to be alive, black, and South African is a tremendous lesson.

ZOLA MASEKO is an award-winning filmmaker born in exile in Swaziland in 1967 and attended school there and Tanzania. In 1987, he joined Umkhonto we Sizwe, the armed struggle in the African National Congress. He graduated from the National Film and Television School in the United Kingdom in 1994 and returned to South Africa in time for the new, democratic government. He was honored with the Best Newcomer Award at Sithengi in South Africa. Since then, he has become one of the best-known film directors in South Africa.

FILMOGRAPHY

***The Foreigner* (1994).** Xenophobia is exposed in this seventeen-minute, fictional film through the relationship between an immigrant street vendor and a homeless child.

***Ghetto Diaries* (1997).** The lives of urban dwellers are depicted.

***The Life and Times of Sara Baartman* (1998).** A Khoi Khoi woman taken to Europe in the early 1800s was exhibited as a freak because of her buttocks and genitals.

***A Drink in the Passage* (2001).** Based on the apartheid-era short story by Alan Paton, a young black man wins an art prize but is denied it because of his race.

***The Return of Sara Baartman* (2003).** The remains of Sara Baartman return home in ceremony.

***Drum* (2005).** The real-life events of black writers and intellectuals of 1950s Sophiatown, Johannesburg, are featured in this fictional film.

Khalo Matabane

Khalo Matabane

I will never be a model for national identity. I don't really think that I am reliable enough for black people to think, "Oh, there's a black filmmaker who deserves [to be known]," because I'm so unpredictable.

AUDREY THOMAS McCLUSKEY: Khalo, tell me about your latest film. The last one that I know about is *Love in the Time of Sickness* [2001]. I haven't seen it yet, but I have read the reviews and they are good.

KHALO MATABANE: That's actually not the latest. The latest film is called *Story of a Beautiful Country* [2004], a feature documentary. It's completed, and I've been screening [it] around. I just finished another fiction project, which I produced myself about displaced persons.

ATM: What can you tell me about it?

KM: It's called *Conversations on a Sunday Afternoon* [2005], and it's basically a crazy project about refugees and what it means to be displaced by war. It's bizarre because it uses fiction and also borrows from a documentary style. It's about two people who meet at a park, and one is an African writer, and the other is a Somalia refugee. She tells him about her life and how her father and brother were murdered in the Civil War in Somalia. She breaks down and cries, then disappears. He goes on this journey in search of her. He asks people he meets if they have seen this woman called Fatima. The film approaches the whole idea of what is fiction[al] and what is real. The people that he comes across are mostly refugees. These displaced people start telling him their own stories—personal stories about the realities of war and what war has done to them. The Somali woman becomes [the vehicle] to explore the bigger issue—the whole idea of war and what it has done to peoples' lives.

ATM: What is the inspiration for this story?

KM: I was traveling in Germany on a bus going to Holland, and I came across a young woman who was from Eritrea. We started having this conversation, and when I told her I was a filmmaker, she said to me, "Would you make a film about people like me who are displaced by war?" This film is my response and my love letter to her.

ATM: You have never seen her since?

KM: No. I have never seen her again. I think that it's really weird, because in the contemporary South African social-political landscape, the response of white critics to black film is very interesting. The criteria by which white critics respond favorably to black films are when they have nothing to do with politics and have nothing to do with any substantial social issues. Yet, black people are in some of the most terrifying conditions in the world. I come from a background where my ideas and thoughts have always been really political. For me, I don't think that making political films is actually a terrible thing. I don't think it's boring. Films are either great or not great. There is a tendency for African people to not want to make political films because the political film seems to be boring. I come from an experience that shows my disgust with oppression.

ATM: Why did you choose filmmaking as the way to convey your political ideas?

KM: I don't have any tangible answer to that. I can make up a reason.

ATM: No, please don't. Has filmmaking always been a passion?

KM: No, because I never watched any movies until [age] sixteen.

ATM: You never saw any images?

KM: No phone or television until I was sixteen.

ATM: Why was that?

KM: I grew up in a rural area where there was no television. It was simple. There was however, a very strong storytelling tradition. Most families, most parents, most grandparents tell stories. The notion that storytelling is particularly African I find a bit romantic. People tell stories. Period. The question becomes what kind of stories do people tell? When I am asked how I became a filmmaker, I say my grandmother used to tell me stories. She told me stories during the height of oppression in South Africa. She used to tell me stories that you wouldn't get at school. I can't write, still I can't. At age seventeen and eighteen, I was trying to be a painter.

ATM: What deterred you from that?

KM: I'm terrible at it! I like the *idea* of painting, but you have to actually paint yourself. With filmmaking, you can have an idea and get other people to execute it technically. I'm not really a technical person in that way. I come from [a place of] feeling. I never look at film as a business, and I don't understand the dynamics of film as a business. I am terrible at it. I don't understand these talks that people have, these conferences where people talk about filmmaking in Africa. I don't understand this discussion.

ATM: So what is the essence of filmmaking to you?

KM: It's a response to injustice. I think that if I was a true revolutionary—sometimes I think that I am really a coward or [I'd] be like Che Guevara and go into the bush. I think if I were a true revolutionary, that's what I would do.

ATM: You'd give up filmmaking and go into the bush?

KM: No. I won't give up filmmaking. What else would I be doing? I am making political and philosophical films, and I like making films. I like the artistic side of making films. There is a whole range of things [that explain my interest in film]. All of the notions of injustice in the world, the idea that I feel so real about is my own existence, even in black South Africa. What do I feel about a world that has so much inequality in it, so much injustice, and [such] a lack of compassion, even from black people? My films are like a little guerrilla warfare. That's how I like to think about filmmaking—war against [oppressive] systems.

ATM: You didn't take this route through film school?

KM: No. I didn't go to film school.

ATM: What was your very first film?

KM: It was a documentary I made about a couple of black South African filmmakers. My memory says it was about how black filmmakers are trying to reconstruct their own image, history, and memories onto film after years of seeing themselves through the lens of others.

ATM: So your agenda has not changed. You've been straight ahead from the get-go.

KM: Yeah. I'll never be a trendy filmmaker, although people may think that I am, but I don't think so. I will never be a model for national identity. I don't really think that I am reliable enough for black people to think, "Oh, there's a black filmmaker who deserves [to be known]," because I'm so unpredictable.

ATM: Well, do you depend upon a certain audience? Who are you making these films for? Beyond yourself, do you think about audience?

KM: Who knows about those things? I found those questions really complex, because there isn't always an audience, but there are always people. When I was young, I used to have this arrogance and this sense of wanting to make the kind of films that people would [want to] see, but now I know there is an audience all the time. I didn't have to go out and identify it. [My] last documentary has been screened in more countries than any other documentary made in the last ten years. I don't think there has been as much black response to a documentary in an artistic and intellectual sense than the one I just finished.

ATM: *Story of a Beautiful Country*?

KM: Yes. From Cape Town to Copenhagen to New York. It's scheduled in Washington on the fifteenth of June, then in Germany and Guinea. The response has been incredible.

ATM: In South Africa as well?

KM: There has been a legal action against it, so there hasn't been a full screening of it [here]. The response has [still] been so good. It has been amazing.

ATM: Like good literature, it will find its audience?

KM: I think the film will find its audience, and if it doesn't find its audience, that's okay. We live in such an abstract world and crazy world that I can not put my hand on anything. Sometimes, I think that my films are not tangible. When people look at my films, they have such a strong emotional reaction. I try to deal with something abstract, something that is so difficult to put your finger on.

ATM: Maybe that abstractness is from your life as a painter. It's those ideas on a canvas coming out.

KM: I think that is the problem. People who love the work that I do overcriticize [it], and people who don't love the work that I do sort of underestimate what I am trying to do. Filmmaking is hostile. Except for the very rare great filmmakers, most filmmakers in the world who are very smart and have interesting ideas cannot put them into cinema. They make terrible films. Some of the greatest thinkers who really understand how to articulate cinema and the relationship between the image and the reconstruction of the image and the idea make very terrible films. Why? Because film as a tool is a very simple.

ATM: Do you think that film has been overtheorized?

KM: No. I think a [good] film portrays the best ideas that one has about the world. Sometimes, it cannot capture the depth and psychosis of the world, of history. When I was making *Story of a Beautiful Country,* one of the things I was trying to capture was the psychosis of the physical thing—who was rich, poor, whatever. When you go through the history we have gone through in this country, what happens in your mind self-consciously? Who are we as a people? Film is very good at the image, the physical, but once we try to deal with the psychosis, something that is really strong, but it is also abstract, and it becomes very difficult to convey that in film.

ATM: How do you approach such complexity with the camera?

KM: I say to myself how do you frame memories, how do you color pain? I think those are significant questions when you film. How do you frame something? How do you frame the past? How do you frame someone who has gone through whatever they have gone through? How do you color that? Most filmmakers don't think about that. If you're a good filmmaker, you realize that the aesthetics are also political. So that's my argument, starting out with the subject that is political, but the aesthetics, the way you make the film, even the way you finance it is [also] political. That's why with my latest film, I went to people who were in the struggle before and asked [for financial support]. Some of them have become very rich, and some of them have become completely reactionary. They could be anywhere else in the world. I don't want to go into that. Some of the people are completely, completely disgusting.

ATM: Yet you asked them for money?

KM: Of course! Some of the people are really disgusting and have no sense and place of what happens in the world with black people and that we have gone through a history ten years ago. Today they are no longer engaging in it. I find that completely disgusting.

ATM: How do they respond to you?

KM: They were fine. I showed them the film.

ATM: Maybe it ignited a suppressed memory?

KM: I don't know, but in every society, you find a few people who give you money. I mean it depends on how much. I didn't need so much money. I produced the film, and I own it, and I have some friends who help me out, but I own it. Those events all affected the way I make films. I've been watching women filmmakers, and there is something very sensitive, even when there's violence. Even among filmmakers I don't like who happen to be women, there's something still pretty gentle [in the way they] shoot the film. There is something in the way they position the camera, a softness, how they take interest in the details of the characters they are dealing with. While I say most men do not care about the details, they care about the bigger picture. If the person is Arab, he's Arab. That's what the men care about. While filmmakers who happen to be women will be sensitive and care about the details.

ATM: So how did you instruct your cameramen?

KM: When we started shooting, I said to him, "Shoot it like a woman." I don't know if it was successful or not, but that's what I said.

ATM: You told your camera person to shoot it like a woman?

KM: Yes. That's what I told him. Someone that I've been seeing says that she hates intellectuals. She hates people who spend time with theories and all those kinds of things. She thinks it is not necessary. She has no respect for people who call themselves intellectuals. I always argue with her, because I do regard myself one way or another as [an] intellectual. I regard myself as an intellectual filmmaker. That's why I concern myself with the economics and how I finance my films. I understand, to a certain level, what I am doing. Lots of filmmakers just want to make a film. For me, the *idea* of making film is not enough.

ATM: Sounds like you understand the business of film quite well, despite your protestations. How did you raise money now for this new film?

KM: That's how I raised the money for the new film. For the documentary, I got the money from Canada.

ATM: Did you get any money from the South African government?

KM: They gave me a little, but I got most of the money from Canada.

ATM: On our way over here, you mentioned having a party in order to raise money. Could you speak more about that?

KM: I've been doing all sorts of things. I've been such a maverick. We live in such difficult times and not only in the U.S. but everywhere in the world. South Africans would like to think otherwise. Everywhere you go, there are the right-wing conservatives. This noncompassion, this greed, this materialism, all continue to manifest while the majority of people in the world remain poor. It doesn't matter that we have the best constitution [in the world in South Africa]. One hundred years from now, people will still be poor. My interest in film is informed by these political issues that I am grappling with. Now it's time to make significant and substantial films about black people, and that is under attack. There's so much attack that people are in denial, and we have become an ahistorical people. The films that are coming out, even in the black communities all around the world, have become so ahistorical. There is this kind of thing where the white cultural system, the economic and financial system is so strong that it reminds black people all the time that the best way to become part of us is for you to move forward and not to mention slavery, apartheid, or your oppression. I realize that the trend among the most successful black people, including South Africans, is to indulge less in what has happened to them or what has continued to happen to them. They [become] in a way an enemy of their own success. It would be like Oprah having an interview with Mayor [Rudy] Giuliani and never asking him about the [Amadu] Diallo case. As a black person, you can't do that. I think that the white system has made it impossible even in South Africa for black people to raise significant issues about what has happened to us. History continues to repeat itself even in countries where black people are the majority, and they seem to be in power. The history of black people—of repression, of inequality, of injustice—continues.

ATM: Are you optimistic about the future in South Africa today?

KM: What is optimism? I mean, it's my country, I don't have to search for optimism. When you see a best friend or a family member, and you see them not interested in anything. . . .

ATM: By rejecting the lure of material wealth—corrupting elements—does that become a message or warning in your films? How does an impoverished and oppressed people reject materialism when it is all they see? In other words, can you ignore your own privilege and financial access as a filmmaker?

KM: No, but I do see this. I was in a friend of mine's [high-rise] apartment in Manhattan, and when I looked out of the apartment [window], I was dizzy for a long time, because I realized that this is what I want. I know, but the point about it is I'm halfway through my life, and I like to look at my life as meaning so much more [than having a fancy apartment and a nice view]. I say to myself, "What is my human existence, what is the meaning of my human existence? What is my significance?" When I do that, it changes my perspective about the way that I do things and the things I want to do. People are still making films about the Second World War, still writing books about the Second World War and what happened to them. No one else in the world ever forgets what has happened to them. We are the only people in the world who somehow are asked to forget. . . .

ATM: Your earlier comment about Oprah interviewing Giuliani is a case in point.

KM: It's a pattern. When I was seventeen and eighteen, I was so naïve about what it means to be a black person. Now, I have come to understand that some of the most reactionary people I have met in the world are actually black. I have come to reconcile with that notion that we are not homogeneous. We are not one people. There is Condoleezza Rice, and there's Spike Lee. Yet, a white person will say that a film by a black filmmaker is "refreshing" because it does not deal with the history of South Africa. Something is so weird about these dynamics.

ATM: How do you respond to being put on the defensive as a filmmaker?

KM: I really don't care. I find it more complex. I think that's why as a black filmmaker, I have come to understand the complexity of the world. My films have to be, too. Films should never attempt to provide answers, because the world that we live in is too complex. That's a very bizarre position to be in. Sometimes, I feel like I'm living in a country that is schizophrenic.

ATM: But you redirect those anxieties into making films. Does the process of filmmaking make you feel whole? Does completing a film make you feel whole?

KM: I never want to complete a film. [Italian auteur Federico] Fellini said something interesting. He said that when he is on the set, he feels protected. I feel exactly like that. I never want to finish a film. I'm so emotional because I don't want to stop. The kind of films I make are a reflection of the kind of world [I live in] and my experiences. I would like to be in a privileged position where I could move from one film to starting another film three days later.

ATM: How have conditions changed in the last ten years [since the end of apartheid] in South Africa?

KM: I'm really convinced that we are living in one of the most terrible periods in human existence. Maybe there were more terrible times, but in these times, it doesn't matter where I am in the world, I feel a real sense of displacement. I feel completely like a refugee. I feel that I don't belong. I cannot talk about the national consciousness anymore. I cannot talk about all those big things because I feel out of place. . . .

ATM: Less so or more so than before democracy?

KM: It's not a comparison. One cannot compare the apartheid regime with what has happened. This is a different level. This is a level of people's refusal to engage, people's denial of memory. The Truth [and Reconciliation} Commission is not the end of history; it's not the end of apartheid. People live their lives; they live with those memories. I think that the honors and the celebrations are ritualistic; they're not real. Lots of black South Africans don't really care about who have made it, and lots of black people who haven't made it don't care about each other. The rich want to be richer and keep the poor and the working class [down]. It's messed up. The poor are the same; they [just] don't have the money. There is the idea that the poor are much more compassionate. They're not more compassionate. It's a surreal experience to have just gone through apartheid and to [now] see people ten years later being so trivial—so indifferent, so uncompassionate, and uninterested in anything. I have never been to any country in the world where people talk so much about possessions than in this country. Absolutely! I've never been anywhere else in the world where people talk about material things [so much], where people talk about their BMWs [more] than anything else in the world. It's so revolting!

ATM: Do you think that's because of the unique way of which apartheid functioned? Gross materialism is not unique to South Africa. Do you think that South Africa's history makes it different?

KM: Jewish people, wealthy Jewish people understand one thing. It's not just about Ferraris and yachts and P. Diddy [American hip-hop entrepreneur] going to Holland throwing twenty dollar notes to poor people. [Jewish people] know there is a political and historical significance to material wealth. I'm not a social scientist. I don't have the answers. I look at SKG–DreamWorks [studio], and I'm like, "Why can't Oprah, Denzel, and Spike or Will Smith create a [film] company like that?" Why is it so difficult for black people to get together? Not just [get together] when the white cultural system marginalizes and humiliates them? Why should Spike battle to make the kind of films that he wants to make? Why should Charles Burnett [a gifted African American filmmaker] or anyone else battle to make those films when they can create their own financial framework in the U.S.? It's bizarre, but it's like that all over the world. It doesn't matter whether black people are the majority or the minority. I think the trend is the same, and people are asking, "Why is it so impossible?" When I look at the number of white people who responded to giving me money . . . shocking. A lot of them have given me money. It's not just simply the equation that white South Africans have [more] money; it's also the idea of *how* people use money. Some people will use all the reasons in the world to not advance you the money. They say, "We want to make you professional." But they are actually closing doors [on you]. They want to be the only ones [to make it]. I have never seen such self-hate. Yes, apartheid, colonialism, slavery, I don't care what it is. Black people cannot excuse themselves from progressive involvement and engagement in sociopolitical issues and the everyday issues of black people. There's no reason why they can't change their response. Of course, that is why I make these films.

ATM: What you just said reminded me of a Chris Rock joke about the difference between being rich and being wealthy, which black people sometimes confuse. Rock joked that if Bill Gates woke up with Oprah's money, he would jump out of a window! I liked what you said before about film being your weapon.

KM: That is my real existence. A friend said to me that Jewish people are always having memorials to the Holocaust and what has happened to them. It can get a little tiring. Maybe they've got a point. There are so many films coming about the Holocaust. I've realized that the problem is not the Jewish people who constantly remind us what has happened to them. It's the other [oppressed people] who do not remind everyone else what has happened to *them.* I don't think there's enough protest or enough engagement by black people. I hope that the films that I make will be artistic, but I also hope they will start to engage [people] in sociopolitical dynamics. I want to give young black people, especially young filmmakers, writers, artists their say. When I am sixty or seventy, I'll look back at all the kids who say, "I can make the film that I want, and no one will stop me." I hope that my films are saying that, too.

KHALO MATABANE has established a reputation as an innovative filmmaker whose work places him among the "new wave" of African-based filmmakers. His passion and dedication to film as a "weapon" are reflected in the timeliness of his storytelling. He participates in film festivals and travels throughout the world.

FILMOGRAPHY

***Two Decades Still* (1997).** Postapartheid South Africa is the subject of this documentary.

***The Waiters* (1997).** Families of freedom fighters who disappeared in exile attempt to survive without them.

***Young Lions* (1999).** Former comrades in the struggle against apartheid now find that they have little in common.

***Love in the Time of Sickness* (2001).** Sexual relationships during the devastation of the HIV epidemic are complex.

***Poetic Conversations* (2001).** This short-subject study focuses on black-consciousness poet Ingoaplee Mandingianee.

***Story of a Beautiful Country* (2004).** The filmmaker equipped with a handheld camera goes in search of his "new country" and whether it is now the promised land.

***Conversation on a Sunday Afternoon* (2005).** A chance meeting in a park sparks deeper questions about nation, war, and identity in a time of crisis.

Teddy Errol Mattera

Teddy Errol Mattera

When the past and the present meet,
it enlightens people.

AUDREY THOMAS McCLUSKEY: How did you become interested in filmmaking?

TEDDY ERROL MATTERA: Interestingly enough, it started when I was about seven years old. I was in primary school and my father worked for the *Star* newspaper in Johannesburg. School was out at two o'clock; he finished work at five o' clock, so he dropped me off at the cinema almost every afternoon for about three years of my life. I developed an interest beyond just what was on the screen, I started [repeating] the dialogue, and I used to get kicked out of the cinema by lovers sitting in the corner. I would run behind the screen to be with the projectionist—very much like a *Cinema Paradiso.* I got to know the projectionist and ushers, and eventually they didn't even notice me when I walked in. That was the beginning for me.

ATM: What kind of films did you watch?

TEM: I watched everything. I watched *Sounder* [1972]. I watched Bruce Lee films. I watched *Valdez Is Coming* [1971] and *The Sound and the Fury* [1959]. I saw Sidney Poitier for the first time. It was amazing stuff. I actually ended up making a film portrait of my life as a child growing up. It is called *Waiting for Valdez* [2002], which was based on *Valdez Is Coming.* It is story about my growing up. I was living with my grandmother, like [most] African kids, especially black kids. You know, as we grow up, our grandmothers play an important role. Mine was really strict. One weekend *Valdez Is Coming* was going to be showing at the cinema. What we kids used to do when we didn't have money to go the cinema was to pool what we had and send two of our friends to watch the film. Then they would come back and perform the episodes for the rest of us. They would recite the story. One would do the visuals, and one would do the sound. So a guy would go "Valdez cocks his gun," and the sound goes "Crrccckkk." They would perform the whole movie for us.

ATM: These kids were very talented!

TEM: Yeah, it was a beautiful talent. You had to graduate into doing the visuals, because that guy had the most important role. It was all boys, usually. For the most part, I didn't get to see many films. I was just lucky when my dad was working that I got to go to the cinema a lot. Most of the films I knew were retold in our own way—in Zulu, Afrikaans, Sotho, as it suited us. The dialogue was irrelevant because we couldn't do American accents very well. The guy would just do it in Zulu as it suited him. It resurrected language in cinema for us because we came to understand it in our own language. That was really my beginning in cinema.

ATM: Did you decide to be a filmmaker at that age?

TEM: I wasn't sure, but I knew that I had something else going on that sparked my interest. I would sometimes go behind the screen and watch the movie. I never wanted to be anything else—maybe a professional football [soccer] player, because I was good at football—but other than that, I may have wanted to be a bus driver.

ATM: You grew up in the era of apartheid. Did that affect your aspirations?

TEM: I come from a very powerful family, and that's what saved us. My dad was a Black Consciousness leader, poet, and journalist, and at no time did he or my mom allow us to ever give up on our dreams. I was reading when I was four years old. That happened with most of my family, because my dad used to sit us [children] on his lap and make us learn a new word every day. [He made us] read the news. We didn't understand what it meant, but we still read. The circumstances under which we grew up were definitely austere. There were hurdles in front of us but never insurmountable ones. I never imagined that I wouldn't [succeed]. It reminds me of what Martin Luther King said about not getting to the Promised Land with you but getting there just the same. For me, it was always that vision from my family. My dad was banned for ten years by the apartheid government but he never gave up.

ATM: What is your father's name? Tell me about your family.

TEM: Don Mattera, Donald. He's a poet. And my mom's name is Judith. I spent my primary school years here in South Africa and then went to school in Swaziland. I was in semi-exile in the sense that my dad was being hunted down by the police, and because [my family valued] education, and I was involved politically, my parents sent me to school in Swaziland. I spent my high school years there.

ATM: What happened afterwards?

TEM: I came back here for a year. Then in 1983–84, I got a scholarship to go to the U.S. I spent my undergraduate years at Colorado College [Colorado Springs], where I studied sociology and film production. I ended up in Chicago where I had an internship with Kartemquin Films, the people who made *Hoop Dreams* [1994]. I spent my first internship working on a film that was nominated for an Oscar. You can't get a better start! Eventually, I came back home, and I started working for ABC News in Johannesburg in 1990. I decided that it wasn't really what I wanted to do, because the way South Africa was being sensationalized, especially by American television, soaked me in depression, and I couldn't see what my contribution was to all of it. So I left and joined Afrovision, known as Video News Services, an underground video collective. A lot of the footage that the world saw happening in South Africa came from us. I worked on documentaries for the trade unions. Then I started getting interested in feature films. I went to the London International Film School to develop my craft more. I came back here again in four years and then went to Holland. I made 150 documentaries for television.

ATM: You have amassed a lot of experience, and you're still so young.

TEM: Yeah, I'm forty-two years old [in 2004]. It comes to a point where you start really feeling the pressure of wanting to make your documentary participants or interviewees act or say things in a certain way. Then you realize that fiction is calling. It's time to move on and write your own characters, because the real world doesn't actually live up to your expectations.

ATM: As a documentary filmmaker, did the political climate inspire you?

TEM: Yes, it was deeply political, never anything else. Even doing profiles of musicians or profiles on public institutions was very volatile. After my first feature film, the politics haven't really changed. The subject of the film is a professional mourner.

ATM: Why did you choose a professional mourner as a subject?

TEM: It is a man who has been given a gift by his ancestors, which is the gift of mourning. The mourner leads the grieving process. In this case, when he starts to abuse that gift, the curse comes around.

ATM: How does he abuse it?

TEM: He starts crying just to make money out of it. That's a gift that you cannot misuse. His gift is to help poor people with their grieving process. Once he starts using it to make money, the curse [descends], and he loses his ability to cry at the wrong moment—at the township gangster's funeral. It's a comedy, by the way.

ATM: It sounds highly allegorical.

TEM: It is. I mean, it's comical but has very serious comical elements to it. At the moment, it's called *Max and Mona* [2005].

ATM: Will it have international distribution?

TEM: We're looking at it. My producer is at Cannes [Film Festival] at the moment. He's looking to score us a deal. Hopefully, Miramax or somebody will pick it up.

ATM: Are you working on any new projects?

TEM: Yes. I've just finished writing part of a series for television and a commercial. I started on another manuscript, which will probably take me four or five months because it is quite a tedious process. In between, I'm catching work here and there. It's the typical life of people in our medium. I hope to do some university teaching.

ATM: What is your view of the present arts and cultural landscape in South Africa?

TEM: On the whole, it is quite a difficult situation because there's a strange dualism in the sense that the way the world previously came to understand what was going on here under apartheid was primarily through artists—Miriam Makeba, Hugh Masekela, people like Peter Gabriel in the U.S. It was through black Americans such as Randall Robinson and the TransAfrica Movement. Although many of the people who brought South Africa's plight to the attention of the world were artists, I find it quite interesting that after our democratic elections, the government that's now in place saw fit to give the arts and culture portfolio to one of its prime enemies—the IFP [Inkatha Freedom Party]. That party had been supportive of the racist government and had participated in the apartheid [regime]! It was almost like a punitive portfolio. As punishment, they gave arts and culture to a political enemy! It says a lot about what our government thinks about the arts.

But slowly there's been [some] change. I've just received major support for my film from the National Video and Film Foundation. There's been increased opportunities for people like Teboho [Mahlatsi] to direct television programs and other developments that I have participated in. Slowly, our people are seeing images of themselves on screen. This does a strange thing to people psychologically. It is one thing seeing heroes that are always white, but to see black people as film heroes and she-roes is psychologically empowering. The landscape, as far as that is concerned, is changing incrementally, with congruency developing between the political development of our country and social participation in the arts and culture. They seem to be slowly coming nearer to each other. At some point, one hopes that they will be on the same track.

ATM: Why do you think the government has not given higher priority to the arts?

TEM: It was not a clearly thought-out process. I think it came out of the notion that houses and water and education are more important than arts and culture. They didn't necessarily see that the arts are part and parcel of it. It was always thought that people need houses more than they need art. For me it is more than that. The way a woman dresses shows what she thinks about herself, how she raises her children. Art and culture are the pride of our people. It is what gives the people the ability to fall or stand.

ATM: How does that notion stand up against the globalization of culture and the homogeneity that it oftentimes produces? Aren't you afraid that native stories will lose out?

TEM: I now understand the reservoir of stories we have, and that makes me no longer afraid. I will definitely defend the appropriation of our stories and our culture, but I'm less afraid now because I actually think until we go out and present these stories, we will always feel victimized. God, how boring it would be if you didn't have your experience as the basis of your art! It would take away the color, if you know what I mean. I feel less afraid than I did before. Remember how hip-hop became a universal culture? The essence is in the roots of black people, and that's its connection with Africa, even if it is Japanese hip-hop. Everybody tries to imitate us.

ATM: Very true. Now I have stopped calling for reparations [for slavery] and started calling for royalties for all that has been stolen from black people. [*Both laugh.*] That is the trajectory of black culture and its expropriation. Our cultural gifts are valued, but the people are not.

TEM: Absolutely! You can go to Louisiana to the roots of [jazz]. If you are going to trace where blues comes from, it's that journey between the South and Chicago. We are in the [African] diaspora from where you live, you are in the diaspora from where we live. We are reclaiming those connections, and I think that's why the initial onslaught of American cultural imperialism is [weakening]. Suddenly, people's stories about who they are and where they live are actually becoming more appealing on their own terms. There are only so many *Rambo* films you can make before people start seeing the light. We have to be really careful that we don't trample or discard the potential of being a unifying factor on the continent.

ATM: Do you think that's what South Africa offers the world?

TEM: I'm sure. I think we have that unique possibility. There's a thin line between arrogance and having affinity, though. Affinity is being able to learn and teach at the same time, but arrogance is what makes people forget the meaning of this trajectory that you spoke about, this journey. It's what could really destroy a people or make them stand up. This comes back to my theory about what the arts are about. They are about giving people grounding to keep them from falling and [about encouraging them] to stand up. That is where that journey for me becomes significant.

ATM: Given your ideas about politics and culture, how do you respond to the discourse of multiculturalism in this postapartheid era, how it affects the gross disparity in economics?

TEM: I think the so-called second revolution will come. My theory is that, for a while, it was important to entertain white fears in this country. We never came to challenge the economic disparities among our people. Fifty-four percent of our people live and die in poverty in this country. Those of us who have been silent or deliberately headhunted and pulled into the comforts of the world will somehow have a reawakening, [even if] it is by being forced out by the reality of the situation—it is really difficult for me to watch black people almost unconsciously adopt something that was never theirs. To disregard the places they come from, the languages that they speak, the relatives they have, the people [who] fed them both emotionally and psychologically, and, to some extent, educated them—this is difficult to [understand].

ATM: You see that happening here?

TEM: Yeah. It is really scary, but I feel less defeated by it than I did by the deliberate attempt at dehumanization that we were meant to feel. I have a sense of hope that there may be some point of reason that will come into black people's lives.

ATM: Do you see part of your role as an artist to help bring that about?

TEM: Yes. Primarily. Even if I just make one film that will change one person in that cinema, I'm quite happy with that. I hope it will change a lot of people's minds. But for now, we're on a long journey, and I think we just started learning how to walk. There is a white South African filmmaker whose films are so obviously racist, yet our people watch them because they have not seen different images of themselves.

ATM: How do you know that *your* work is making a difference?

TEM: People tell you. They say, "I saw this television program of yours about township soul in the seventies, and I remember the time I learned about jazz." I myself learned jazz because my dad used to make me shine his shoes, and he would play Miles Davis in the background. That was a strange way to have me listen. I didn't want to clean the shoes, but with Miles in the background, it was okay. So I know Miles Davis. People start making connections. When the past and the present meet, it enlightens people. That's what I want my films to do.

ATM: Speaking of connections, when I visit South Africa, until I reveal my American accent, I seem to go unnoticed and to fit in. This is not always true for me in America. You attended college in the U.S. How did you feel as an African in America?

TEM: I was in the U.S. from age nineteen through twenty-six. Beyond childish attractions to certain things, it was the music that connected with me—I matured during my time in the U.S. I remember landing at JFK [John F. Kennedy International Airport, New York], and one of the security men in the airport asked us, "Where did you get them jeans?" I replied, "I bought them." This [black] man replied, "You have jeans in South Africa?"

ATM: Uh! I have heard a similar story from another filmmaker visiting America.

TEM: It happens. He went on to ask if we still "live in trees." I replied, "Yes, we live next door to the American ambassador." I threw it back at him. That experience was contradicted by the African American family that took me in. They came to visit me just four months ago. They treated me like a son and a brother. It was a deeper experience than most African students would have when they come to America. So despite all the B.S. that's going on in the U.S., I still feel, strangely, very connected. When I go back there, I'm also going home.

ATM: In South Africa, there is the sense of a movement towards a unified culture in the official discourse. But I wonder if that is actually true at the ground level. I see a difference from four years ago, perhaps a little more ease in relationships across cultures and races. But underneath that, I wonder if those changes are real.

TEM: Wow! That's interesting. The strange thing about people is what Einstein said, "Gravity cannot be held responsible for people falling in love." It translates as we can try to envision a society that we want, but it's ultimately [up to] the people who live in it. I think people might be involved in the wrong discourse as far as race and the economy are concerned. We should not be so arrogant to think that [people] can't make up their minds or see the truth before them. I trust our people because they are the ones who brought this [last] government to its knees—the apartheid government. It was not Mandela. It was the people whose sons and daughters died on the frontline.

ATM: I really appreciate that. It is a very hopeful viewpoint. Again, it goes back to what you said about trusting people. However, I worry that part of the present discourse may function as a diversionary tactic.

TEM: I have the same worry. I'm saying that if we weren't worried, then I would be really worried. [*Both laugh.*]

ATM: The arts can also become very commercialized. You seem to have a clear sense of who you are and what you are doing. How do you stay focused on the larger issues?

TEM: I did a commercial for the Department of Labor but I have serious problems with doing commercials for just any industry. It is primarily still white run. Some black people have been seriously bought off and bought out. You see people making [television] commercials about what they know to be racist and then say it can't be racist because a black person directed it. It's a trap. Ideally, we would like to be focused all the time, but because we live in this society, we sometimes falter.

ATM: Artists are human, and the ground in South Africa is shifting as we speak. I understand that. That is what's so interesting about South Africa.

TEM: There's an interesting saying—that you can understand a society by the way it treats the artists. The Spanish celebrated Picasso. You look at Duke Ellington and see that America was forced to celebrate him, but the point is that it happened. You see jazz celebrated in Europe with jazz festivals, et cetera, so the home country begins to see that Ellington and Ella Fitzgerald are forces to be reckoned with.

ATM: Having said that, Teddy, when I came to the country just five days ago, all the news was about Brenda Fassie's [a South African superstar recording artist] untimely death at age forty. Talking about how a society treats its artists, what does her story tell you?

TEM: That is a great example. It tells you that there's an awakening, if not a resurrection by our people, because whether she was a drug addict or not, she was the first one who fed the people through her music. She introduced the idea of a black president in this country. She actually made a recording about it. She may not be the most politically sharp woman, but it's not always how politically sharp you are that defines your character. It is whether you have a message that motivates people.

ATM: What gives you the most optimism about film culture in South Africa?

TEM: For the first time, we've got at least twelve films made in this country this past year by black filmmakers. That is, if nothing else, a motivating factor and something to celebrate.

ATM: Do you think South Africa is beginning to appreciate its artists?

TEM: Oh, yeah. Absolutely. I mean, I'm nervous as hell for the opening of my film in the cinemas, but I'm also quite keen to actually show our people that you can laugh at yourself but not feel laughed at. There is a difference between feeling mocked and abused by how white people see us, because they see us as chicken-loving, watermelon-eating kind of Negroes as opposed to us eating chicken and watermelon [on our own terms]. So, I am very optimistic about our future. I can't wait.

TEDDY ERROL MATTERA studied sociology and film production at Colorado College, Colorado Springs, in the United States, where he earned his undergraduate degree. He worked as a trainee on *Hoop Dreams* in 1993 in Chicago. He also attended the London International Film School. He returned to his native South Africa to direct several film and television projects. His first narrative film was *Waiting for Valdez.*

FILMOGRAPHY

***Waiting for Valdez* (2002).** A childhood fascination with performing the movies is recalled.
***Township Soul* (2004).** The music of the 1970s infuses the spirit of the people and fuels their survival and protests.
***Max and Mona* (2005).** Mattera's first feature film is a comedy about contemporary South African life as experienced by Max, a professional mourner who abuses his gift of empathy.
Numerous television documentaries

Jyoti Mistry

Jyoti Mistry

While the gender imbalance needs urgent address, the diversity of filmmakers—not just from a racial mix—but from various ethnic and cultural backgrounds, has produced an exceptionally exciting variety of content.

AUDREY THOMAS McCLUSKEY: I understand that you have been out of the country for an extended period. Will you briefly talk about what led you away, and what led you back?

JYOTI MISTRY: I have always been interested in filmmaking, not only from a production point of view but my particular concern is the connection between theory and practice. While my undergraduate and graduate studies offered me an incredible foundation in film history and theory, literature, and literary theory, I was unable to pursue my research interest at a master's level in South Africa at the time. Film practice as a theoretical inquiry, I would argue, is still a relatively new area in South Africa, and even though an awareness and demand for this approach is developing, there remains a dearth of practitioners who are interested in filmmaking that is informed by a theoretical paradigm. I left South Africa to pursue a master's in cinemas studies with a certificate in culture and media offered at New York University. It was one of the few programs at the time that very self-consciously and self-reflexively was involved in pursuing a series of inquiries dealing with culture, identity politics, multiculturalism, and its relation to production. In short, I left to study and work in an area that was not readily available to me in South Africa and stayed to continue with the doctoral program in cinema studies.

I think one always feels some trepidation when returning to one's homeland. Manthia Diawara captures it eloquently in his book *We Won't Budge* [2003] when he describes it as a feeling of nostalgia, of wanting things to be the same and yet recognizing that in part one feels like one does not belong anymore. My desire to return was also about my own personal development as a filmmaker. The films I was making in New York and the scripts I wrote in Vienna dealt with geography and time, and it seemed like I was constantly on the outside, living in cultures that I observed anthropologically. The fascination with returning is about being able to be on the inside, and yet, as Diawara describes, "One recognizes that one is never fully part of the community one once belonged to." The privilege is that one has the opportunity to navigate such enriching spaces, but the sense of belonging is incrementally eroded. My interest in return[ing] to South Africa is about trying to work through the ideas of belonging. [It was also a] feeling that I wanted to be part of the community that is reinventing itself and to participate in that process.

ATM: How does your work as a scholar intersect with your work as a filmmaker? Are there natural disjunctures or symmetries, and how do you reconcile them?

JM: I think there is a tradition of scholars who are interested in practice as a theoretical exploration. I have in mind people like Isaac Julien, Trinh T. Minh-ha, Manthia Diawara, to name a few, that have taken on issues of representation, identity politics, post colonialism, and multiculturalism in their filmic texts while exploring them in their written texts. The challenge is recognizing the limitations and strengths of each form. A written text can explore and develop an argument that is sustained and contained by the philosophical paradigm that one is writing in. A film has other competencies—whether we define them as technical, narrative structure, using and subverting filmic codes—that it must fulfill in order to make the filmic text "accessible." And, of course, at the heart of filmmaking is the love of the image and a desire to work with images as a language system and move out of the realm of words—not that the two are exclusive. For me, the natural symmetries are about ideas, concepts, and story. The disjuncture is about issues of form and treating each medium distinctly. It's important not to expect a film to be an essay in a traditional literary sense nor to make literary demands on films.

What I find interesting over the last ten to fifteen years especially in Europe and now increasingly in North America [is] the increasing number of scholars who are interested in developing philosophical inquiries not just through written texts but through a practice of some sort whether it is film or fine art. This is important because films and fine art can reach broader audiences, creating opportunities to widen the debates that would otherwise remain in the realm of academia.

ATM: I have visited here twice in the last four years, and I'm struck by the pace of change in the country. On the one hand, so much has changed so fast, but, on the other, there is so much yet to be done. Given the continuing problems of economic inequality, educational deficits, and infrastructure issues, why should the problems related to South African film culture even register at home or abroad? Specifically, I am referring to the ongoing debate about how and to what extent the government should involve itself in the television and film industries and the pros and cons this entails.

JM: When art and culture are separated in civil society from issues like economic inequity, education, and sociopolitical transformation, it is a dangerous oeuvre that positions film and art in the realm of the elite. In some ways, it harks back to the debates about art as a high-culture practice which is an "enlightenment" project once a society has reached a certain social and civic development. In the case of South Africa under apartheid, theater and documentary were important instruments of social and political commentary to draw people into political consciousness and to facilitate self-reflection about the conditions of their existence. In this respect, it is dangerous to make the assumption that issues of education deficits and economic inequity are *more* important. Yes, there is a hierarchy of priorities in the country, but at this stage—ten-plus years into democracy—we need instrumental change in the representations and interpretation of the history and experiences of the country that work concurrently with the other transformations in South Africa. Regarding government initiatives in film and television, these have been systemic, and there is a fabulous momentum which is developing exponentially. In this respect, the National Film and Video Foundation (NFVF), mandated by the government to facilitate and institute change, has been a remarkable instrument to pledge government support to enable the film industry in South Africa. The ongoing problem globally is that governments are expected to pledge increasing resources to the arts, and film is a particularly expensive medium, whether one is shooting film or video, which requires high levels of skill development, training, and expertise. It is not as simple as expecting governments to allocate more funds, but it's also about supporting the creative, intellectual, and "freedom of expression" ideology that film and television offers. In this respect, overregulating can also be dangerous, because where finances come from and what provisions are placed on them shape how a production might be created. This is true not just of government-funded projects; evidence of this [extends] all the way from coproduction finances to how "studios" and production companies determine content based on the ideological framework of their institutions.

In that respect, government support is not simply about money but about infrastructure and ideology.

ATM: We have a discourse of multiculturalism in America that often gets co-opted by politicians and denigrated by conservatives. South Africa with its eleven "official" languages would seem to be the poster child for multiculturalism, yet people always aren't satisfied with the programming of it. You have stated elsewhere that the ideal is often not what people really want. You also noted that English is "the aspirational language" in South Africa, which suggests that *that* is what most audiences want. How do you address this seeming contradiction?

JM: Contradictions are important in society especially for one such as ours not only on account of its history but with its desire to claim reconciliation and transformation. Having eleven "official" languages is a fundamental political gesture that addresses the history of nonrecognition of cultural and linguistic diversity in South Africa. In that respect, it has an instrumental function that speaks to your observation about how multiculturalism in South Africa facilitates the recognition of diversity. It ties in well with the national rhetoric during and after the first elections dubbed the "rainbow nation" campaign. However, my feeling about American academe's discussions about multiculturalism raises a number of inherent contradictions as well. I have in mind here the seminal text by Ella Shohat and Robert Stam [*Unthinking Eurocentrism*], which suggests that the term is used strategically by the left and right to advocate particular political ideas and goals. But I would say that South Africa interprets multiculturalism differently. Generally speaking, the difference is that in American politics, the multicultural discourse—whether on the left or on the right—is informed by assimilation politics, and after 9/11, this has been even more pronounced. The difference is that multiculturalism in South Africa is neither about assimilation politics nor integration politics, as is common in language of European countries, but rather I take up the idea as Shohat and Stam suggest that multiculturalism is polysemically open to various interpretations and subject to diverse political force-fields. If we use the definition of multiculturalism as having no inherent essence but one which points to debate, then the idea that South Africa can have eleven official languages with English as an aspirational language sits comfortably as a contradiction. So, for audiences to aspire to speak English better or study at an English medium school is about the socioeconomic advantages and sense of internationalism that English as a language represents. At the same time, to demand the right to have content created in all languages that represents cultural and ethnic diversity is about exercising the right to have representation and claim recognition of this diversity that was previously denied. Multiculturalism in this context is not about positioning diversity underwritten by assimilation politics but about multiculturalism as a discourse enabling differences and diversity to coexist with equal representation and opportunity.

ATM: In your role as head of television at the Wits [University of Witwatersrand] School of Arts, do you accept responsibility for advancing the transformation of the elite, white cultural establishment in S.A. to reflect the majority of people in the country, who are black? If so, how? Where do you begin, and what are you most proud of having accomplished to date?

JM: Transformations at universities in South Africa have been complex and highly debated, not just at a government level but within the institutions themselves and at a number of different levels—from the people employed in their areas of expertise to the disciplines, canons, and paradigms those departments educate and train in. I returned to South Africa at a time when the debates and restructuring were at their zenith, and university mergers were being evaluated. My appointment as head of television is part of the university's transformation process. My area of expertise and interest brings to the fore alternative questions and practices of filmmaking that address alternatives from a strictly Western paradigm. The changes that I have been responsible for are to bring television studies and film production into the Wits School of Arts as an academic division and to bring a vision to the division, to redesign the curriculum and program at an undergraduate and postgraduate level that serves the changing sociopolitical and industry landscape in broadcast and filmmaking. Having accomplished this in the last two years, I am currently forging international exchanges and research initiatives which focus on issues of cultural production and reception of film. What makes this next phase particularly important is that it challenges canonized conceptions of representations and interpretation and brings different institutional paradigms in conversation with each other.

ATM: We are pleased to have one of your films, *Yoni* [in the Black Film Center/Archive (BFCA) collection] and hope to have more. In this film, your political and aesthetic instincts are intriguing. I wonder how the film with its feminist orientation has been received in S.A.?

JM: *Yoni* has not really been seen widely in South Africa because I have not really had an opportunity to show the film here much. In light of your question, though, I would be curious to show it more widely to glean responses to the politics in the film. I have, however, had occasions to show films I made subsequently, like *B.E.D.* and *Another NY Story*, which deals with women's issues and more specifically with a woman from a minority background as professional in a white-dominated environment on SABC [South African Broadcasting Corporation]. The film was received enthusiastically and raised questions for a South African audience about transformation in the workplace.

ATM: Clearly, the notion of female-centered love and the erotic nature of those encounters, layered with racial representation, invites controversy. Do you intend for your films to be controversial? Are you telling people to get with it or get over it or just try to think and feel differently?

JM: I don't think one sets out to make a controversial film in and of itself. Much has to do with how a filmmaker interprets the material and what ideas and concepts inform the story. The wonderful thing about film is its ability to elicit emotions and inspire thought and reflection through voyeurism and interpellation. The context of the film and the audience's reception "to get with it or get over it" is also about what meaning and interpretation they bring to the text. In various contexts, I have been fortunate to have audiences reflect on the films differently. And in the case of *Yoni* particularly, the genre of this film inspires much debate and controversy because it forces an audience to create meaning through the ellipses, and this discomfort of not having a fixed meaning offered to you creates room for controversy. At the same time, I hope that the film does inspire an audience to feel something.

ATM: Please talk about your present project and the kinds of films you intend to make in the future.

JM: I have just completed a twenty-six-minute film called *We Remember Differently*. The issue of memory, personal and collective memories, and their reconstruction and reconfiguration over time is extremely interesting, particularly as it offers resonances to the construction of histories—official, resistance, or even revisionist. Specifically as it relates to South Africa, the very conscious move to redress the historical record after the dismantling of apartheid and to offer a revisionist view not just around events as was previously recorded under Afrikaner nationalism has forced a radical reassessment of political, social, and cultural identities. In the wake of this very important and necessary move to reconstitute the political and social landscape of South African identity, we have seen that all aspects of identity formation have been thrown into question. This is an exciting opportunity for artists and filmmakers to not just celebrate the possibilities of creating new representations in South Africa but as a space to play what Jacques

Derrida referred to as jouissance. I see this jouissance as a wholly new potential in this country. Under apartheid, South Africa was so regulated and burdened by its political responsibility to make political art, and while art is political, there is now the freedom to be open in the Derridean sense when making art and films.

Many contemporary South African films are about historical events or are observations and reflections of the socioeconomic conditions of South African society. I think these films are important and invaluable in taking on the challenge of using cinema as a means of redressing representations of history, people of color, and minority groups. My interest, however, has been to move away from the politically obvious. In making We Remember Differently, I wanted to question race and identity from within personal and collective memories—perhaps recalling the adage "the personal is political." And rather than evoke the metanarrative of South African history, I tried to work from with the smallest units of personal experience and expression to destabilize the metanarrative.

We Remember Differently uses original 8 mm archival footage from an Indian family shot during the 1950s, 1960s and early 70s as the memories of a woman in her thirties and her mother. The story is of a daughter who comes home after years away to take care of her mother who is recovering from hip surgery. In the course of an afternoon, the daughter questions the foundation of her mother's marriage and their relationship. While the memories of the mother and daughter are Indian, the two women recounting their memories are white. Using racial and cultural dissonances and universal memories, the films tries to evoke questions of identity and identity formation and the assumptions we make about race and racial identities. I was inspired by the spaces of the archival footage and their resonances to the contemporary geography of South African society. I hope to continue making films inspired by my surroundings—what I observe and my interpretation of those spaces.

ATM: Who do you see as the audience for your films? In talking with other S.A. filmmakers, many are trying to reach a broad, untapped audience who are not inclined to go to the cinema because of economics and distance. Are there any restraints on your intended audience?

JM: At the offset, I think there is a distinction between a broad audience and an untapped audience. I would like to imagine, as most filmmakers do, that I can reach a broad audience by the stories I choose to tell. But I have come to recognize that while the stories I choose might have a universal resonance, the modes or form in which I choose to tell those stories are not always easily accessible to an audience who is seeking a classical (perhaps Hollywood) narrative structure. My audience therefore seems to be an elite, art house, or academic audience who are not easily flustered by shifting conventions or who are schooled in the cinematic tropes of the experimental form. Broad audiences in South Africa are reached through television, and the success and popularity of local content in this regard is testament to this fact. More important, the landscape, language, and aesthetics of South African film are created through the production of local television content. Increased television production can only enable the development of a South African national cinema and not just an industry, so the value of local television content can not be overestimated. There is a tension between forging a South African *national cinema* and the commercial aspiration for a successful South African *film industry.* This is where I think your question is a pertinent one. In terms of broad-based audiences, films made for television or South African films that are televised is the space where local content can be accessed by a broad audience. This is different from the question of untapped audiences. This is about the economics and infrastructure of distribution and exhibition. What distributors are prepared to exhibit is based on what they consider to be financially viable and profitable. Distance and economics are about the socioeconomic conditions of potential audiences, and this is being addressed through outreach programs like that developed by FRU [Film Resource Unit], and certainly there are initiatives to develop more theaters in the townships and rural areas. Of course, there is also the issue of audience development, in some instances even visual literacy. The aim is to create an awareness and support for South African product. The competition with global products—I mean Hollywood—remains the essential deadlock between local filmmakers and distributors.

I think the issue of reaching untapped audiences is also about content, not just form. It seems that in this pursuit to create a South African industry, much energy is spent on creating products that will travel internationally and showcase South Africa, whether it's history, politics, or social issues rather than consideration for local viability. This is evident from the numerous case studies over the last five years, for example, *Paljas* [1998, Katinka Heyns], *Yesterday* [2004, Darrell Roodt], *Promised Land* [2002, Jason Xenopelous], *Forgiveness* [2004, Ian Gabriel], *Drum* [2004, Zola Maseko], and *In My Country* [2005, John Boorman].

The expression gaining currency is the breakout film—the idea that one film will launch South Africa on the international cinema scene. It is here that I think the issue of a national cinema is more important. The idea of a national cinema evokes questions of identity and repositions the focus on the local—local stories, local audiences, and local distribution—and not in relation to international or global conditions of production and distribution. Rather it emphasizes local cinema for local audiences! Provocatively speaking, then, this makes the larger South African population an untapped market.

ATM: What has ten years of democracy meant for the film industry here? Where would you place South Africa now in terms of [the] world cinema [market]?

JM: The last ten years has been an important moment to change the privileges of filmmaking. By this, I mean that filmmaking has historically been the privileged domain of white, mostly male South Africans who have controlled images, representations, and narratives of black and white South Africans. In the last ten years, a new generation of black South African filmmakers has emerged. While the gender imbalance needs urgent address, the diversity of filmmakers—not just from a racial mix but from various ethnic and cultural backgrounds—has produced an exceptionally exciting variety of content. In terms of infrastructure for promoting filmmaking, there have been numerous institutions that have secured instrumental support to ensure the development of the film industry. The NFVF, IDC [Industry Development Corporation], DTI [Department of Trade and Industry], and the National Lottery are vital avenues for filmmakers to secure funding. Also significant are the various coproduction agreements that South Africa has garnered with various countries to ensure not just contribution to expertise and funds but to enable channels for distribution and exhibition. In the last ten years, these very internationally visible initiatives have taken South African film production from its pariah status to a much sought-after location and coproduction player as well as a market for distribution and content. The most recognizable difference over the last ten years in South Africa is the volume of films being produced, and this has far-reaching and overarching implications. In 2004 alone, approximately twelve feature films were made which received broad-based distribution, probably the highest number of films to date made per annum in the history of this country. This impacts the general public's awareness of South African content and begins to create an interest and support for local content. For this reason, the value of television cannot be overemphasized. As long as South Africa continues to have distribution problems, and, as you suggested, untapped audiences for theatrical releases remain a problem, then television offers an alternative space for promoting local content and audience development. There remains a desperate need for local content on local broadcast networks. I would like to point out, though, that volume at this point has been the target, and with volume, the quality of content will improve exponentially.

Over the next ten years, we will see more filmmakers making better films as the industry and infrastructure start maturing. Related to this is the foundational support or the feeder for the industry, which are tertiary institutions, and training programs that are qualitatively improving and, furthermore, developing a focus on the cultural context of filmmaking in the country. In other words, a conscious move away from emulating dominant cinematic forms is the next imperative step to developing cinema in this country. Here again my concern is the difference between an industry and a national cinema. This relates to your question about South Africa in terms of a world cinema. National cinemas are about relations between national film texts, national and international contexts, and the sociopolitical and cultural contexts of production and reception. National cinemas are important because they offer a distinguishable alternative to dominant international cinema [Hollywood]. While I would be cautious and not simplify the vices and virtues of Hollywood, national cinemas offer an authentic, indigenized, and evolved—sometimes subversive—alternative to dominant global film practices. My observation is that South Africa is seeking to create an industry, perhaps right now at the cost of a national cinema, that appears on the surface to be readily enamored with dominant cinematic forms, and this relates to the issue of the breakout film.

Once again, this is where training programs and tertiary institutions are absolutely relevant, because they will enable the next generation of filmmakers to address the authenticity of South African experiences, historical and contemporary, and this will be the phase when South African filmmaking will be truly idiosyncratic. Capacity building has been the real focus over the last ten years, and I imagine that the next ten years will be about finding the unique, indigenous narrative, aesthetic and cinematic language which puts South Africa films in the league of other world cinemas. South African audiences are open and ready for this intervention as is evident from the positive responses to local television content.

JYOTI MISTRY is a filmmaker and senior lecturer at the University of Witwatersrand, Johannesburg, where she is head of television at its School of Arts. She teaches a range of courses in television theory, production, film analysis, and history. She is a council member of the National Film and Video Foundation (NFVF) and is on the board of the Johannesburg-based monthly *The Media*. Mistry received a PhD in Cinema Studies from New York University.

PARTIAL FILMOGRAPHY

***Yoni* (1997).** Female power and desire are provocative in this video pastiche presented in a mix of cinematic styles.

***We Remember Differently* (2005).**The dynamics of a mother-daughter relationship is set against the backdrop of displaced memories in Johannesburg.

***i MIKE what i LIKE* (2006).** The work of poet Kgafela oa Magogodi is the basis of this spoken-word film, done in collaboration with Kgafela oa Magogodi.

Palesa Letlaka-Nkosi

Palesa Letlaka-Nkosi

In South Africa, young filmmakers know [their work] will be broadcast on state-funded television. There is not always the incentive to be innovative.

AUDREY THOMAS McCLUSKEY: Palesa, what is your view of what is happening in film and television culture in South Africa?

PALESA LETLAKA-NKOSI: As you know, I'm back in the academy at the moment to become a historian, and I'm not really working [in film] that much. What I see is as an evaluator at the National Film and Video Foundation [NFVF]. My big interest is in eliminating the barriers to black people working in the [film] industry in South Africa, especially black women. Our industry is very television heavy. I'm worried about the lack of diversity in the stories that are being told in broadcast and the kind of submissions that are coming through and the ideas people are pushing. That really is more of a concern. Documentaries that have been made in South Africa about black life are pretty much the same. I'm much more encouraged about the feature films that have been coming out. Everyone is not dealing with political themes.

ATM: Are narratives more advanced than documentary-based films in presenting the diversity of South Africa?

PLN: I wouldn't say it's more advanced, I'd just say there's more creativity, because, first of all, the format of a fiction film—the heart of the film—is very different. My worry about the documentaries that are being made is that many are formulaic. It seems that people are being made or being told to do certain things. There is a conservative push at work. Content is important, but it's a visual medium, and we have to use the images to make films that are graphic and just move away from actuality. Documentary for me is not about certain cameras following people around to see what's going on in their houses.

ATM: What is it about for you?

PLN: It's about the way that people choose to represent reality. Documentaries can tell stories. It's still a construction. People are trying to move away from talking heads, but they don't know how to do it. It ends up being someone standing in their kitchen making tea as opposed to a fixed, filmed interview, which would be like a talking head. They must try to interrupt that way of seeing people so predictably.

ATM: Why would you choose one or the other format? Do they have a different purpose?

PLN: It's all storytelling. Documentaries are still constructions.

ATM: One of the concerns that I hear expressed is that the past is being lost or distorted, and one role that film has is in maintaining a certain level of honesty in the presentation of South Africa's past. What's your view?

PLN: I'm going to have to answer you as a historian. [Documentary filmmaker, teacher, and author Alan] Rosenthal says that any film that is made about the past is still a film about the present, and I do subscribe to that. When people say the past is being lost—it's not being lost, it's *been* lost, and I don't think that everybody needs to make a so-called documentary [to preserve it].

ATM: Yes, I think [William] Faulkner also said something similar—that the past is not dead. Can filmmakers really reclaim the past without having it drag them down?

PLN: I think that it is quite a heavy burden to put on young filmmakers. A lot of people are making films who have not been afforded the opportunity to go to film school. It's about learning on the job. In South Africa, young filmmakers know [their work] will be broadcast on state-funded television. There is not always the incentive to be innovative.

ATM: So they have access but not necessarily authority?

PLN: Yes. They definitely have access. The most likely only way you will make something is if it is commissioned, which means it will be broadcast. Now this may be your first attempt—

ATM: —if it's not good, you probably won't be called upon again.

PLN: No, you *will* be called because of certain types of confirmation, and I think that that is what I find quite interesting about this country.

ATM: Low expectations? Is this an encouraging environment, then, for young filmmakers?

PLN: I don't think so.

ATM: They are getting access to a national audience. That is less likely to happen for young filmmakers in America.

PLN: But it's not access. Being broadcast is not access.

ATM: What is it then?

PLN: It's distribution for a product that you've made, and you may have access to the means of production in another environment where it's just easier and cheaper to get your hands on a camera and into a production facility. Maybe in America you'd go a different route, which is more festivals. To be broadcast on television does not mean access, because you have to ask, what does that access depend upon? Can a young or new filmmaker with a good track record and maybe a good story and proposal make a film without that? No. They would have to go to an established production company. More than likely, that production house is going to be [run by] white [people], and the kind of nurturing for black stories in those environments seems dismal. First of all, you have to do stuff rather quickly. You do need [to have] a creative producer who has more of an understanding of local black history. Oh, I can be a good filmmaker, a good producer, but to be a creative producer—how do you really help the director in the choices to be made? You need critical input and guidance about black life, which means it's going to be about history, whether it's gender or class in the stories that are being told. That's the last thing these people don't understand—that if you are making something that fits within a context, [you need to know] that context. The big problem is the lack of contextualization in the stories.

ATM: Is that because of ignorance?

PLN: I think it's ignorance. It's not about making films where you're explaining South African life. People have different experiences, so it's this kind of thing where [they ask,] "Oh, what's township life?" There's no *one* township life. I'm telling about XYZ and the minefields of the silences, because there will be silences. You have to make choices. You can't put everything in. You have to see where the clear, blue line is.

ATM: What are the implications for the emergence of a particularly South African cinema with multiple voices and multiple issues?

PLN: It's a bit psychological with that question. Of course, there are going to be multiple voices. I understand that in a way that I understand history. First of all, multiple voices are important—life, history—it's not harmonious. It's about the different strands that are there, and I believe that people are caught in history, and history is caught in people. I wouldn't call it nostalgia, but there is a South African movement—black and colored stories that people want to tell. South Africa has had the attention of [world] media. So, you are expecting a product.

ATM: The world is intrigued with South Africa right now and what you have accomplished and overcome.

PLN: Well, what does the world see? The world sees [the surface], the top. What floats to the top is not necessarily always going to be the best story.

ATM: South Africa seems particularly eager to show the world what it has accomplished. Whatever [Nelson] Mandela does becomes a news event. [President Thabo] Mbeki, particularly his earlier controversial views on the HIV/AIDS pandemic, certainly garners worldwide attention. Now, the great news that South Africa will host the 2010 World Cup seems to be setting this country up to represent the whole continent. Will cinema reflect this kind of grand ambition, as well as the problems and nuances it presents—even with other African nations?

PLN: I think it's unavoidable. There's a process that we've lived through, but it has not necessarily inspired an analytic [view]. I think that the kind of setting—the choices and the ambiguities; the traditions around black and white living together in this country—is more ambiguous. I don't know if you'd even call it tolerance, but that is in the stories that are coming out. It's very different. It's not as black and white. It is about these individual choices that people make which inform the narrative in film fiction, all the arts.

ATM: Can you give me an example?

PLN: There are different films on the subject of identity. I programmed a post-apartheid film festival in Amsterdam. The festival was called "Screaming in the Present, Tense?" These included ten-minute shorts and others, mainly around notions of identity. These ironies are beginning to be addressed in South Africa, and it is more open ended.

ATM: Even your title seems to be a negotiation with history—"Screaming in the Present, Tense?" These are young black filmmakers?

PLN: Well, not white. People of color.

ATM: What was your goal for this project, and were you happy with the outcome?

PLN: It was very, very well received. It was done in an area that's supposed to be multiethnic in Amsterdam, and the cinema had a funding mandate to encourage diversity. They hadn't been successful because multiethnic means different things in different parts of the world. There wasn't a lot of films made about race even though when you walked in the area, you saw that it was multiethnic.

ATM: Who was the audience?

PLN: There was a very large turnout of people of color. There were visiting black groups, Asians, and others and a lot of discord in discussion. That was the whole point of putting together that compilation of films.

ATM: Have you done the same thing here in South Africa?

PLN: No, I haven't.

ATM: That seems surprising. Why not?

PLN: I probably shouldn't put it on tape—but, first of all, it was easier for me to program, because I was part of a South African festival—dance, theater, and film—that was put together by a South African who lives in Holland. Here, it has been a lot harder because we don't have those [resources].

ATM: But you do have film festivals here?

PLN: No, not really. We don't really have annual film festivals. That kind of thing I'd love to put together for the new films that have come out of AFDA [School of Motion Picture Medium and Live Performance]. They are producing very well-made films with well-trained filmmakers, but I don't see a lot of black directors.

ATM: Do you mean graduates coming out of that program?

PLN: Well, I don't see them. I'd be curious to know the success rate for the students being absorbed in the industry, because the people who are working very successfully, at least the ones that I know, are white. I do want to know what is happening to the black students that they are turning out.

ATM: Your observation that you don't see many black graduates getting opportunities would seem to dampen the enthusiasm a bit, I would think, particularly if you don't have a sense of who is being trained to become filmmakers.

PLN: I must ask them if they track their students. That's what I mean. It's not always about who you see as a main-credit director.

ATM: That leads me to the question of audience development, going back to your earlier statement about not being able to do such a festival here in South Africa. Do you think that because South Africa is a multilingual society your idea of identifying an audience poses a linguistic as well as ethnic problem?

PLN: Exactly. That's not a problem that I have in Amsterdam. It was the public. It is very difficult to get [these films] out to the black public. This is a big problem—audience development and reaching the largest number of black people.

ATM: Do you think the government has a role in [promoting] audience development and funding in order to put films in places where they can be seen by the people that we are talking about?

PLN: Yeah. I do think that the government has a role to play in terms of audience development. I worked in theater about twenty years ago, and it's the same problem. It was how do you get people to the Market Theater [in downtown Johannesburg] at night? If you know there are no more functional cinemas in townships and that the emphasis on where new cinemas are being built and new screens is not in the township, then there seems to be an expectation that if they want to see films, they have to come to the shopping centers.

ATM: Can you imagine another paradigm that would accommodate this reality?

PLN: I know of some initiatives such as Scipati Dulane's *Video Suitcase* that tried to take films to the townships and got funding for it. There are two different publics. There are the types of films that went out to townships and more rural areas, which I think was good. There was another initiative, which was much more successful but it was market driven—they'd have a big truck and set it up with a big screen to show films. It was stereotypical kind of stuff [shown], and that was a problem.

ATM: Can we now turn to your work and where you are headed with it? Everywhere I've gone, people have mentioned your name as one of the pioneers, particularly as a black woman filmmaker, but now you say you are not doing much film work. Can you explain this?

PLN: Suddenly, I have a new direction—becoming a historian. It's still storytelling. I'm interested in telling stories about black life, first, and South African life, second. I always find it curious when people ask me why am I doing South African history—that's the question that I always get asked—have I dropped film? There are few people who will see that there's a very intimate and important connection between those two.

ATM: Would you explain the connection that you make between the two?

PLN: Well, you have the condensing nature of the medium at making television documentaries, and what becoming a filmmaker has made me do is really look at how I can work around that condensing. The limitations of the condensing may be in telling stories through television or documentaries and [forgetting to] look more at how important context is. Context is everything. There are two documentary projects that I have been working on, and I don't think I could have made them before now. One of them is an animated documentary, and in the other one, I'm looking at an era in South African history—the early eighties—through the music and character of a cultural activist who was very well known at the time. I'm very interested in the intersection of memory and history, which is an important debate right now. You can also see with the Truth and Reconciliation Commission [TRC] how personal testimony can conform to the so-called record and how the private became public. The woman is a singer who kept politics in her work, even as a nation engaged in fighting its neighbors. Her themes include lots of black stuff. She ends up being one of the first women members of parliament.

ATM: What is her name?

PLN: Jennifer Ferguson. I think it's a close examination of her albums becoming more and more African. As a woman, she was concerned with the impact of [apartheid] on ordinary lives. She put her poetry in her songs and commentary. I get asked by white South Africans, who are usually old, why I am doing this. I must say that the younger people don't ask.

ATM: Maybe it's generational. Why *do* you want to tell her particular story?

PLN: It is another angle of vision not usually talked about.

ATM: Interesting. Does it have a title yet?

PLN: I've got a working title, *History Was a Song.*

ATM: An arresting title. Have you begun?

PLN: Yes, I've already commenced. [I should mention] that Jennifer is also a very good friend of mine. When I came to Johannesburg and was working at the Market [Theater], that's when I became exposed to her music. It was the dying days of apartheid, and everything was just [crazy], but our friendship began. I have a lot of respect for her.

ATM: What are your views on the work of the TRC?

PLN: The TRC has shown victims and perpetrators. It's much more complex than victims and perpetrators. There are victims, perpetrators, bystanders—I mean we all are victims and perpetrators and bystanders at the same time within our lives, within our ordinary social settings, and that, to me, is the debate that I don't see coming out. In one of my [stories], I have the character—a black woman journalist—watch white Afrikaners being killed. Later in the story, she interacts with a character who was part of the death squad. She becomes his only link to some kind of humanity. In the fiction script, she's hesitant. She is there on assignment to do a series of interviews.

ATM: That brings to mind this book that I just read, *A Human Being Died Last Night,* by Pumla Gododo-Madikizela, which is about a black woman psychologist who interviews an imprisoned, apartheid death-squad leader.

PLN: Yes, excellent [book]. My working title, and I'm not happy with it, is *Redemption Song.* I'm trying to look at how in using that power, he becomes the victim, and she is like a perpetrator who holds the power to represent him. She's no longer a bystander just a journalist watching the death of an Afrikaner. I think that's why we need to find ways to break free of the perpetrator-victim [syndrome].

ATM: Paul Gilroy was lecturing here this week at Wits [University of Witwatersrand], and he said that South Africa is leaving America behind when it comes to dealing with race. America's notion of race is simplistic, while

South Africa and Brazil, he said, have more complicated notions of race and can offer the world new insights. This was interesting to me, because I have visited Brazil and found the racism there unbearable. But he sees South Africa as a kind of a laboratory, an experiment that the world is watching to see how it turns out.

PLN: But it's not about race. I think the lessons that we have to teach are much bigger than that. If you are talking about what I think is important about this so-called reconciliation, I do think that the politics we are talking about are the politics of the heart, and I can only put it in visual references that I have. I don't have the theoretical references.

ATM: Like postcolonial theory or poststructuralist film theory?

PLN: I don't have that discourse. It's not mine. It's not the language that I speak in, so what are the things—if we are talking about the evolution—that we have to teach the world in South Africa? It's about the evolution of aspects of human consciousness and [if] we are going to talk about forgiveness and living together, where do we look for that? [It is] not forgiveness in the binary way that is being presented by the TRC. Individuals have to reconcile themselves with their past. At a microlevel, we all have to work to forgive ourselves. Forgiveness is not just about people who were perpetrators and did terrible things, because it is possible for things like genocide in Rwanda to happen. Here, reunification has to also consider [class divisions]. Blacks could become the new whites in the way the disparity now exists.

ATM: Yes, these are not simple matters, and they are sometimes blurred by the binaries that we are force fed. Do you think something is lost in a discourse of forgiveness that flattens all of this out?

PLN: Sure, but it's not just about that either. I'm talking about the next stage and the question of who needs to pay. There will become a time where it's not just whites who need to pay, you know? It's those who can. What I'm talking about is not just pay as in pay the price, but I'm talking about rebuilding society after war. When I talk about the responsibilities that we have to one another, that also impacts the economics and the choices that certain people of great means will not be making. I think what happens is that it's not just about forgiveness it's about, "OK, what are our responsibilities to one another within the society and within our sphere of influence?" It is also [about] social justice.

ATM: That remains a challenge, I think, for your country and for all of us.

PLN: Yeah, for all of us. I'm not really seeing a lot of things, like the growth of social justice. It's not just about white people. We all have a responsibility to rebuild society however we can.

ATM: You are certainly treating these issues as complex and raising tough questions that will impact the kinds of films made and the [film] industry itself. If people were to grapple with what you are doing in your work, I think South Africa and the world would be better for it.

PLN: I hope so.

PALESA LETLAKA-NKOSI is a graduate of the University of Witwatersrand in Johannesburg, where she studied African literature and philosophy. She earned an Advanced Production Certificate in Film and Video in New York. She returned to South Africa in 1991 and began working in television, directing socially conscious documentaries, and producing commercials. Her work as a producer and director has won international acclaim and made her the first black woman to direct fiction films in South Africa. *Mamlambo,* her best-known work, has won several festival prizes.

FILMOGRAPHY/VIDEO

Short Hair, Flat Nose **(1994).** Beauty standards and their effects on young people are examined.

Mamlambo **(1997).** Magical realism is revealed as Mulusi, a street child, spins the tale of Mamlambo, a half-human spirit that can change its form.

Golden Girls **(1998).** The first women in the mining industry in South Africa are documented.

Music Saved My Life **(1998).** This documentary focuses on South African musicians.

Akin Omotoso

The South African public still needs to be convinced that they must support their own films, and I don't know why that is.

AUDREY THOMAS McCLUSKEY: Akin, I want to get a sense of your feeling about the current state of filmmaking in South Africa and how it has changed in the last ten years of democracy.

AKIN OMOTOSO: I'm originally from Nigeria. I came to this country about thirteen years ago. I studied drama and acting, but I've always been interested in storytelling. To answer the first part of your question, I have to link it to how we made *God Is African* [2003], because that to me illustrates some of the differences and the change taking place. In the current state, everyone is excited because there is a tax rebate that has been introduced [by the government for filmmakers]. Then you have the National Film and Video Foundation and other entities like the Grand Merchant Bank that are trying to build a popular South African film industry both locally and internationally. We want to make it viable for local producers and for international producers.

ATM: That's a positive development.

AO: Of course, absolutely. I think it's amazing. What I want to say is that when I made my movie four years ago, those structures didn't exist. We had a climate here that was agonizing. It was hard. I think it's hard to make a film in the best of times. So we went out and shot a film guerrilla style. We begged, we borrowed. We put together this movie in a climate of what I call apathy—where people weren't making any films. People thought we were crazy. They asked, "Why are you making this film without money?" For us, the people associated with making *God Is African,* it was about getting it done. For me, as director, I took my cue from what was going on in other places in the world—people were making films. Here [in South Africa], filmmakers would sit around the table and complain and complain. I saw that as a waste of energy. "Go out and make the film," I would say. We argue about the kinds of films we are going to make, but what was important to me was to go out and make the film. When we showed our film digitally a couple of years ago, people were laughing [at that]. Now, you can't talk with any filmmaker in South Africa without them asking, "Can we shoot it digitally?" I feel like we were right. You can say whatever you'd like about *God Is African* whether you like it or not, we got it done. My father always reminds me that we made our film at a time where nobody was making anything. [We] went out and did it in the face of everything. Today, if I want to make a film, I am much more comfortable. I feel like I've learned a lot. I feel that I have a chance to get support. Four years ago, I felt it was hopeless, even though I was making a film. Now, I feel like there's a lot more hope.

ATM: Well, does that mean that you are moving ahead and making more films?

AO: Yes, yes, yes! I'm working on two separate projects. One is a documentary about my mother, who has West Indian heritage. She is from Barbados.

ATM: Oh, OK. Your personal history is truly representative of the diaspora—born in Nigeria, living in South Africa, mother from Barbados—

AO: —Yes, it is! When people talk about the African diaspora, they forget the West Indies. In my experience, everyone talks about African Americans or Afro-Britons. Nobody ever talks about the West Indies or Barbados.

ATM: So your project will address that.

AO: This documentary is about me looking at that side of my African heritage.

ATM: Have you been to Barbados?

AO: Yeah, yeah. I've been there as a child and even as an adult. I was there last year. I've managed to go almost every year.

ATM: Have you seen [Cuban filmmaker] Gloria Rolando's film about West Indians in Cuba—*My Footsteps in Baragua* [1996]?

AO: No, I haven't.

ATM: It's about the descendants of Barbadoans who went to Cuba in the 1920s to work and now still retain their West Indian heritage, despite pressure to assimilate.

AO: I will see if I can find it.

ATM: So that's one project you are working, You mentioned two.

AO: Yes. I am also shooting a short film called *Rifle Road.*

ATM: What's that about?

AO: It follows the gun culture in South Africa. Guns are so easily accessible here. The film is examining gun culture amongst the youth.

ATM: What kinds of financing did you have to put together for this?

AO: Oh, well, I applied to the National Film and Video Foundation, and I just heard yesterday that I got the grant.

ATM: Well, congratulations!

AO: It's quite fresh news!

ATM: Will that be the totality of your finances, or will you have to go somewhere else to raise money?

AO: No. It will be the totality. It's enough—it's an eleven-minute film.

ATM: What is the market for short films? What do you intend to do with it?

AO: It is [all] about growth. One of my motivations was to continue to hone my craft by making short films. I didn't go to [school to be a] filmmaker. Before I made *God Is African*, I made three short films. I really wanted the opportunity to work with a proper budget and have my vision realized. I wasn't sure if people would show up on the set. I had to worry about so many things. "Are we going to have this location?" All the stuff that distracts from the creative process. I wanted the opportunity to show what I'm about as a filmmaker, with the freedom and the financial backing to do it. I would like the film to travel [everywhere]. It has something to say about our society that is very relevant.

ATM: I am wondering about the fact that a lot of the films made in South Africa actually have more international rather than local distribution. Am I wrong about that?

AO: Well, no, you aren't wrong. I think there are things that need to stay on the agenda. I don't know if you noticed while you were here that the majority of the people live far away from the cinema. It is easier for the guy in the township to just sit at home and watch television. In order to even get there, he has already spent one hundred bucks and hasn't even watched the film. There's a whole lot of things that have to change in terms of distribution outlets and who the audience is. South Africa has to build a cinema-going audience, and that is still in process. I don't have all the answers. In my experience, we still have a ways to go in convincing South Africans to come to the cinema to support their own. Coming from Nigeria, it is a shock because if you know about the Nollywood situation—Nigerians watch their own!

ATM: Do you see that as a model for South Africa?

AO: The Nigerian film industry is able to survive because Nigerians want to see Nigeria. The American film industry is able to survive because Americans want to see America. The South African public still needs to be convinced that they must support their own films, and I don't know why that is. I just know that it is something that filmmakers continually moan about. But as the films are made and as they are better, I think it will all change.

ATM: You think it will find an audience.

AO: Well, yes, it has to change. It is easier once you've made the film to take it overseas. A South African journalist asked me the same question you did. I said, "Well, let me ask you a very simple question. What's the last South African film you watched?" She couldn't answer me. I said, "That's the problem. You are South African and you can't even remember the last South African film you saw, but I bet you saw *Spiderman II.*"

ATM: No doubt.

AO: I'm not South African, so I don't understand the psyche. I think it might have a lot to do with the past, but I think as the film industry has grown over the past ten years—I think the audience will also grow over the next ten years.

ATM: I think so, too.

AO: I think everyone should be patient. The other thing I want to say is in South Africa—I don't know what it's like in the States—but here, every article you read will start by saying, "Is this going to be the next great South African film?" Like, every filmmaker has this pressure of being asked, "Is your film going to be the great South African film? Is your film going to be *The Whale Rider* [New Zealand, 2002] for South Africa? Is your film going to win awards?" That pressure is unfair.

ATM: Why is it unfair?

AO: Because it can't be.

ATM: I understand, but I'd like to hear you explain why you think pressure is unfair. Other segments of society face pressure, too. Why should filmmakers be exempt?

AO: Like I was saying earlier, making a film is hard. Period. You do not need the pressure of making the next *Whale Rider.* What should be asked is, "Am I making a good film?" That should be first and foremost. If I [screen] it in Poland, and the Polish people get it, and the same thing happens in Barbados and Los Angeles, that is what's important. That's what needs to be done. Here, it's like if the film flops, you can never make another film again. I just think that's wrong. Give me a chance to start. Give me a chance to fail. Give me a chance to learn.

ATM: What is the definition of a flop? Is there such a thing for South African films?

AO: Well, if it doesn't become this great international hit! That's how it's defined.

ATM: Anything short of that is a flop? In other words, it's still the audience outside of South Africa that determines the success or failure of a film?

AO: Well, I don't know. My [belief] is if it is a good story, it resonates, especially if it comes along at the right time like *City of God* [2002], for example. In 2006, they are probably going to release four South African films. This year they are going to release like six. Some of these films will be good, and some will be bad. That's the nature of the beast. Instead of wasting our time waiting for this messiah to come and save us, I think we should spend our time trying to make good films.

ATM: I hear that. How has *God Is African* been received in this country? It is about xenophobia—South Africans' hostility to African immigrants. Has it generated much conversation and discussion about this state of affairs?

AO: Yes, it has. When I attend screenings, we have a question-and-answer session afterwards, and that has always generated debate. I'm from the school of thought that believes that films are entertainment, mainly, but they can also have a deep message. I think our film helped stimulate a conversation, a dialogue that should be happening. Some people hate the film. Some people like the film. For me, it comes from a place of honesty. It's a personal story. It is my story. I am passionate about the continent and issues important to [its people]. I meet a cross section of people—from security guards at the bank to ministers who thank me for making the film. Zimbabweans in South Africa say they know that my film is about Nigerians but it speaks to their experience, too.

ATM: Where does the title *God Is African* come from?

AO: We had a caucus about what to call the film. I remember we were saying it deals with themes of unity, African renaissance, and such weighty topics, so we should have a title that unifies everybody. The Nigerian president, [Olusegun] Obansanjo, had said that Nigeria has gone through bad times but is still standing, so God must be Nigerian. That comment ignited my thinking in that way. It progressed from there. I remember thinking at the time that everybody's going to think that this is a corny title. Little did I know that it has become a greeting card. I meet people, and they say, "Ah, you are the one who says, 'God is African.' We like that."

ATM: Talking about pressure, that title puts pressure on you for the next one!

AO: Yeah, I suppose it does, but I never think about those things. I think what's important is trying to get the story out and trying to get your vision back—everything else is secondary.

ATM: As a Nigerian living and working in South Africa, do you find that there are differences in terms of your viewpoint from South Africans?

AO: Well, I think that there are—you've got different tribes. I'm from the Urhobo [a main ethnic group in the western delta] in Nigeria. I work with a friend who is from the Zulu tribe. I think that you acknowledge your cultural upbringing. But there's always this attempt to say, "Hey, we're all black, so that means we all know what's going on." I think on some levels that's probably true. We all share [some issues], but we are also individuals from different backgrounds. I think it's not so much whether we are all South African or all African. We are people who live on a specific continent at this time. I'm sure that's what you found since you came. South Africa is a mixture of all these different people with similar goals, and in a way, similar to the States and to parts of London, where people are attracted to a place to come and build it. The only thing I would say, coming from Nigeria, is that I don't have the baggage of the apartheid past. My father wasn't dragged out at four o'clock in the morning, beaten up, and humiliated in front of us. I don't have that experience, but I can share a bit of the pain, but there is a difference. Nigeria was independent in the 1960s. When I grew up, black people were ruling. With my mother being from the West Indies as well, I have a very [expansive] world view.

ATM: What is multiculturalism after all if it's not about respecting and acknowledging other people's culture?

AO: Yes. That is what *God Is African* is asking—what is an African? Well, you sound American, and you are not African enough. One character says, "Just because I sound this way I'm not this, I'm not that?" For me, being African is everything that you are. It's not just walking around in a dashiki and speaking with some exotic accent. It's everything that encompasses your being.

ATM: Those things really go throughout the African diaspora because we have conversations like that in the U.S. around issues of authenticity and identity. People often want to simplify blackness as a category of things they recognize. I think it's really interesting to look at it from an international perspective. How do these issues become challenges for the African filmmaker, wherever she happens to reside?

AO: A lot of South African films are coproduced, and they have to bring in international actors. With that comes a certain dilution, because you are no longer making the film about the guy in Soweto. You have to make it so that the guy in Massachusetts can understand it. The real challenge is how do I convince someone to support the kinds of films that I would want to make. How do I convince someone to give me the money to say, "Listen, this can work if you stay true to what it's actually trying to say as opposed to trying to dilute it because it makes financial sense"? Having said that, I do understand that it is a business, and it's very much the devil you choose to dance with. That's the challenge, really—how far you are willing to compromise.

ATM: I like that. I think you have given me my [book] title—The Devil You Choose to Dance With!

AO: Well, I don't think I have a copyright on it. I'm sure I have heard it before.

AKIN OMOTOSO is a native Nigerian, who now lives in Johannesburg. He received a performer's diploma in speech and drama in 1996 from the University of Cape Town. He has extensive acting experience on stage and television, the latter of which includes stints in popular programs such as *Double Shift, Generations,* and *Big Okes.* He won M-Net's Best New Director award for *God Is African* in 2003. He had an acting role in the Hollywood film *Blood Diamond* (2006).

FILMOGRAPHY

***God Is African* (2002).** The mistrust and hostility that many South Africans express toward immigrants from other parts of the African continent are the focus.

***Rifle Road* (2005).** The lives of young South Africans are caught up in the world of risk taking and gun violence.

***A Gathering of Scattered Cousins* (2006).** His mother's origins in Barbados are examined as the filmmaker acknowledges his diverse roots and revels in family lore through interviews with relatives.

Bhekizizwe Peterson

Bhekizizwe Peterson

We find it extremely important to look beyond the glitz and the glamour of the industry. That is why it's precious to tell those stories, and as we complete each one, it is a profound moment—just exhaling in order to pick up again—because no one story is going to encapsulate what we have been through.

AUDREY THOMAS McCLUSKEY: Bheki, thank you so much for meeting with me here in your office in the African Literature Department at Wits [University of Witwatersrand]. I want to begin the interview by asking you about your latest work, *Zulu Love Letter* [2004], for which you wrote the screenplay. From previous conversations I've had, I know that some here are calling this the first true historical film about conditions in this country.

BHEKIZIZWE PETERSON: Well, I've not heard that. It is really difficult to assess one's work against what has come [before it] and what other people are doing. I always think that you work modestly and work from the things that you are passionate about. [Film] is a fairly young industry [in postapartheid South Africa], and I'm not keen on claiming to set any sort of milestone. I'm still moved by the very same issues that moved me before 1994. It's always been about doing work that's fixed on our experience and the human condition in South Africa. I just hope to remain true to my own artistic and political vision. I do think *Zulu* was an important story for us to tell at this point and time. Because, as you know, societies do change. I think certain stories can be more impactful if they come out at the appropriate time and moment when the society is still searching, [exploring] certain issues and questions. That is what people have tended to appreciate about *Zulu Love Letter.* It is looking at two mothers' search for their daughters—and for truth. The main protagonist is a woman who is a journalist trying to reconnect with her teenage daughter. The distance between the [mother and daughter] is because of the journalist's connection to the public issues in the past at the expense of the private ones. While she is trying to reestablish the relationship, a much-older woman comes to the journalist and says, "You need to locate the remains of my daughter." The older woman wants to give her daughter a proper burial. These are the two mothers in search of truth. It looks at the tension between private and public commitment. There are a lot of movies coming out with the TRC [Truth and Reconciliation Commission] as the backdrop to their narratives. Whether coincidentally or not, the movies have tended to come from a very mainstream point of view. Our movie is distinct in that it looks at the whole issue of personal costs, how people deal with posttraumatic stress, and how the ordinary person struggles to find a moment within this huge public discourse, to say, "Look, I also have a particular sense of this experience." That is what people seem to appreciate. There hasn't been enough of that angle or perspective in looking at what the violence of the past has meant to people in the small, intimate spaces of their lives.

ATM: Some theorists, Sylvia Wynter in particular, have said that film has been complicit in the subjugation of black people, but that it can also be a tool for liberation and rebirth. Do you think films like *Zulu Love Letter* can be part of such a project?

BP: Hopefully, because we are in such a marginal position in this society. When it comes to issues about the number of films that focus on black stories or the dominant ideas and images that we see, they do not tend to reflect black people from an independent sense. The South African film industry hasn't really changed that much. There have been some interesting developments in trying to increase output from black directors and black producers, but against the backdrop of an industry that is over a hundred years old, we're just starting to scratch the surface. We need to create a body of work that will contest the past on many levels. Every film that we do adds to that body of work. I don't think we can learn to effect different processes of liberation—mental, social, or cultural—to start to control the industry—unless we have that kind of orientation. Secondly, we need to push stories that are going to affirm that. It is very easy and fashionable in this new context to suddenly see yourself as being exceptional and distinctive, so you're going to set your own template and not be burdened by the past. I don't think that way. In the company that I'm with, we see our work as adding to a collective project. We want to do work that will bequeath something different to our children ten years from now. We find it extremely important to look beyond the glitz and the glamour of the industry. That is why it's precious to tell those stories, and as we complete each one, it is a profound moment—just exhaling in order to pick up again—because no one story is going to encapsulate what we have been through.

ATM: How do you deal with resistance to the imperative that you just articulated, particularly when it comes from other once-subjugated people. Shouldn't they have a voice in the matter?

BP: Yes, well, that's their dilemma to resolve. What I argue is to say, show me a film industry that does not feed off of its own experiences. Look at the number of Hollywood products in the last few years that have had a historical theme. Our work wants to move forward. I think we are really committed with blasting the future open, so we don't look back out of any sense of nostalgia. But we know that we cannot move forward from a position of amnesia. That's the difference.

ATM: You cannot move forward from a position of amnesia. That is a power axiom.

BP: You cannot move forward from a position of amnesia. We are not prepared to go into any future which is to be based on forgetfulness. It's not about being scared about the future. I find it ironical because before 1994, our artists and writers were concerned about opening the future. We were the ones that were trying to open the future. We realized that at this point in time with the changes and the installation of a democratic government, that part of extending the gains that we've made is to at least cast one eye on our past experiences. When you do get a chance to see *Zulu,* [you'll see] it's not about pre-1994 events, it's about how we carry the past into the present. The way that we are trying to find a filmmaking language is [by] asking, "How do you make the past and the present exist simultaneously in a frame without having a flashback?" In terms of the writing, I was thinking there is a sort of interlude. I think when you're going through stressful periods in the present, you see images of the past. That sometimes [can] create this attack of paranoia, of recalling things. It's not that you've gone backwards—it's walking down the street and seeing cops today searching someone they assume is an illegal Mozambiquan. I see that, but I see another layer to it—what we went through not so long ago. I hope I'm making sense.

ATM: Exquisite sense. The past is lived in the present. This building where we are sitting now has a history. Who could enter, and who was denied access? For whom is it named? That is part of the history that I engage as I enter, whether I acknowledge it or not. I'm always intrigued by continuities as much as by the ruptures of history, how on some level things continue to be what they were.

BP: Continues to be. [Among] the people who advocate what I call new strategies of containment, there is a refusal to deal with the living baggage that we carry. They find other ways of trying to cast themselves as new redeemers. Again, in a very ungiving way, there's never space allowed for you to express whatever it is that you are concerned with now. It's always a case of "I am the light. I am the leader." If you don't follow, there is something wrong with you. It is not even a generous attempt to create space for people with different focuses. So, on the level of content, I really don't subscribe to this. We moved into post-1994 issues, which are simply assumed to be somehow fundamentally different. There are still struggles in this country about mothers and families who are basically trying to survive: where the kids will go to school, the degrees of violence that surrounds them and so on. The watershed of the political transition does not necessarily mean that there has also been a watershed on other levels of societal experience. To me, that's what the artist should focus on. That's always what the artist should be preoccupied with—you cannot confuse political change necessarily with changes in peoples' lives, their daily experience.

ATM: What has been your experience as a participant in the community of artists? Is there enthusiasm about addressing these issues or at least having a conversation?

BP: I think different artists will be differently positioned. For instance, I think our musicians and people in the performing arts have always had this huge repertoire. If you talk now about an African renaissance, it doesn't make sense because it's been there for decades. These are the artists that, against all odds, have created compelling, incredible work. Because they have that body of work behind them, the way in which they're trying to expand their work is very different from black filmmakers. We're just starting out, trying to [establish] a presence, to see what kind of cinematic language we can evolve that suits us, one that is based upon our experiences. That is the big difference between what filmmakers are doing and where other artists are in terms of the growth and creation of a black aesthetic, if I could call it that.

ATM: Yes, as in music. Black music worldwide has always been a trendsetter. There has never been a problem in finding an audience for black music. We want other art forms to catch up aesthetically, to be able to travel and reflect the energy and innovation that is there is black music. What will it take for black film to reach that level?

BP: I think it has to do with a number of things. First, it is the mindset of people who work within film. They have not yet understood on a deeper level that there is so much that you can create that will be liberating, both in form and content. Secondly, [filmmakers] have to reject the sense of always aiming to write and think as if Big Brother is behind your shoulder. I find that there's a tendency to aspire toward something that will be acceptable within the conventional norms of what film [has] been.

ATM: Could it be also that music has always been closely identified with black culture, whether we are talking about Africa or America, while film has always been a colonial enterprise?

BP: It's on those two levels at least. As I said, it's a mindset. The second part of what you are referring to is also very important, because what it means is that because we have so little control of the means of filmmaking, you always start with a sense of disadvantage. If you want to have your film made, you should listen to those who can make it possible. That's where you start to lose what should be an equal commitment to your characters and story. I think, increasingly, we will start to think of other ways of making films. There's still a set formula to how you make a film. If we are starting to feel frustrated with the ways in which mainstream cinema works, we need to find people and start to do our own movies independently, even if that means taking four years, shooting every weekend.

ATM: You think that filmmaking is too rigid. Well, Adolphe Sax probably did not envision a Charlie Parker when he invented his saxophone, if you know what I mean.

BP: Yeah. You have to [defy] convention. If you don't, it means that you're going to have to defer, not only to those conventions but to those who confer those conventions.

ATM: Is South African film ripe for such a tour de force, at least at the germinating stage?

BP: I think so. There are one or two projects in which people have really tried to shoot in a very underground manner. I respect that, because it's not just that you are defending the integrity of your work but also rewriting the processes of production. Even if we go through periods where we do more work like that of any quality, for me, just the fact that you could just create the sense that there is another way that one can go is important. We will [become] more efficient. We'll get better at [it].

ATM: Can you speak about those two examples or say more about this oppositional strain of filmmaking?

BP: No, it's just that [I believe] that you always have to make certain [decisions] about how you are going to do the work. I think because South Africa is tending to be a service industry and becoming proficient with good crews, everybody assumes that is the only way you need to make a film. I don't think so. We try to work with smaller crews because we need to. We work as tightly as possible because that creates a different ethos as well in terms of the creative team that you have. It doesn't mean that you need to follow the classical textbook as to what an ordinary production team should be. You have to find new ways of doing it. You have to decide where to put value in the project. Do you want to move away, strip the production machine to the bare essentials so that we all see everything as much as possible, every cent on the screen? That's where our focus should be.

ATM: How did that ethos inform your collaboration with director Ramadan Suleman for *Zulu Love Letter?*

BP: Well, this is our second project together. I think in both cases it was the same. At first, we would know that there is no such a thing as an ideal budget. So again, you set yourself up in a manner where you're going to try and maximize money that you get. He is the director of the movie, he is one of the partners, but he has never been given a separate allocation or any of the trapping that comes with production—which is very common in South Africa. The director travels with everyone else. He's got to find space on set anywhere that he can. We make sure that he gets what he needs, because he has got a lot of things to do and to concentrate on, so you have got to give him as ideal circumstances as possible. But he doesn't come with a designation. He knows the struggle to make his own films so he's got to think differently. We try and do that with the rest of the cast and crew as well, because at the end of the day, it's about creating a space that is creative, dignified, and is going to give people full respect. It's not about the glitz and the glamour. If there are any cents to spare, it is directed towards those things that are meaningful to the cast and crew, either as individual people or in terms of reinforcing their faith and commitment to the production.

ATM: With this collaborative creativity, what happens in postproduction? What happens when you begin to think about marketing and audience? Are there other paradigms that you are envisioning to break through the established conventions in those areas?

BP: Yeah, it's obviously a very complicated process and experience that we're just starting with. For instance, with *Fools* [1997], which I worked [on] with Ramadan, one of the things that we did was to devise an outreach screening project so that we do not think in terms of the way in which we roll out our movies, simply in terms of the standard commercial circuit. Because of the kind of paradoxes that we find ourselves in, and there is so little African content on our screens, we think that it is politically imperative to try and change that. This does not necessarily refer to South African films. We would like to see film from West Africa and from [other African countries] start to be represented in our cinemas. That's one level of struggle that we need to engage in. But in the same time, you know that that's still on the symbolic level, it's not just about putting our films in some of these multiplexes when you know that ordinary people can't afford the tickets or to travel the long distances to see them. That's another level.

On one level, we are fighting to get our prints [shown], and on another level, we are starting to rethink what we understand about distribution and ask, "How do we create new audiences in this society?" So with *Fools,* after the mainstream screenings, we—Ramadan and one of the actors—took two prints to high schools. I designed a booklet for high school students which looked at the original short story and the film and tried to teach [students] about the kind of choices made in both. They took it to over thirty-seven township schools. We try as much as possible to give them the big-screen feel at the high school. It was important not just for them to see the film itself. We're also faced with the challenge of trying to bring different forms of cultural richness into the township schools. The schools tend to be extremely barren, not just in terms of the bricks and mortar, but there is a sense that we have to make our audiences also feel special, that they are a part of our mindset.

This same thing [will happen] with *Zulu.* The township audiences are not just a byproduct of PC [politically correct] reasoning. We know that's where the future of our cinema is going to be [with the upcoming generation]. It's not going to be easy to turn it around, but we don't think that there will just be this one hit, and everybody starts running in [to the cinema]. We have to create those audiences. Especially as black filmmakers, there is a responsibility that we cannot run away from. We have to try and find ways. We have to rethink distribution.

The government is investing in multipurpose community centers, so [we want to see] if those are able to have digital screening equipment as well. We have that, so now you ask, "How do you exploit that?" For me, it's not just again about the cents and figures in terms of recruitment, but it's also trying to act as a catalyst and a stimulus for new writers and performers. I think many times our kids are in environments where they just feel suffocated. There's a lot of ability, will, and desire, but I think sometimes you need someone just to lift, in a sense, the veil a little bit, and you see a completely different perspective. Outreach and community screening are not just something that you need to commit to for the right political reasons. That is where the musicians and the performers are so strong. You can go any weekend, anywhere in Soweto, and you—

ATM: —Find some music?

BP: Yes. You find some music, and you'll find people rehearsing plays, too. It's that kind of ownership of the arts that one is seeking.

ATM: I would like to conclude by asking you to talk briefly about your present project. Do you plan to continue to work with Ramadan Suleman in your company? What is on the horizon for you?

BP: Well, yeah. I am working with Ramadan, but I've not yet decided. It takes me quite a long time to make up my mind what my next project is [going to be]. I'm working on things, but if you ask me what it is about, I find it very hard [to say]. But we also do work with other outside projects that people want us to get involved with. We're open to that. One of the things that we've done after *Zulu* was work with Rehab Desai on *Born into Struggle* [2004]. What we need to do is to create a loose association of artists who are able to pull together in order to make sure that more work gets done. I think that when you look at cultural movements across the globe, many times part of the stimulus is when like-minded people are prepared to submerge their egos and be able to help a kindred spirit wherever they find one. That is what makes so-called movements. It is groups of people that feed off each other, and they don't all necessarily need to think the same way or do the same thing, but I think that you can recognize integrity when you see it. For me, fortunately, I have this job here at Wits [University of Witwatersrand]. It means I'm not as hard-pressed as most of the other artists in terms of how I pay the rent. That is an incredible opportunity, because it means that I can be more selective in what I do and pursue the projects that are important to me. It doesn't always necessarily come down to bread and butter.

ATM: That almost sounds like a luxury.

BP: It is a luxury. When I observe what other artists have to go through, it's not something I can be light[-hearted] about. But my situation allows me to keep working.

BHEKIZIZWE PETERSON is a senior lecturer in African literature at the University of Witwatersrand. His recent book is *Monarchs, Missionaries, and African Intellectuals: African Theatre in the Unmaking of Colonial Marginality.* Peterson has written several screenplays and collaborates with filmmaker Ramadan Suleman, their latest being *Zulu Love Letter.*

FILMOGRAPHY (SCREENWRITER)

***Fools* (1997, with Ramadan Suleman).** A once-respected township schoolteacher rapes one of his students and exposes the moral frailty of personal and political structures.

***Zulu Love Letter* (2005, with Ramadan Suleman).** A journalist and mother of a thirteen-year-old deaf-mute is haunted by past events and is called to action by another mother's loss during the apartheid era.

Dumisani Phakathi

Dumisani Phakathi

All I knew was that I had a story to tell and a camera.

AUDREY THOMAS McCLUSKEY: Dumisani, thank you for meeting with me here in your office overlooking the lovely Rosebank Mall. A very nice space. For people who may not know your work, can you tell me about the films that you have done up to this point?

DUMISANI PHAKATHI: Quite a few. I've done films in association with an initiative called New Directions. It's sponsored by a pay-per-view channel in this country. I've directed three films for that particular initiative. My first one is called *An Old Wives' Tale.* It's about a white farmer who decides he wants to take a second wife. His farm laborer, a black man, has more than one wife, and the farmer thinks that if his farmhand can have a second wife, then surely he can, too. This comedy has this cultural theme. Christian culture doesn't allow this [practice], but in a small town, you can create your own values. This was in 1999.

ATM: The concept is hilarious, but it also debunks the notion of cultural superiority. What are some other titles?

DP: The second film from this initiative was called *Christmas with Granny.* The English title is not mine. I did it in Zulu and Xhosa. The story is about an old woman who is about to die, and the last thing that she would like to do is to baptize her grandson. Her own son didn't have faith. "Before I die," she says, "I will make sure the boy is baptized." She goes to Jo'burg to take the boy from the mother, and she can in our culture. The whole scene happens on the train. About 80 percent of the film takes place on the train, returning to the rural area.

ATM: What was the inspiration for that film?

DP: That was actually written by somebody else. The writer used his own experience. I was asked to direct the film.

ATM: Do you usually write your own stories?

DP: I have not written most of my own. The only film I have written and shot myself was my first film.

ATM: That was *An Old Wives' Tale?*

DP: No. It was *Tribulation.* It was what led me to *An Old Wives' Tale.* I did not know much about filming, I hassled [people] and found my first camera and a cameraman. He kept telling me, "You can't shoot against the light." All I knew was that I had a story to tell and a camera.

ATM: You hadn't studied filmmaking at all? How does the film look?

DP: Actually, it's not bad. Of course, it is my first film. It's got poetry in it. There is a guy who commits a robbery, but you never see that.

ATM: Oh! And he's shot?

DP: He's shot. He writes to his mother, and he say he's going to act in a play about [Nelson] Mandela, which is very funny.

ATM: What was happening to him while he was telling these lies to his mother?

DP: The mother is always in the bedroom, but all we ever hear is her voice, and we see the picture of Mandela. I was working with some ideas that I didn't [completely] realize at the time. You only hear the voice saying, "Where are you going?" "Don't go!" The son says, "No, I'm going to act in the play. I've got Mandela."

ATM: And he dies?

DP: Yes. But I have misplaced this film.

ATM: Oh, no! I hope you find it!

DP: I hope, too. I'll look for it.

ATM: So how many films have you made to date?

DP: If I calculate it, one, two, three, four . . . four short films and one, two, three . . . about five documentaries, if not six.

ATM: You've done all that in less than ten years?

DP: Oh, yeah. I just take the chances as they come.

ATM: What has been your most interesting project?

DP: It's really hard to say because I think all of the projects—and I'm sure you hear this all the time—have their place and have importance.

ATM: Is there a certain film that expresses your core beliefs as a filmmaker?

DP: I still haven't done that film. You see a glimpse of my values and what I think about in some of my films. But there is no one film that expresses it. That is because of the funding structure. My last film, for example, I edited it in France.

ATM: Why France?

DP: Because that's part of the deal. In exchange for financing, I had to agree to go to France for postproduction.

ATM: Which film is this?

DP: It's called *Don't Fuck with Me, I Have Fifty-one Brothers and Sisters.* Yeah, that's about my family—my late father had fifty-two children. The film is about searching for who he was, through these relationships. It's a documentary.

ATM: It is a full-length feature, eighty-four minute film. What has the response been?

DP: People love it a lot! I think that it is my most loved work.

ATM: Do you see yourself as a documentary filmmaker primarily?

DP: I see myself as a creator. I see it all as one thing. If I wanted to, I could learn how to paint. I could acquire the skill and then paint.

ATM: Yes, I can see your love of art from the paintings on the wall.

DP: Yeah, that one was done by my friend, my favorite artist. His name is Samson.

ATM: I like it. Tell me about the political environment for filmmaking in South Africa.

DP: If you talk about any industry, you talk about the whole country because they go together. I look at what the hurdles are. I look at them in relation to where the country is at this time.

ATM: What are the hurdles?

DP: The hurdles, the obstacles are not about film but the country itself. [You] have to know the reality and choose your fights. That what I tell my fellow filmmakers. I'm not saying that you mustn't fight—you must fight—but you must look at the broader picture. It's not very difficult to complain or rejoice about the industry.

ATM: Can you give me an example of what you mean?

DP: Yes, it's very difficult for me to sit here in front of you and say it could be better, because I know it's where it's supposed to be at this moment. Because it is a development that takes years. Even in France today, it's still hard to make films.

ATM: In other words, you shouldn't expect film to be ahead of education or other developments in the country?

DP: No, I don't want to oversimplify it. Let the country develop, and try to fit in. It's not enough to have great ideas. It's useless to *not* make films. The [film] industry needs to look at where the country is going.

ATM: Useless to *not* make films?

DP: Yeah. If there are these great ideas and this amazing artistry, why not make films? [Otherwise,] we're going to remember you as the guy who had amazing ideas, and we can't afford that in this country. We need to be telling stories. We have to try as much as we can to film our stories. If the country has a relationship with the Congo, why don't I go there and do a coproduction with the Congo? I think there has to be more effort to make it better. I think we are on the right track. Some filmmakers will not agree with me.

ATM: I know. Some would say that film is not where it should be, that there are so many reactionary forces at work—

DP: Yeah. Reactionary forces are reactionary forces, and they will always be there. You can't become a victim in your own country or talk like a victim. It is your landscape, after all, and surely the list is long of those who have died to create it. We have to find ways. Life is about negotiating all the time—negotiating space, relationships. You can't be like Van Gogh and say, "It will be this, or I will cut off my own ear." Not at this time, not in this country. I know some filmmakers that I like, and they want to cut *my* ear off. I think that's good. I'm just not like that. It's not like I'm curing cancer.

ATM: No, you're making films. And where does film fit in?

DP: It's got its place. Part of the exciting thing is to make it happen. We don't have a *Citizen Kane* [1941] or *Do the Right Thing* [1989], but what we have, though, is a system for making sure that it *can* happen some time. I might not be the one who does it. I think every filmmaker wants to make a film that everyone talks about. That's the struggle to be the first one. I don't have that ambition.

ATM: You don't want to be the first one?

DP: No. The struggle is bigger. The struggle is everything, more than making one film.

ATM: It is important to have a community of filmmakers?

DP: Yes. Every time I read about a new filmmaker, I feel great. I welcome him. I'm not thinking, "Oh, another one is going to take my place," or "Fuck, I'm going to lose my work." You know, that does exist here . . . that perception.

ATM: Also, you work on another plane. You have called yourself a creator, an artist, who is not exclusively a filmmaker. You told me earlier that you are producing a Chinese cookbook! Are these projects related in any way to your filmmaking?

DP: Very much! Filmmaking happens to be the first thing that I learned because I taught myself. Cooking is one of the things that I love, and somehow I am able to do quickly. . . . For my other ideas, I call upon other people.

I called this painter and said, "You're a painter. Let's do an exhibition of doors." I wanted to exhibit doors that are in different spaces in different parts of the country—wooden doors, zinc doors, every different kind of door. I spoke with him, and he said, "Okay, I think it's better to frame them." I say, "Ah, that's even better." He says, "Let's call it *Deur ammaa Deur.*" That's how I do it.

ATM: Collaboration. *Deur ammaa Deur?*

DP: *Deur ammaa Deur.* It's means "Because of the Doors" in English. But it's Afrikaans and Zulu.

ATM: What field did you study?

DP: Nothing. I didn't train to be anything. I did theater. That's the only kind of training I ever received. I loved it. It was three years of having fun.

ATM: What about your schooling?

DP: I went to a township school. I didn't speak English until I was a teenager. I spoke only Zulu. I met the first white person in 1992 when I was digging in a mine.

ATM: How old were you?

DP: I was eighteen. That's the first time I considered a white person not as a cop or as someone on TV. We were not on equal footing, because I couldn't speak English then. I taught myself to speak English, because it wasn't taught at school.

ATM: Did you speak Afrikaans?

DP: No. I didn't know anyone who didn't speak Zulu.

ATM: What is the inspiration for your, so far, unusual career? What propelled you to do what you are doing?

DP: I think it's a mixture of things. I'm where I'm supposed to be. I [have] spiritual gifts. I know it sounds very [strange], but [this is] in a Zulu African ancestors' kind of way. I look at my father, I look at my grandfather, then I look at myself. There are quite a few similarities. I am in a place where I can influence, to a small degree, how people look at themselves and what they think about themselves, which is what my father did. In a different way—not art but in music and soccer—he helped the community. It's in my system.

ATM: What about the influence of women on your life?

DP: They are there, of course. I grew up with my mother. I didn't like [women] for a long time because my father stole me when I was about six years old, and I lived with men [in a hostel] for two years. I had not seen a woman for two years. I came back, and they said, "This is your mother." I had forgotten her somehow. This is your grandmother. I was like, "Oh, I want to go back," because [I liked] living in a hostel with only men. All these men loved me. To them, this was an opportunity to be with a son of a man they respected—my father. So they used to take me to their workplace. When I left there, I had a tin full of money to spend.

ATM: Were there other boys there?

DP: No. Others would come visit their fathers and go. I stayed.

ATM: Did you go to school? Did your mother know where you were?

DP: I went to school. My mother didn't know where I was, but she knew I was with my father and [that] I was fine. Of course, I don't think she wanted it that way.

ATM: In the few minutes we have left, tell me about your current work and the direction you are taking with your film projects.

DP: I'm at a turning point in my work. I can only get better by doing films. I've always loved making films, but I'm respecting it [more]. I'm the kind of guy who never sticks to the story. I think the work that I'm going to do is a step toward finding something a bit different.

ATM: Different in what way?

DP: Different in visual presentation, different in how I deal with the ideas or the themes. To give an example, I'm doing a film about a boxer who lived in the eighties. I tell myself I'm doing a documentary. Someone else is doing a feature film, because I never thought it was a story for a feature film.

ATM: Tell me about this boxer.

DP: I did the documentary three or four years ago. I talked to family, used archive material, and it became more about remembering him, about what he meant to people. Now, I'm into representing more than that. I'm interested in codes.

ATM: Codes?

DP: That guy wasn't a great boxer, not great enough to make a film about [his boxing skills]. His greatness was the fact that people loved him so much. I want to create a film that searches for that greatness through his relationship to people.

ATM: What was his name?

DP: Mayisela, after the fighting Zulu Prince Mayisela. The film is about the icons of the time, what people see as a symbol of the time. What did they look like? How did they smile? How did they dance at a party? He was a common man, but he was an icon of the time, like a Michael Jordan. He rode the train, he didn't drive a car, so he was with the people all the time. He worked a very menial job as a packer. He was a man's man.

ATM: Who plays his character?

DP: No. It's a documentary. I'm going to have dancers playing his role, doing his movements. It's not just an acknowledgment or a memory of him. You should be able to watch it and react. There are certain things I'm going to put in your face so that you cannot run away.

ATM: Do you think of such a film as making a political statement?

DP: Yeah, of course. All films are political. One of the things I've always said is that for me the mere fact of *me* is political. I've always said that. My work will always be that, because I don't think [being] political is doing a film about apartheid. No, I once put a black woman in [a film]. She was quiet, looking into the camera, not saying a word. That is political. What is not political is having her just cooking. As an audience member, you [engage] by watching the whole film unfold.

ATM: Is it political because it's a different kind of representation?

DP: No. It is [political] because it makes you look at an everyday situation in a different way. If you take it further, it makes you want to read and understand the connecting factors to that particular story. This particular story happens on the train, but on that train, there's a white ticket examiner who does something. There is a Christmas party on the train. The boy is traveling with his grandmother. There's a compartment with only white people, and there's a party—kids are blowing balloons, et cetera, and this kid, by mistake, ends up in that compartment. He is not supposed to be there, because it is segregated by class and by race. That statement is not overt. For me, there is a danger in wanting to limit the stories to the big political themes like apartheid. I think interpersonal relationships amongst people in this country are important for our stories. It used to be only black people, but all the relationships across gender, race, class, et cetera, are more interesting and critical. If I want to talk about capitalism, it's going to be on a very simple day to day basis, not . . . Nietzsche or Karl Marx. It's going to come in a personal relationship between two people or a person in a certain situation. I don't choose it; it happens because I love people. Because I love people, I find that I am more likely to tell the story from a people point of view, not from the top down. I do see it from the top, but I don't have to tell the story from the top. It's not my instinct, and it's not my mission. My initial instinct is to tell the stories from this country—that guy standing there, where is he going? The security guy—what is his life like? Where does he live? Is he happy today? The politics are there in people's lives everyday. It's just such hard work to capture those politics. It's much easier to say, "He's like this because of his background, or this country's like this because it chose capitalism over socialism." That's old for me and not even the real story.

DUMISANI PHAKATHI was born in Soweto. After high school, he worked as an intern at *Die Beeld,* a leading Afrikaans newspaper. From there he joined a television production company as a director trainee, where he conceptualized a long-running youth television program called the *Electric Company.* He next tried theater as a member of the Market Theatre Actors Training program. He performed in several plays, including a tour of Europe, before entering the Young Directors Competition sponsored by M-Net Television. Thus began his award-winning filmmaking career.

FILMOGRAPHY

***An Old Wives' Tale* (1998).** In this comedy, an Afrikaner decides that like his black helper, he should be able to take on a second wife.

***Christmas with Granny* (2000).** A boy and his grandmother are depicted in this short film.

***Rough Rides* (2000).** The adventures of minibus drivers are documented.

***Wa'n Wina* (*Sincerely Yours*) (2003).** HIV/AIDS survivors are interviewed.

***Don't Fuck with Me, I Have Fifty-one Brothers and Sisters* (2004).** Phakathi searches for his family in his deceased father's many, many children.

Bridget Pickering

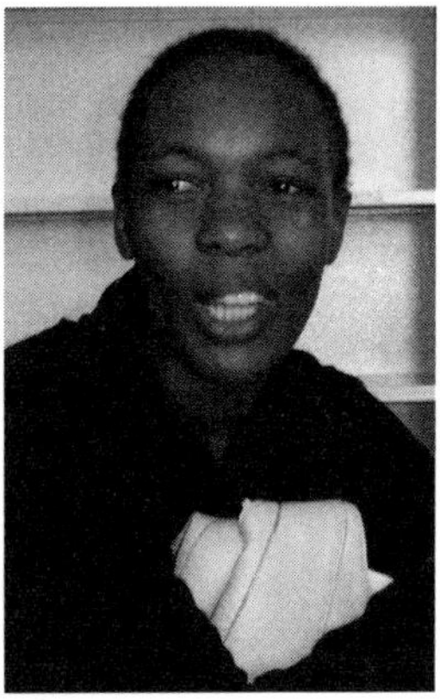

Bridget Pickering

> We haven't had enough authentic filmmaking. Now, it is almost like the Wild West. [Filmmakers] want to try to find their own space, their own position. There's also an acknowledgment that we haven't been making the films we want to make, the definitive South African film.

AUDREY THOMAS McCLUSKEY: Bridgette, my first question is about your own involvement in film, primarily as a producer. How did you get started?

BRIDGET PICKERING: I studied politics and film at Syracuse University in the U.S., and then I worked at Universal Pictures in New York. I did that for about two or three years, then came back to southern Africa, particularly Namibia—my father is Namibian, and my mother is South African—and worked in Namibia, making films. The films were about governmental issues that promote basic political and social literacy.

ATM: When was this?

BP: This was between 1992 and about 1998. Namibia had just become independent, and NGOs [nongovernment organizations] really needed films that dealt with land and social issues like childbirth and health—which were needed by the new country at that time.

ATM: Did you return with the idea of making films?

BP: Yes, I came back with those intentions. My parents went into exile to England [during the apartheid era], and a lot of my influences came from watching British television and the BBC. I decided that I wanted to make films, particularly documentaries. When I went to university, that was my intention, so I studied film and politics. I needed a job to stay in the U.S., so I got a job at Universal Studios, and I decided to stay. Being involved in that highly commercial environment doing feature film productions made me think quite differently about film but confirmed my desire to do documentaries. Also, I became very interested in fiction storytelling. When I left Universal to return to southern Africa, my intention was to work between those two fields. I always thought that it was possible to make films that were interesting creatively but also had a message that would get ordinary people excited—whether it was trying to promote better health care or better sanitary conditions. In Namibia, there was a lot of excitement about the possibilities and challenges that it faced as a new country. Making films in that kind of environment was very exciting. There was a real sense that these films could change lives.

ATM: Do you still feel the need to go in between the two genres?

BP: Very much so. I've worked as the South African producer of *Hotel Rwanda* [2004], and I've just finished two much lower budget documentaries that I made with two young filmmakers here in South Africa.

ATM: What are the documentaries about?

BP: One film is called *Morris Fynn Goes Native* [2005] by a filmmaker whose father is South African. He moved to Canada in the 1960s and married a white New Zealand woman. The other filmmaker is from the colored community in South Africa. Her film is about her uncle who was given land in KwaZulu-Natal by Shaka Zulu. When apartheid came, the Fynn family, who had become colored in the South African context, lost their land based on the fact that they could not be chiefs, and therefore they could not own this land. In the last few years, the present South African government created a Traditional Authority Act that is allowing people who lost land through apartheid policies to reclaim their land. The film raises a very big question about what makes someone African. It is about race and history in South Africa.

The other film is one called *Vuwani* (2005) by a filmmaker from Venda.

ATM: What does *Vuwani* mean?

BP: *Vuwani* means *awake.* It's about a young filmmaker who has grown up in a very rural environment with a very strong idea of clan, family, and community. When he moves to an urban environment, he begins to question the meaning of these concepts and the value of what is lost as one generation passes to the next. It's really about generational struggle and what it means to be a modern man.

ATM: Do you think that film in this evolving society should be, in part, about reclaiming some of those lost stories?

BP: I feel that so much of the past has been denied and vilified that, to me, an important part of film[making] is about people reclaiming who they are. I've never really thought about it very consciously, yet as I look at the body of work that I've done, it's all historical. I think that history, especially in southern Africa, is such a recent thing. It's been scarcely ten years since apartheid ended. Yet, if you ask my daughter, she knows nothing about it, and she has no sense of what you are talking about when you tell her that ten years ago this country used to be very different. We are the generation who have our feet in both periods. We grew up in a world with a very repressive political system, and now we are being offered all the opportunities of a new society. I think that we are constantly struggling between these two kinds of experiences. What do we take, and what do we leave behind? There is a constant pressure in South Africa to leave the past behind. We're told it doesn't matter, move on. I think that's a terrible thing to say, because you cannot deny people who they are. I want to tell stories about what it was like for me as the only black student in a white school. That's a very important story. It's a part of who I am. I cannot deny and pretend because it makes someone feel better.

ATM: This feeling of wanting to forget is shared by many—both blacks and whites, isn't it?

BP: Well, you hear that a lot. They [blacks] don't want to think of how bad things were. The white population doesn't want to know; they don't want to deal with it. They feel that people will use that against them. I think artists should resist that and use [the past] in their art. When you look at other societies, whether there is Iranian film or other countries, you see how they use history. It can be done very creatively. You can't pretend that it all started in 1994! You've got to find a way of acknowledging the past with all its complexity and richness. You can look at the body of work, and in the last year of South African feature films, they've all been about apartheid, specifically about the past. It's about truth and reconciliation. It's about forgiveness . . .

ATM: Do you mean films by South African filmmakers? Another development that I see happening in Africa is that the continent is being used as a backdrop for Western stories.

BP: Yes, that is true. A lot of these films are being made by white filmmakers. There are also South African films like *Forgiveness* [2004], which have their own problems. Obviously, that may change. The flood of films that will be released in the next two or three years will be different, but how you incorporate history into art forms is still very important. When people say it's not helpful to [incorporate history], I wonder what they mean.

ATM: You wonder why that issue isn't raised about films about the Holocaust.

BP: Absolutely, no one asked us if we've had enough of the Holocaust.

ATM: It's the same about slavery. We're told to move on. It's interesting.

BP: I think a lot about the content of film. Even among the traditional French filmmakers, the new wave, there was a strong critique of content. What kind of content do *we* want? What are the stories we want to tell? How do we find the [right] language? What is missing is that we haven't taken film and made it our own. In West African films, there has been a very strong French influence. Yet, there is a language of storytelling, a quality that makes [those films] West African. That is something that I don't think we have found yet.

ATM: What will it take to get there?

BP: I think it's a combination of different things. It is about new voices. Unfortunately, South Africa has a very heavy Western influence and [is] very infatuated with the outside world, especially in filmmaking. I do find it problematic that the references and influences that we are getting now, at this very critical time in our development, are very Western based. I also think that young filmmakers are insisting that they want to tell their stories their own way. They may say, "This doesn't feel like a South African film. Is there another way to do it? The content may be South African but that's not how people behave and speak and walk and talk." They think our films should reflect who we are as people. There is constant friction between these poles.

ATM: Do you find that there is much conversation about this among South African filmmakers as a community?

BP: No, no, no. It's quite a divided film community. I feel it has to do with issues of race. But I think it's also because this is a new industry, and people are jostling for position and defining who they are. In other countries, there are often [film] masters who have made great films and are looked up to. I don't think we have that yet. We haven't had enough authentic filmmaking. Here it is almost like the Wild West. [Filmmakers] want to try to find their own space, their own position. There's also an acknowledgment that we haven't been making the films we want to make, the definitive South African film. This creates a sense of unease.

ATM: It is a competitive environment. But is this a good type of competition?

BP: It is a competitive environment. I think that's probably true of most filmmaking communities. But here [it] is not necessarily along the lines of wanting to make the best films.

ATM: That would be good competition. [*Both laugh.*]

BP: That would be great competition! But [here] it is about who gets money, but there isn't enough. There never is enough. There are also issues among black filmmakers about filmmakers who come from outside of South Africa. There is a lot of friction around who is South African and who is not. This won't help to build the kind of confidence needed for us to understand that the filmmaking community is a worldwide one and that we are all part of that community. This is especially true for African filmmakers. I feel like there are too few connections among African filmmakers.

ATM: This gets back to your point about filmmakers looking more to the West and not to Africa.

BP: Absolutely.

ATM: There is a solid tradition of filmmaking in Africa.

BP: Completely. Absolutely. Most South African filmmakers, if they've completed a film, rather than thinking of the African market and saying wouldn't it be great for [other] Africans to see my film, their imperative is, "Wouldn't it be great if my film gets seen at Cannes?" It is also about money. Where in Africa will my film get seen? Where is the market? I think that it is a psychological state of mind. Even if you know that your film won't make money, if you thought of an African audience as your primary audience, that would influence the content of the film. A lot of times people think their film is going to be seen in New York or London, and that begins in the writing process.

ATM: Can that be a healthy development if filmmakers are constantly thinking about a foreign market? What a foreign market likes about Africa often invokes a heart-of-darkness mentality, although South Africa is accorded a special status.

BP: That's the problem. With South Africa being in the world spotlight and having so much wealth, it is able to do so much more. Its economy makes it possible to be more connected to the outside world than most other African countries that don't have access to capital or financing from places like the IDC.

ATM: The IDC?

BP: The Industrial Development Corporation is the financing body in South Africa. West African films still have to consider France because the French are giving them money. Maybe it's not much different. But I think there is this possibility in South Africa to be more inward looking, especially in terms of finding and telling our stories. We have a population from which a profitable film market could develop if we make films that majority of people want to watch. It is possible here.

ATM: Are you thinking about audience when you make your films?

BP: When I look at American filmmakers, I know that they constantly think about audience. With my training, I don't think of it as much as I should. I am sort of like Europeans who just make the film and then worry about the audience later. I think that is something that is changing. Certainly, South Africa is not going to be able to sustain an industry where it is constantly giving money, and the films don't make money back. There is a huge initiative by film distributors and cinema owners to bring black audiences in. The reality is that black people are not going to the cinema. Black people will see films on DVD. There is a huge gap between what filmmakers create and the audience that they are creating for.

There is constantly this discussion among people I work with, but I am not sure how wide spread this is—about who the audience is. In television, that audience is much nearer because you've got those very clear audiences in SABC-1 [South African Broadcasting Corporation channel 1] for young people between the ages of eighteen and whatever, and you make programs for them. In film, that audience is not very clear. In time, it will come. I'm talking about feature films. These questions will be answered. It is a very interesting time.

ATM: How did you come to produce *Hotel Rwanda* [2004]?

BP: When I was approached about the project, it was to come on as a trainee producer, because even though I had done quite a lot of work in documentary and some short film, I'd never really done a project of that scale. I was approached to work very closely with the American producer on the project. However, what happened was that the South African producer was no longer available so I was asked if I would step in. That's how I became involved.

ATM: It is interesting that South Africa was considered a home site for this film about Rwanda. Perhaps a comment about the region's politics and Western perceptions. Were your experiences positive or negative?

BP: Both. It was such a huge project with so much at stake. I found it very difficult to have a sense of power and to feel like I was contributing to the film. In most films that I work on, I am a very important part of the film, mostly because there isn't a lot of money, and I am really involved in getting the film made, including contributing to the writing process.

ATM: Were you called upon to do very much in making *Hotel Rwanda?*

BP: Not really. There were so many people doing everything. As a producer, you're there to watch and make sure that if there is a problem you solve it, but on the whole, most of the people are highly experienced and do this all the time. There isn't really a lot for you to do.

ATM: But did it open doors for you?

BP: Well, sort of. The doors that have opened are purely on the level that connects you with a film that has done really well. There is a confidence that people may have in you. That's what it has done. But I have done a lot of the other [film projects] which in terms of content have been very exciting ways that are more risky and interesting. That is the kind of work I like to do. Although *Hotel Rwanda* is a Hollywood film, it is an important story, and I thought the story was very well told. It really didn't play down the Africanness of it, which a lot of those films do. It was authentic, very rich. The actors really came across as African. It taught me a lot about filmmaking and gave me a lot to think about. The film told the story of Rwanda in a way that probably would never have reached so many people except for its scale. We make these films that we think are great, these documentaries, but who sees them? At most, maybe ten to twenty thousand people will see them. I am not sure *Hotel Rwanda* put the spotlight on Africa, but that is the most any film can do—get the story told. Being involved with *Hotel Rwanda* did make me think a lot about the audience and the world.

ATM: Could that be one of the models for the development of film in South Africa—partnering with other nations?

BP: Well, yes. You always want to make sure that you are equal partners. Because what often happens is if one partner is still very new and on a learning curve, the more powerful and stronger people end up taking over. South Africa is obviously planning treaties with a lot of countries—Germany, Italy, the U.K.—these kind of partnerships are inevitable. A project like *Hotel Rwanda* is obviously a good example in that it was written by an American. It was directed by a British-Irish subject, the talent was British and American, and most of the actors were South African. But key talent was American/British, and yet the film stayed true. It didn't try to be American. It didn't try to be Hollywood. In that way, it was a success. Another film like *Drum* [2004]—I haven't seen *Drum*—but I think one of the [questions it raises] is whether Taye Diggs is believable as an African. I think it depends. Obviously, the idea with *Drum* was that Taye Diggs will bring an American audience to that film. I'm not sure if he does, but that was the goal.

ATM: What does it say to the African audience? They may think, "no way"?

BP: Yeah, I know! They may say, "We don't believe this guy."

ATM: It is a tightrope to walk.

BP: It is absolutely a very difficult one. If you are looking around at what is happening in other countries, it's not purely a South African problem or African problem. It's a problem in Britain, too. How do the British make films in relation to Hollywood or other European countries? The British are working more closely with the Americans. The French, Italians, and the

Spanish are doing so less. One of our issues is we haven't decided where we want to go. There has not been a very clear direction. We need to position ourselves and say our primary goal is to make films about ourselves that are very strong and authentic. That doesn't mean we can't make a *Hotel Rwanda*. We can make *Drum* or those kind of films, but the primary thrust has to be *our* films. When we do those films, are we constantly selling ourselves? Defining ourselves on our own terms? This is especially important for a new country that is still trying to find its values. There's so many questions that we are still struggling with. There is constant debate about whether white filmmakers make [good films about blacks]. Are we making films only about the black community? How do you make a film about this new country that is coexisting among all these different racial groups? All of that stuff is so complicated, and we have to struggle with that content. It is very important that we do that. We are trying to find a way of telling those stories that are very important for our own development. These debates are happening, but I think they should be much stronger.

ATM: Can film leapfrog over other pressing issues? In other words, should where South Africa is now be reflected in the films it produces? Do you expect film to lead the way or simply follow what exists?

BP: I guess for me it is both. What filmmakers do well is raise questions. Film can provide a vision, suggest answers, and find a way of saying that this is the way it could be. I think it's therapy to work out who you are and who you could be as human beings. That's what film can do. It's a way of working out the confusion in this society which exists at the moment.

ATM: Is there any one or two things that you would look to in a few years and say, "Aha, this is what I'm hoping South African film will be about"?

BP: If you look at documentaries that were made almost ten years ago, they were very much about the struggle. They are incredibly beautiful films because they are about that, but they are also about the power and strength of people. Dumisani's [Phakathi] work I like a lot because he shows the beauty of the people. There are people who laugh and people who fall in love, people who desire. All of that is about pain, but it's also about beauty, it's about laughter, it is about the many layers that exist in our lives. We are not just one thing. It is only a work of art that can [make] people sit in front of the television or in the cinema and laugh and cry. I can't imagine one kind of film, but I do think about the people. I think about creating interventions in a body of work that will make people think. That is why I became a filmmaker.

BRIDGET PICKERING is a producer and director who has been working several years in the film industry. She served as South African area producer for the internationally acclaimed and Academy Award–nominated film *Hotel Rwanda* [2004].

FILMOGRAPHY

***Uno's World* (2002, director).** Part of the *Mama Africa* anthology, a young woman lives an active social life until unwanted pregnancy complicates things.

***Hotel Rwanda* (2004, producer).** The Academy Award–nominated film shows genocide in Rwanda.

***Morris Fynn Goes Native* (2005, producer).** The question raised is whether a mixed-race man can become a Zulu chief and explores broader questions of race and identity in South Africa.

***Vuwani* (2005, producer).** Tensions arise as a young man is torn between his traditional upbringing in rural Venda and the pull of the modern world.

Maganthrie Pillay

Because only 10 percent of the population goes to the cinema in South Africa, and a very large proportion of the other 90 percent has never been to a cinema, it feels like we are at the beginning of creating a local industry.

Dingi Ntuli and Maganthrie Pillay

AUDREY THOMAS McCLUSKEY: You are a pioneer of sorts. You have discussed the fact that your film *34 South* [2005] is the first feature-length by a black woman in South Africa. What in your background prepared you for this breakthrough?

MAGANTHRIE PILLAY: I have been tracking the creative contribution of women and of black women in particular in all artistic fields for many years. I am on a mission trying to encourage women to do their thing! Whether it is as directors of theatre, film, choreographers, artists, or composers. After being a cultural activist, I realized that the only way to change things is to create the change yourself, if you are in that particular field. I took my own advice of "Just do it"!

Making movies was only a dream growing up. Up until 1990, the advertisements in South Africa, for example, only featured white South Africans, and even today, diversity is a new idea that constantly clashes with the "universal" idea, which is still white. In any English drama, [blacks] are typically not [present]. I thought the theater was a more immediate setting for telling stories, so I studied English literature and education. That experience taught me that there were no published texts that reflected my reality. We had to make it up and create our own stories. We didn't want to just do Shakespeare and [Harold] Pinter.

My producer, Dingi Ntuli, happens to be a pioneer as well. His tenacity and determination have been a constant source of inspiration. South Africa was isolated for such a long time, and black people were oppressed for the last four hundred years. We should all be pioneers [in order] to create a more normalized environment where our children can dare to dream.

ATM: You are of Indian heritage, and in South Africa, I note that some Indians identify as "black," which is not true of Indian Americans in the U.S. Can you explain this from a South African perspective?

MP: One of the main liberation ideologies in South Africa has been Black Consciousness, which is what created unity among black people and was critical to the formation of the United Democratic Front. This was a mass movement that created awareness and fought a common system of oppression. Identifying as black did not negate anyone's particular cultural practice, but it certainly created more pride in who we are. My identification as black is also not unique. For decades, the institution of higher learning that I attended, even though it was created to further divide people, actually drew people together. It was a site of much political activity. I have a poem that I often use to explain how I feel about this.

ATM: Would you share it?

MP: I'm a so-called Indian in a so-called new South Africa
More a Red Indian than a South Indian
More an African than an Asian
Living in the Bo-kaap
More a Muslim than a Hindu
It took a Steve Biko, though, to bring me back to my roots.

ATM: Excellent. I see what you are saying. Your film actually deals with questions of racial identity, which seem to be in flux in S.A. What inspired you to do this film [*34 South*]?

MP: Many things, I suppose. I raised my own questions about how I fit into the country in a postapartheid South Africa, where I was officially classified as Indian—I rejected that, because I am South African—and now I am being reclassified in a so-called nonracial society! Yet, there are others who would cringe at being called black, because apartheid was about hatred of the idea of blackness altogether. This is a notion that is inculcated in people. We must deconstruct that and [ask,] "How can we get to that elusive rainbow nation?" Most of all, "How do we accept who we are and also be allowed to be South African?"

ATM: Makes sense to me. What has the reception been for your film? What did the "best" and "worst" reviews say?

MP: We have had an overwhelming reception for *34 South.* I sat at the premiere in a darkened theater with over three hundred people who from the second scene on laughed and were totally in tune with the film. This was definitely an experience that is etched in my heart. Many [people in the audience] came out saying they had goose bumps. Others were just so glad to see themselves on the screen in such a normal way. We have a great response. I'll send you some [of the reviews] from South Africans of all racial descriptions. On the other hand, the worst [review] was from a few white reviewers who said it was racist. Although the white crew who worked on it are still trying to see what they meant.

ATM: That is interesting, but my visits to South Africa have shown me that there is an active resistance to black cinema among some, while others simply have disengaged. Do you feel that you are part of a larger national filmmaking community? What defines that community for you, if it exists?

MP: Making local films in South Africa has been a real feat for [every]body the last ten years. There is a community [where] we meet at festivals and at Sithengi market and exchange war stories and encourage each other to keep going. But we are also inspired by each other. Every film that gets made is important, even for television. We hope that the new processes will finally bring more equality. Having only one public broadcaster has meant that we are all trying to get a piece of the pie.

ATM: Some film critics say that films are political even when the subject matter is not easily categorized as such. What political ideas do you embrace as a filmmaker?

MP: Generally, my work pushes a diversity of voice and perception, which is a contentious notion in South Africa, it seems. Politically, in *34 South,* for example, most of the characters are black or brown, as some like to call themselves, previously classified colored, but not white. That is a statement in and of itself. Was it intentional? Yes. I was trying to tell the story of a particular group of people who are grappling with being of mixed heritage. I try to subvert all kinds of stereotypes around gender, around who can be a surfer or a hacker, et cetera. The film also dealt with the legacy of slavery—a subject that is hidden in the midst of shame and denial. Now, what many people said that they liked about the movie was it was not filled with hate. If anything it was [more of] a celebration. But it is all relative, isn't it?

ATM: Yes, I would say so. What is your view of the present state of national film culture in South Africa?

MP: We are at a very exciting moment in South Africa as black people in particular are coming into their own and want to tell their stories. With the number of South African films that have been released this year, people here are being made aware of the industry, not only as a service industry but are also beginning to [appreciate] South African stories. Because Hollywood has had the market share of entertainment, for the first time we have a variety of products [that are homegrown]. As we make more films, we will find our own cinematic voice, and our audiences will be able to see themselves more often. Because only 10 percent of the population goes to the cinema in South Africa, and a very large proportion of the other 90 percent has never been to the cinema, it feels like we are at the beginning of creating a local industry.

ATM: What is your primary source of funding?

MP: The only grant one can get is from the National Film and Video Foundation. Their investment assisted in most of the feature films being made and certainly contributed to a historic number of film productions in the last decade, perhaps fifteen. This thirty million rand [US$4.5 million] is their total budget for all genres and all stages per year, although this year they will not be making any grants due to the government not renewing the budget. This is going to have serious implications, but the flip side is it might get us to unite and lobby together as an industry in a way that we have not been able to before. Television does not regularly invest in feature films and getting them to buy your film or do a pre-sale just does not happen. It is not automatic either.

ATM: What keeps you inspired despite the obstacles?

MP: What shall we do? We have equipment, crew, and private resources. My hope is that we can continue to make more low-budget films and create an independent movement.

MAGANTHRIE PILLAY, the youngest of five children of a Hindu shoe-factory worker and a dressmaker, was born in Durban, South Africa, in the early 1970s. She grew up in the township of Chatsworth and studied teaching at Westville University, completing her studies with honors at the University of Cape Town. Maganthrie belongs to WEAVE, a black women writers collective, and has directed television documentaries and theater productions. She is considered the first black woman to direct a feature film in South Africa, *34 South,* a comedy about self-perceptions of racial identity in postapartheid society.

FILMOGRAPHY

***34 South* (2005).** A group of "coloreds" decide to take a car trip from Cape Town to Johannesburg and encounter different cultures along the way.

Numerous television documentaries.

Isabelle Rorke

Isabelle Rorke and Dumisani (Dumi) Gumbi

> It has great, new story content that's never been seen. Fresh, different stuff. That's the level that we are at now—the Africanization of the animation industry.
>
> —Isabelle Rorke

> Yes, but also we are business people. We realize that this is a business.
>
> —Dumisani (Dumi) Gumbi

Dumisani (Dumi) Gumbi

AUDREY THOMAS McCLUSKEY: How long have you been making films and involved in animation?

ISABELLE RORKE: We founded the company in 2000 but actually got started in 2001.

ATM: Isabelle and Dumi are partners in a company called Ana. . . .

DUMISANI (DUMI) GUMBI: An-Amazing Workshop.

ATM: An-Amazing. That's a cool name. How did you decide to come together and do this?

IR: Dumi was involved in live action at another production company and wanted to animate the story of the African hero Shaka Zulu. I was, at the time, an editor for a children's magazine, and I was doing cartoon strips for kids. We wanted to pitch a project to ETV [Educational Television] for an animation series they were doing. Dumi asked me if I had some ideas to pitch, and I created Black Forest, which is a black female superhero, and the other one was based on a comic strip in my magazine called "Roland, the Funky Green Teen." That was pitched, and ETV, of course, didn't have a budget for it, so with three great ideas, we decided to look into the world of animation. Our research made us realize that it was a hell of a lot more lucrative than live action! It was our passion for our children, the kind of stories they have access to—that inspired us. None of the [stories] are African. There's no representation of African culture or African people in any of the animation that is broadcast out there. Part of our motivation was to be able to use the media for edu-tainment and to capture our culture, our stories, and folktales. That was our motivation to go into animation, even though we were both firmly entrenched in the live-action industry. I was producing live morning breakfast shows that are still on SABC [South African Broadcasting Corporation]. Yes, we completely changed careers. We were convinced that we had the passion for it and that it was financially viable.

ATM: You bravely stepped out although neither of you has a background in animation?

DG: No, not at all. We looked at where the local industry was and found that it is pretty much based in the commercial industry. Animation doesn't really exist even today. We don't really have capabilities to produce a television series or a feature film. Broadcasters don't really commission any long-term animation in South Africa because of the expense that is attached to production. There were really no black people in the animation industry. It continues to be a handful of black people in the center of the film industry. That was one of the things that propelled us. We said, "Well, let's see if we can make something out of this." We realized that there are a lot of live-action productions going on in South Africa, but even with a script, the acting isn't really that great. We looked at it as a plus for animation. [In our productions,] we can use stage actors who have a great deal of background and experience.

ATM: How does animation actually work? Conceptually, is it similar to developing a documentary or a narrative film? What are the major differences?

IR: This is one of the things that we have been working on over the past four years. We are finding all of the problem areas, and one of them is the shortage of writers in animation. We just had an experience with our *Lost African Folktales* series, where they [hired] a live-action writer, and this person went completely haywire. It was the set, the characters. It was just too much, way too expensive. We had to get an experienced animation writer to cut it down and put it within animation parameters. People think when you're in animation that you can completely go wild, but you've also got limitations on what you can do. The production pipeline is similar but also different from other genres. Once you have completed the script, you're going into visual drawings of characters and sets and putting storyboards together. One step is different—we're working with computers instead of cameras. It all depends on the kind of animation you're doing. There's 2–D animation, which is the traditional style of animation, but it is becoming computerized and [has] moved away from paper to drawing onto tablets directly onto the computer. Then with 3–D, you are building the models in the computer, so it's all computer based.

ATM: What are you each responsible for in your company?

IR: We are the producers.

ATM: You contract out the animation?

DG: Yes. We identify material that we think will be suitable for an animated project. We then develop the content. Developing means putting it together, getting the scripts and treatments done, working with the art director and illustrators to make sure that we come up with a good, nice-looking design, as well as character development and set design. Then we put together a pitch document, which is what the brand is really about; the target audience; whether it's a 2-D or 3-D project; and identify who the creative people are. All the different aspects of the project go into that document, which we take to broadcasters, film markets, or investors.

ATM: I'm sure you have been successful, but has anything surprised you about your success or the obstacles along the way?

IR: Obstacles have been humongous. We've had to develop an industry while we develop our business at the same time. We have even had to start an animation-industry organization because one did not exist. Everyone was in little companies, and nobody spoke to each other about a unified vision of what we're doing in the industry, such as lobbying government or having broadcasters to take us seriously. We have been doing animation festivals now for a couple of years. This is a platform to showcase work with experts from around the African diaspora, including South Africa. We've had to buy respect by doing all of that, because it's a white male industry. Once they saw the success of the festivals, they realized that we have a vision for what we want to do for the industry. A lot of what we are doing is very industry focused. This animation-production training program that we're doing is industry [driven]. It's about training professionals and directors to become animation directors, writers to become animation writers, doing production, short films. All of that is to move the industry away from the commercial and start to think about doing stories.

DG: The great thing about the animation sector is that it is very new. The obstacles are great, but the opportunities are even greater. The situation with the broadcasters, like I said earlier, is not commissioning animated content, because there is a lack of knowledge among them. It's too expensive and nobody is working together. It's a dog-eat-dog world, where everyone is competing against each other. If an advertisement agency puts out a brief, Studio A and Studio B are actually going against each other to get the work. So there is not going to be a collaboration. What we are saying to people is, "Let's come together and work together so that we can build an industry." Everyone says, "I hate doing commercials. I'd rather be doing television series and feature films." That's what everyone wants to do in our industry, but you can't do it by yourself.

ATM: Is there a role for government in building the industry?

DG: No one really cares. Animation is like the ugly duckling that everybody has forgotten about. We are trying to champion the cause of animation and say, "Excuse us. We're right here, and if you invest in this sector, it's going to benefit the country as well as the broadcasters." There is a lot of local programming that doesn't sell outside of South Africa, but if you look at animation, especially children's programming, it's doing really well internationally. The growth has been great over the last five to ten years.

IR: Africa offers an opportunity for new eye candy. It has great new story content that's never been seen. Fresh, different stuff. That's the level that we are at now—the Africanization of the animation industry.

DG: The great thing about it is, the government has started listening to us.

IR: It has been a long road.

DG: Now the National Department of Communications is commissioning our company to do a feasibility study on the status of the South African animation industry and the viability of the industry. We completed that last year. It is really sort of a game plan to build a snapshot as to where we are, what the problems are, and what the potential is. We are looking at a one hundred million rand industry [US$13 million] in South Africa, whereas globally, it is a seventy billion U.S. dollar industry. We should be with our capabilities and infrastructure in this country getting a much-larger slice of that. Places like India, the Philippines, Korea are a getting a huge chunk of the global animation revenue.

ATM: Isabelle, you mentioned that you are anticipating the Africanization of the industry. What would that mean for your content? How would it be different from, say, *Shrek* [2001] or some of the other blockbuster animation internationally?

IR: It's African! It is based on historical figures like Shaka Zulu. It is folktales, African folktales. It would be original ideas. For example, we coordinated the AIDS series that is in development. It is based on growing up in Africa in urban situations. The subject matter is different, not to mention, of course, the look and feel are also different.

DG: I think it's more about its content rather than a different look. We use African mythology, African literature, and other subjects that are important to us, so we can draw a lot more from what Africa is about. I think a lot of these stories are being concealed. African literature is [widely] consumed. I know it is studied in the States. I saw it when I attended university there. I had African literature in high school. We are a company that wants to create African animation for the global-market spacing that would use works by Chinua Achebe—his novel *Things Fall Apart*, for example. There is so much great material for animation that will be consumed by the world.

IR: We have to find a balance between just finding and taking any old story and taking stories that have a brand value that are recognizable around the world. You want it to travel. Animation is an expensive medium to work with, so you have to use something that's going to help build the project.

ATM: Certainly, African folktales are universal. There are so many collections of folktales and African proverbs and, as you said, African literature.

DG: Yes. That's what our business plan is based upon. But also there are other very creative—

IR: —book properties.

DG: Book properties that exist that are from other cultures as well. We are trying to leverage content that already exists, that's already been consumed locally and internationally. We will eventually be in a position where we can do things like *Shrek* ourselves. The design, the look, and the feel of the characters will be highly experimental. The South African industry will have to come up with its own identity the way that Japan has come up with its own anime. Mongo [animation] style, that's what we're going to have to do. The same way that Disney has come up with a very different look, as well as Pixar. You can see what a Pixar film looks like, and you can see what Blue Sky productions look like.

ATM: How close are you to having that South African identity or African identity in your work?

DG: Not close at all.

IR: Not close at all. That's why we put this animation-production training team together—to give a platform for experimentation to take place. The challenge we are dealing with is that the schools are teaching Disney animation, they're teaching Mongo. Every kid wants to be a Mongo artist these days, and it is the most frustrating thing. These kids come to us with these portfolios of this, and I just want to tear it up.

ATM: They have lost their identity in them?

IR: Exactly, none of them have experimented on creating something unique, something different, something African, which is really frustrating. That's when we realized there's a problem. That's why one of the things we have got to encourage the university to start pushing the unit's standards and making changes so that experimentation is expected and encouraged. Right now, that is not happening, which is a real problem. These are the kinds of things that need to be addressed.

ATM: It seems to me that that creativity and experimentation would be part of the larger educational system, given the need to transform the curriculum from what existed under apartheid.

IR AND DG: Yeah!

ATM: Do you have allies in the public sector who also see this kind of transformation as imperative?

DG: Yes, definitely. Stakeholders are buying into this [vision].

IR: But they weren't in the beginning.

ATM: Was there active resistance?

IR: We will say we had to educate them.

DG: But what is also happening now is we used to have corporate clients when we started the business. We had the animation business as well as a communications business. A lot of our corporate clients found out we were also doing animation and would say, "Wow, that's great, because our kids are consuming this Eurocentric, this Western animation. We need to create our own African style." We were getting feedback from black corporate leaders, black CEOs as well as our own Department of Education. Artists will also help us because we see the different painters' styles which are great style for animation. I think it is changing slowly but surely.

IR: Slowly.

DG: Even the SABC. Two days ago, we had a great meeting with the SABC, and that's exactly what they want as well. They want to start producing content that [reflects] African identity.

IR: Finally, it's a new breed of people in these positions. People we were friends with years ago are now commissioning.

ATM: Your generation now is coming in to its own. Have you had any luck with getting your productions into the schools?

IR AND DG: No.

IR: Why in the schools?

ATM: You mentioned that you wanted to also use animation as you said, for edu-tainment. Couldn't these be great teaching tools, to accompany, say, a unit of African literature?

DG: We haven't done that yet because we are literally just setting up. We are producing our first television series.

IR: It has taken two years to penetrate the Department of Communication and get them to understand it. We are working through each department.

DG: It is an interesting point that you bring up. About a month ago, we had the idea about the possibility of taking some of the school curriculum and making that into animated stories, especially for the grade naught [kindergarten] to grade three or four. We're still putting that proposal together. In my research, I have found that the National Department of Education sets the curriculum, then each individual province or state chooses books for each grade. That is the problem. We are determining how we can get around it. But it is something we are thinking about doing.

IR: For our main edu-tainment, what I was thinking is that African folktales are universal whether they are studied in many schools or not. The fact that they could actually be watching those stories—just imagine! But for now, we had to outsource the project we are working on to India. The nature of a lot of African stories has subliminal educational elements in them. Part of my thinking was to get this guy who teaches mathematics on Saturday morning television. He sits there like a teacher, and he bores the hell out of everybody. Take the concepts, give it to animators, and it would make learning math a lot more fun, more interactive. Slowly, we'll be able to open these other doors.

ATM: What project are you working on now?

DG: There are a couple of things that we are involved with over the last year. One of them was a cartoon strip. The guy who actually created the film strip came to us and asked if could we help him produce this. He then created twenty-six, one-minute episodes [from the cartoon]. I produced a short film, also based on a folktale. It's called *Un Memo* [*The Echo*]. It was a part of a thirty-nine country coproduction called *Animated Tales of the World.* It won an award about six weeks ago.

IR: We were called in to help produce it. They had overspent the budget. God knows what they used it on. They called us with this minuscule budget, and it had to be done in three months, with half the money [needed]. It was a nightmare. But for what we had to work with, it's okay.

DG: To show you where we are as an industry, the other producers that I worked with on the film were sitting around one day, and the director said,

"Well, actually this is going to be the first thing that we are doing that has end credits." Everything else that they had done was thirty-second commercials. This is a great move forward. It will be shown on SABC later this year.

DG: Then the TV series we are speaking about is a twenty-part series called *Magic Cellar.*

ATM: What's your general assessment of not only animation, your own industry, but the context for innovation in film and film culture in this country today?

IR: It's a big problem. It's coming out of a history of domination by whites; of being influenced by white stories and their perspective on black stories. Now, young people are entering [the profession] with different ideas. Then there's the older generation, where any black people who was there were trained solely as technical workers. Blacks could push the buttons to edit or know the buttons to push for pulling the camera, but, creatively, they were not involved at all. This younger generation has been trained as filmmakers, but they are frustrated by the limitations of what the SABC is doing—being put in this box. I had a friend who was in the *Project 10*—the documentary series—and they completely changed her concept. I couldn't understand that. There are a lot of barriers to being creative, unless you've got your own money and can do your project on your own.

DG: I don't think that is really the problem—

IR: —not *the* problem. It is one of the problems.

DG: Yeah, it's one of the problems, but I think there is a problem with the talent. There are a lot of contenders—

ATM: —contenders?

DG: Yeah. Their stuff is bad! It's "I wanna be on TV. I wanna be in film." It looks glamorous. But I think that it is going to happen in any industry, especially with where we come from as a country. The talent is very lacking right now. We don't really have a lot. The scripts that we get, the ideas that people pitch for us are really not good. A young kid was pitching [a film] to us last Tuesday, and he thinks he has an animation feature idea, but before he finishes his pitch, we stopped him and said, "You don't know what you are talking about."

ATM: Is that because of the educational system?

DG: It's because of education.

IR: Yes, education. After ten years even. Bantu education has been irreparable. It's terrible what damage it did. Even in the proposals, you can see the writing problems—

DG: —bad grammar—

IR: —poor story structure.

ATM: Are these people now college graduates?

DG: These are young people with BSE [bachelor's] degrees. They are going to the best schools in the country, going to Rhodes University. These are not people who are off the street or who are uneducated. These are educated people.

IR: Always see that diamond in the rough.

DG: I know that after living in America for a while, what we're competing against are Hollywoods of the world. It's a juggernaut. We can't say that it's OK because it's from South Africa. We have to ask, "Is it good?" If you are watching a television series on SABC, a locally produced one, and then right after that *The Practice* comes on, you can see the difference.

IR: I think that's what really frustrates us is that it comes down to story. When it comes down to the story and the script, they don't put enough time and effort into it. I can see the problems, they're so obvious. These are young, dynamic, people who come up with great concepts for producers, but they haven't thought that if you are producing four films per year, how much time are you allowing for the development of the script. We have to go into production before the script is even ready. People pay money to go watch this, and I'm sitting there, but the hope is gone.

ATM: Are you hopeful about the training you are doing will make a difference? Do you think that in another ten years, South African films will have reached par with some other international films?

IR: I think that in the production our industry—

ATM: —I'm talking about the industry as a whole—

IR: —there has been a huge improvement from the beginning to where we are now.

DG: I think what will happen is the pretenders will fall by the wayside, and the cream will rise to the top. It is becoming very difficult to be in this industry. There are great initiatives, creative initiatives, that are happening through SASWA, through the National Film and Video Foundation, and AVEA.

ATM: Would you say what those are please?

IR: South African Script Writers Association.

DG: The National Film and Video Foundation.

IR: The Audio-Visual Entrepreneurs Association.

DG: They are running a great script training program right now. These are people who have been writing for the industry for a while but still need training. The AVEA program is helping them out.

ATM: How many people are there?

IR: About ten people. The great thing about the AVEA concept is that they're encouraging a culture of lifelong learning. Some filmmakers think that, "I went to school and studied film, I'm going to be doing my films," not realizing that you have got to go back and refine your art and your craft. Professionals who are going through the AVEA program say they have learned so much in two weeks in the workshops. We have trainers coming in from the U.K. and other places. We want to encourage young filmmakers. We have got to have continuous learning. This will certainly pay off in the future.

ATM: This is a good place to end, but I have one last question. The two of you have come together, pooled your different skills, and originated this great concept and created a company. Would you say that you are typical or exceptional?

IR: We're definitely not typical. There is nobody like us. [*All laugh.*]

DG: I think that what she is trying to say is that we are different in the sense that we are—

IR: —we are big-picture thinkers.

DG: Yes, but also we are business people. We realize that this is a business.

IR: Home industries run by creative people who don't know the standard of the business part of show business—this is a big problem. The films don't make money, even the DV-8 guys. We thought, "Wow, we are going to do some really good business," and none of the films can make money. None of the films can travel. That is the scary thing. [An] America[n] company asked for one of their concepts, but they wanted to redo it completely. They just liked the core idea. That tells you that you are not making the quality stuff that can sell. This is slowing your business model. You've got to fix that. It's great doing stories for our own people and for our own audience. There is a market for them, but in South Africa, it's oversaturated. That's all we see. Everybody knows that.

DG: We have no theaters in the townships, so the majority of the people can't even access what you're making. A smaller population who can consume your films, that population doesn't want to see local stuff. They want to see American films. How are we going to make money? It's about finding solutions to this problem. We are the exception to the rule—we are the only black company in animation. We are leaps and bounds ahead of everybody else.

IR: White and black.

DG: Yeah. We are definitely different from everybody else, because we realize what the problems are. You have to know your business side of things, and you need to know the labor. You can't do things in isolation. You can't be creating your pilots, because along the pipeline, you are going to get stuck somewhere. The producers are king. It's the producers who control everything in South Africa because they've got access—to broadcasters [and to capital].

ISABELLE RORKE is cofounder of An-Amazing Workshop and responsible for its strategic plan. She studied journalism at Rhodes University in South Africa and honed her journalistic skills at the East Cape News Agency and *Ebony* and *Tribute* magazines in South Africa. Her professional background as a writer and producer includes stints at the South African Script Writers Association and the Independent Producers Organisation. She cofounded the African Eye Animation Festival and is the 2004 recipient of the Women in Technology Award.

DUMISANI (DUMI) GUMBI is cofounder of An-Amazing Workshop. While completing his studies in filmmaking at the School of Fine Arts of Tufts University in Boston, he cofounded a literary magazine, *On the Make,* serving as managing editor and arts editor. Returning to South Africa in 1998, he joined the International Exchange Film Project as its curator and arranged collaborations with filmmakers from France, Israel, the United States, and South Africa. He also served as a line producer at SABC, the South African national television network, where he produced animation and programs in a variety of other formats.

FILMOGRAPHY

An-Amazing has produced several animation shorts, live-action films, and documentaries. More information about their company and its films can be found on their Web site: http://www.anamazing.co.za.

Xoliswa Sithole

Xoliswa Sithole

My desire is to find a way to assure that film does not remain in the domain of the bourgeoisie. I don't care whether they're white or black.

AUDREY THOMAS McCLUSKEY: Xoliswa, I'd like to begin by asking you about your own journey into filmmaking and some of the projects that you have been involved in.

XOLISWA SITHOLE: I started as an actress in *Cry Freedom* [1987] and then went to work on *Mandela* [1987] with Danny Glover and Alfre Woodard. I also worked on *Dry White Season* [1989]. At the time, I was a doing a master's degree with honors in English at the University of Zimbabwe. I decided that I wanted to go to the [United] States to do an M.A. I went to Penn State and auditioned for a master's degree in acting. I never pursued that. I went back to Zimbabwe—I was in love and crazy—and two years later, broken-hearted. I ended up in London because I had family there. I was penniless and broke, so I worked as a social worker. Then I made the decision to come and visit my father in South Africa. I'm South African but grew up in Zimbabwe. I hadn't met my biological father. So in 1992, I decided to come and see my father in South Africa, and he asked me come back home. He felt that he was getting old, and he wanted to get to know me. I moved here in 1994, and I decided that I wanted to be a producer. Since I didn't have any formal training, I started at the bottom as a receptionist on a television series called *Cecil John Rhodes.* It was a BBC production.

ATM: You took the scenic route. What did you do next?

XS: I went to work on *The Ghost and the Darkness* [1996], a Paramount Pictures film, and I was the PA [personal assistant] for Val Kilmer while working on the film. I was never meant to be anybody's PA, let alone a Hollywood actor's! I decided I couldn't do this, I didn't care how much money they paid me. I wanted to produce. I went to work on a South African feature film called *Fools* [1997] by Ramadan Suleman. I was the assistant director and helped with the casting. I also acted in that. It was like a rounded experience. I worked on two feature films for M-Net [a South African subscription television network], then came under the guidance of Richard Green and Letebele Masemola Jones, probably the foremost pioneers in this country for giving opportunities to black people. I worked my way up.

ATM: You had a variety of incredible experiences along the way.

XS: I also went to work for Charlene Hunter-Gault, who was CNN bureau chief in South Africa, and was associate producer on two documentaries. One was called *Mandela: Man of Our Times,* and the other one was called from *Trans to Transition.* Charlene Hunter-Gault has definitely been my mentor, one of those people who have pushed me to be where I am today. In fact, two people I have to thank are Letebele Masemola Jones and Charlene Hunter-Gault.

ATM: It's good to hear that women are helping other women in that way, particularly in this male-dominated industry. It is inspiring that you are doing the same thing. You're here today at this school, on a Saturday morning, mentoring young women who aspire to work in the media industry.

XS: Yes. I think that you have to do that. South Africa is still a very racist society. The film industry is very much white dominated. I think that black men are coming up, but also I think as a black woman—I have to be honest—we are dealing with issues of patriarchy. I wouldn't say that it's just a race issue. It's also patriarchy that we are experiencing in the film industry. Some of us are fighters, and my being a black woman has never really bothered me, because I'm a very, very strong woman, and I have a very good support network—the women I just mentioned and, of course, God. That's the biggest support network. When white folk and [some of] these brothers try to bring us down—which is something that constantly happens—you can never keep a good woman down. Those are the challenges that some of us are facing.

ATM: When did you decide to step out on your own? You had this tremendous trajectory and maturing experience, but at what point did you say, "I'm ready now to do it on my own"?

XS: After doing my stint with CNN, it was a need to make a film about HIV/AIDS. HIV/AIDS is one of [our] biggest problems. In fact, it is the biggest problem that we are facing in South Africa at the moment. My own mother had died from HIV/AIDS in 1996. I wanted to focus on girls. It was Charlene Hunter-Gault who said that if you are going to make a film about HIV/AIDS—and I'm very committed to making films that are women centered—the only way your film can make a difference is if you personalize it. It was a very difficult thing to do, but I did it. With a friend of mine, we made *Shouting Silent* [2002]. We didn't have money, although we put in our own money initially. Charlene Hunter Gault asked Camille Cosby [wife of comedian Bill Cosby] through a foundation and got money for my film. That's really how *Shouting Silent* was made. Although it was a very difficult experience personally, emotionally, politically, it was also a liberating experience, because I thought no one has made a film better than that!

[Both laugh.]

ATM: You have to think like that.

XS: Yes, I am a woman and I am black—

ATM: —and they better get used to it!

XS: This is the only way to go. That's really what catapulted me into having the strength to be independent. The strength to say, "OK, I can also make films on my own."

ATM: What was the budget for the film?

XS: All I asked for was thirty thousand U.S. dollars. To make this film was thirty-seven U.S. dollars. I never got paid a penny, and also the director never got paid a penny. It was one of those labor-of-love films. The budget could have been higher, of course, but I just wanted to make the film. That, for me, was what was important.

ATM: But the film is making money now, isn't it?

XS: It's only just started making money, with the screening on *Showtime* [a U.S. premium cable channel]. Before that, it had been distributed by Women Make Movies but, literally, four hundred dollars every six months. It's not making money in that sense because people ask for copies. Sometimes, you have to send copies to festivals. I've never been fully paid because I actually put in seven thousand U.S. dollars of my own money. I raised thirty thousand. I'll probably just break even.

ATM: What can you tell me about your current project?

XS: I'm doing quite a few projects at the moment. I am doing a six-part documentary series called *Flowers of the Revolution,* and it's looking at women who were part of making history in this country, during a certain time—women who have not been celebrated. I am the executive producer along with a gentleman named Clarence Hamilton, a wonderful person with a lot of experience who is committed in mentorship and black empowerment. We [work together] in this mentorship project for students who have just completed their media studies. We are helping them understand what it's like making films.

Another project that should be finished filming pretty soon is a documentary called *Return to Zimbabwe.* Hopefully it's going to be ninety minutes. I was brought up in Zimbabwe, beginning at the age of three. The film looks at my life from 1970 to now. But it's not so much about my life. I am interested in Zimbabwe as a country from 1970 to 2005, and I am celebrating a country that created a home for me and for many South Africans who were living in exile [during apartheid]. I want to show the complexity of Zimbabwe as a society. I think that no one has really made us understand how complex the situation is in Zimbabwe. I'm interested in looking at how African countries are compromised when they are liberated, how they get into negotiated settlements, and how those negotiated settlements have negative economic repercussions ten, twenty years later. In my opinion, that's what happened with Zimbabwe. Zimbabwe signed the Lancaster House agreement [for majority rule] in [1980], and that has had salvaging consequences. The war in Zimbabwe was about the land. The war in Africa is about the land.

ATM: But that will certainly be a needed part of the discourse. As you know, the news from Zimbabwe is all bad, and it's all skewed in a certain direction. It sounds like your project will shed some light on this subject, particularly for people outside of the region.

XS: I'm trying to show the complexity of Zimbabwe. I'm not demonizing Robert Mugabe. I have no desire to demonize him. In fact, I believe that [among] the true leaders worldwide, especially in the developing world, that have invested in human capital—in education, in having people develop a strong sense [of themselves]—I can only think of Fidel Castro and Robert Mugabe. I can't think of anyone else who has invested in making education a priority more than those two leaders.

ATM: It's interesting that you don't mention Nelson Mandela.

XS: Nelson Mandela. When I say investing in human capital, I'm talking about investing in terms of budget, to say that we are going to aggressively put aside a certain percentage of money to make sure that our people are educated. I think that South Africa is not anywhere near there.

ATM: Zimbabweans as a whole are more educated?

XS: By far, by far. Zimbabweans are probably one of the most literate people, apart from Cuban people, in the world.

ATM: I saw that investment in education for myself when I visited Cuba. But Zimbabwe? I know that there are a lot of emigrants leaving Zimbabwe for economic reasons and coming to South Africa. They often become street vendors, and there seems to be great resentment of them.

XS: No. South Africa is an economy. You've got about six hundred thousand to one million Zimbabwean people who are running corporations in this country. They have very, very high-powered jobs, precisely because of the education that Mugabe gave them. Nelson Mandela is different. Nelson Mandela gave his people a very strong, very good, positive sense of self. But in terms of the ANC [African National Congress] government, we've got challenges. The ANC government is still working through those challenges, however. I've never felt that education is something they have excelled in. Education in South Africa is poor, poor, poor. That, frankly speaking, hasn't improved much. I support the ANC. I vote for the ANC, but I am very critical when it comes to education. The priority is education if we are going to say that we want to be part of the twenty-first-century economy. In South Africa, education is under par.

ATM: As a filmmaker, a producer, how do you see this issue as being vital to the development and enrichment of the film industry?

XS: I think it's a problem. We are doing a mentorship program now, but we're dealing with kids who have very poor education, which we understand because we are coming from apartheid, we're coming from Bantu education. You find that if you want someone to write a one-page synopsis, the English is terrible. The grammar is terrible. You want people to think critically—and I'm talking about young people who are coming from disadvantaged backgrounds. I'm not interested in black kids who are coming from private schools, because black kids who are coming from private schools are going to walk into any company and get a job. A lot of my work is done in the rural areas. I've been to a lot of schools so I know what I am talking about. I think that it's atrocious that for a child to have a good level of education, the parent must have money. I [find that] unacceptable, but that is what is happening. I've never been interested in being part of the bourgeoisie class, never wanted to be part of the black bourgeoisie. I am working class. I am middle class by virtue of my education, by virtue of the access that I have, and the world that I can inhabit, should I choose to. But my desire is to find a way of demystifying film. My desire is to find a way to ensure that film does not remain in the domain of the bourgeoisie. I don't care whether they're white or black. My commitment is to mentor people from disadvantaged backgrounds. That is a lot more challenging. Their level of education has not taught them critical thinking. It has not taught them a certain kind of analysis. However, I believe that we can [overcome] that with commitment and training. I want to give our children a very strong sense of self and [for them] to say that, "I matter. I am valuable. I have a voice in this country."

ATM: Do you feel that there's a critical mass of people who feel the same way that you do? If so, are they involved in similar kinds of initiatives?

XS: There are people like Clarence Hamilton, people like Mickey Dube, who you should interview. Mickey Dube is one of our top commercial directors. Commercials are so much a white domain. Mickey has cracked it, and he's better than those white boys in there. Mickey probably is one of the few people who has phenomenal integrity. Mickey is the sort of person who, if he were working with the top advertising company, he would be offered seven million [rand; US$97,300] to go and shoot a commercial. He won't do it because he won't make a commercial about smoking. He just turned down a job recently because it was alcohol—with a very high budget—but he reiterated, "I'm not doing cigarettes and alcohol. They are killing our people." I don't know anybody who has as much integrity as Mickey Dube.

ATM: I will soon meet him. He is obviously a positive example for you as a filmmaker.

XS: I don't see how I can be a success and not to help uplift the race. I'm not interested in being a successful black person with elite black people. I don't want that.

ATM: I'd like to talk just a minute about audience. What are the challenges for developing an audience for South African–made films?

XS: That has been a serious challenge. The DV-8 boys [digital video] have been making feature films [using DV-8 technology] films, which is a fantastic concept. It is the best concept that has ever come out of South Africa, in my opinion. They are making fully financed South African films with a 100–percent South African crew for South African audiences. The challenge is huge, because the belief is that black people don't go to cinema. We are saying, "No, you as the distributor must market this film so that black people get to see it." A lot of the cinemas are in areas where it is difficult for black people to have access. We don't have a great public-transportation system to begin with. People don't have access to the public transportation after eight o'clock in the evening.

ATM: How are these challenges being met?

XS: We're trying to communicate whether it is with the SABC [South African Broadcasting Corporation] and with [film] distributors to find ways, but I don't think that we are aggressive enough. Civil society has to be a part of it. It must remind the distributors that we constitute a certain percentage of their total box-office intake. We demand that you show our films. We demand it! In South Africa, people are coming out of apartheid, where civil society was very vibrant. Civil society is still vibrant in this country, but the middle class has become very comfortable. They have access to all the things that they feel they fought for and have achieved. Maybe it is a process.

ATM: Is it understandable that some people, given the new opportunities, have lost the sense of struggle and what it means for all the still-dispossessed people? Or is it, as you say, simply that some people just want a share of the spoils of this rich country?

XS: They might shoot me, but I personally feel that that is what's happening. I frankly don't believe that South Africa needs any more billionaires. A lot of these people who are making this money are not creating work. They are not opening factories and giving people employment. In fact, the hope of this country is the small- and medium-[size] businesses. I think that more money should be invested in decent education. The government will tell you they are doing that. I don't think that is good enough, because the education system is so bad.

ATM: There are adult-education programs that try to remediate this educational deficit, but, obviously, it's not enough.

XS: Not in a country where you've got 50–percent unemployment and eighteen million people living below poverty. That's what, about 40 percent of our people are living below poverty?

ATM: People tend to forget that South Africa is a mix of first and third worlds and rush to make it an example for the world.

XS: It is unacceptable. I don't think that what's happening, especially in education in South Africa, is good enough for our people.

ATM: Your passion seems to extend beyond simply being a filmmaker. Do you see yourself staying with film or branching out into other areas?

XS: My friends always tell me to get into politics.

ATM: I think you would be a natural!

XS: No, I have no desire. I only have one desire in life. Only one—to create images that change the world. That's my only desire.

ATM: Just a real small desire, right?
(Both laugh.)

XS: A small one. That's my only desire: to create images that cross the boundaries, that make people see themselves in my films. Whether they are from Afghanistan or Russia or America, they'll get it.

ATM: Do you think that filmmakers should aim their films toward an international rather than South African audience so that the films will travel?

XS: No, I do see that. That's going to happen, but I also think that making films is an organic process. If today I'm going to make a film because I want it to travel, it probably would not travel. If I make a film[, it is] because my desire is to do something—to the best of my ability—for mankind, not because I'm interested in making money. Money is an energy, and money comes, I am sure of it. Those are my principles. For instance, the film I'm doing in Zimbabwe now, no one has given me money [for it]. I am using my own money. I just go in there and do the work. Do I lead an extravagant lifestyle? No. Am I interested in that? No, I'm not. It's work, and there's nothing phenomenal about being a filmmaker. We need to really drum that into people. Filmmakers—not all of them—have a very strong [sense of] self-importance.

ATM: You were in London recently to receive a prestigious BAFTA [British Association of Film and Television] award for *Orphans of Nkandla* [2004]. Since it is not about personal glory for you, what has that award meant to you?

XS: That I am now more visible. But it means nothing if I'm not visible to those young black women who one day want to be filmmakers. It means nothing. This is what I am grappling with—the invisibility of black women. Many who are doing phenomenal work and being recognized internationally are not acknowledged at home. What do we do about that? It reminds me of how [author] Alice Walker and a group of black women-activist writers had to fight to get the American academy to recognize and include Zora Neale Hurston's work and treat it as they do writers like [William] Faulkner and [John] Steinbeck. They were not prepared to do that. It took that level of activism. But what I also find interesting now is that in South African, a lot of these positions are held by black women. Positions like being editors of the newspapers.

ATM: This is the point you were making, isn't it, about the lack of commitment among some blacks. Why don't those black women put pressure on the newspapers; be activists like you just described?

XS: Frankly speaking, it's a bit too tiring sometimes. I mean, OK fine, this woman is the editor of this newspaper, she's a black woman. I'm having a problem with the black middle class.

ATM: Isn't it enough that your work speaks for you?

XS: Yes. My work speaks for me. But when you choose to not profile me, you are denying millions of other girls with dreams to be the best of what they can be. You are stifling the dream—for black women to create images that change the world.

ATM: What do you think is the present culture after a decade of freedom? Is it a healthy society?

XS: No. When you are living in a society which is in denial about HIV/AIDS, that for me is highly problematic. We are living in a society where more people are losing jobs now. Black people are actually poorer in this country now.

ATM: Poorer how?

XS: Poorer in terms of employment and life [expectancy]. Life [expectancy] has gone down because of HIV/AIDS. Of course, you've got black people who are doing better. Of course, you have a lot more opportunities for black people. There have been phenomenal strides [made]. South Africa is incredibly complex. But, here you are. You are dealing with a society where the disparities when it comes to [wealth] and poverty are just way too huge. And that gap is widening. I don't see how we can call that a healthy society. I don't see how we South Africans can say that we have achieved what we set out to achieve. No, the work is only beginning.

ATM: You would make a convincing member of parliament.

XS: Actually, our president, Thabo Mbeki, talks left and walks right. I've never thought that capitalism has benefited anybody. In a country like South Africa, with such huge disparities, there has to be a certain [point] where you [have to be] uncompromising about empowering your people. We need an economic framework. I want this to be put in where I am criticizing the government. When we gained independence, the ANC government inherited a debt of billions. They had two choices: either to say we are not going to pay that debt off, which would affect the insurance for people and [the country's] international standing, or they could pay it. But paying it meant that you have less money in the coffers for social spending. So, of course, they are paying it. They have reduced the debt now, which makes sense. Now they are spending more on social development. I totally understand and support that. In the meantime, one in four people is HIV positive. In the meantime, Trevor Manuel, our finance minister, is managing the economy very well, but whose economy is he managing? He's managing white capital. In South Africa at the moment, 3 percent of the land belongs to black farmers. We are going to have a Zimbabwe-[type] situation in this country, unless those things are sorted out. When people are hungry, when poverty is accelerating, when unemployment is reaching an unacceptable scale, people are going to revolt. People don't understand these dynamics. I have just mentioned about whether or not you are paying off your debt to the IMF [International Monetary Fund]. That was also one of the reasons why Zimbabwe went down. So for me, when I make films, I am moved by all of the collective politics in this country and the world. This is what informs my work.

XOLISWA SITHOLE is a former actor turned producer and director. In 2005, she became the first South African to win the prestigious British Association of Film and Television (BAFTA) award for *Orphans of Nkandla* as its associate director. She earned a master's degree in English with honors at the University of Zimbabwe and did further study at Pennsylvania State University, in the United States.

FILMOGRAPHY

***Cry Freedom* (1987, actor).** Sithole plays a nurse at a hospital.

***Mandela* (1987, actor).** Sithole is the character Zindzi.

***Shouting Silent* (2003, producer/director).** Sithole, who lost her mother to AIDS in 1996, explores South African HIV/AIDS pandemic as she embarks upon a journey across South Africa in search of female children who have lost their mothers to HIV/AIDS.

***Orphans of Nkandla* (2005, associate producer).** The lives of young children orphaned by AIDS are depicted. That number is around 750,000 children in South Africa. The film focuses on three families in rural Zululand to see how HIV/AIDS has affected the children.

Motshabi Tyelele

Motshabi Tyelele

My mission has always been about empowering self, my people, and more than anything else, the youth.

AUDREY THOMAS McCLUSKEY: Motshabi, as I told you before, I'm interested in your perspective—as a performance artist who works in several media—film, stage, television, and as a writer—and your observations about the film and artistic environment in South Africa in the last decade.

MOTSHABI TYELELE: I'm the right person!

[Both laugh.]

ATM: Tell me, how do you describe yourself? A performance artist, an actor, a writer? Or all of the above?

MT: I think before all the others, I'm a writer. I'm an artist. I'm an actor. I trained as a performer. The writing is only coming now as I challenge myself to develop. I've got things that I want to say, personal things. How else do you express them? It means you have to create them yourself, and that means writing.

ATM: Well, let's come back to that, but, first, I want to establish the trajectory of your career and how you got into the performing arts, particularly in acting, and what roles have you had.

MT: Those who know me say that I started performing from the day I was born!

ATM: [*She laughs.*] You know! Artists are born, they say.

MT: Back to nursery-school days, I don't know what you call it in America, I was one of those who was always in the forefront of everything. If the teacher asked, "Who can sing?" I'd yell, "I can!" It's just always been that. When I got to high school, unfortunately, the education was under apartheid. The arts were not a big part of the curriculum. We didn't even know that we could study the arts. But we would perform in music clubs back at home in the townships. I was one of those who was fortunate enough to be selected to go to Waterford, which is a very prestigious private school in Swaziland. Teachers used to say, "Gosh, you're smart, you should go for science." If you were a clever kid or excelled in science, everybody thought you were going to be a doctor.

ATM: How did you defy predictions and go to the arts?

MT: Well, it's a long story. Madiba [Nelson Mandela] said, "It's a long walk to freedom." It started when I attended school in Swaziland at Waterford.

ATM: All black?

MT: No. No. International. It was a school based here in South Africa, but they believed in multiculturalism, going against the system in South Africa. They must have decided to move the school to Swaziland, and that's what happened. At Waterford, we used to have productions coming to our school, and we'd see performances from all over. I saw a production at Waterford by UCT, the University of Cape Town, drama students. It was so good. I thought, "Wow, now that is what I want to do." I'm not going to study medicine. I went to UCT and graduated in 1990. I remember the head of the department of drama called me into her office and said, "Motshabi, how do you feel that you've completed all your work?" "Oh, I'm fine," I said. And she said to me, "Do you know that you are the first black woman to graduate from our department?" I moved to Johannesburg, and, shortly, I was working in a production.

ATM: You were talking about your first production and getting started?

MT: Yes. It was at the Market Theater where I took you. I'm blessed in the sense that at that time, there were very few trained black actresses—so to a very large extent, I found myself in demand, if I may say that. Even at drama school, because they then suddenly had the chance to do the productions that had a black woman in them.

ATM: You always found work. You weren't ever out of work in your profession?

MT: Professionally, I wouldn't complain, even though I'm not a millionaire now.

ATM: Aw, shucks. I thought you were!

[Both laugh.]

MT: No! No! I'm sure if I were in your country, by now I would be, but the nice thing is that I had a choice. I could say, "No. Yes. No. Yes." And then, of course, television was becoming another choice. I even started with the magazine programs—youth programs that dealt with different issues. Some of my friends worried that I would leave the theater for television. I told them not to worry. Then, in 1995, there was this new television series—that's the one that really made me popular.

ATM: What was that?

MT: *Suburban Bliss.*

ATM: What was it about?

MT: It was a comedy, a sitcom that ran for over a year. It was very popular. It was about a black family living next door to a white family, which was very unusual at that time.

ATM: What do you remember about the response?

MT: I remember that everyone was interested in it, even in the U.S., some magazine did a story on it, I don't know which one it was. The BBC [British Broadcasting Corporation] covered it, and everyone was talking about it. I received an award for it—best supporting actress. Things just kind of moved forward for me.

ATM: When and how did politics intrude in your art?

MT: Knowing what you stand for, you are able to say, "I will not do this one, I will pick this one." I had a choice. There were times when I was very young, I was offered some stupid [roles], but my mission has always been about empowering self, my people, and more than anything else, the youth. I have always maintained that as an artist, there's a responsibility that goes with it. I'm conscious of that. That's why my work is not really about fame. Fame happens to come with it. I wanted to further my studies and go into directing. I had lots of support in no time. I had all the application forms from all the best institutions in the U.S. But then, at that time, South Africa was celebrating me so much—this sounds like, "Whoa, she was a diva!" But you understand?

ATM: Don't be modest. Please tell me, because I don't know. Tell me.

MT: I remember the kids from Soweto—I'm from Soweto. Kids would meet me, and they would scream and say, "Gosh, we didn't think you were from here! We thought you were from America!" That hurt me so much. It really hurt me. Not that I hate America or anything or being associated with America, but it hurt me to see there are people who think whatever is good has to come from outside.

ATM: That made you decide to stay?

MT: That actually stopped me from going to study abroad because—and I know it sounds ridiculous—I remember thinking if I disappear, it's almost like denying them that glory to see themselves [in me]. To me, it felt like I was saying, "I also don't want to be here."

ATM: I understand that. It makes perfect sense.

MT: Particularly at that time [the early 1990s], I felt that black youth needed so much. Even now. We still need so much. I hate using the word *role model,* but we need to see good things happening among ourselves to motivate each other. That's why I believe that even now, kids must still see me in the township. I must not disappear.

ATM: How can artists use their work to promote the interests of children in South Africa?

MT: I remember a scene in *Suburban Bliss* where the black family wants to slaughter a live sheep. Some of the white actors said, "Oh, no! This is so horrible, how barbaric!" I remember asking them, "What are you concerned about? What is it that you don't understand about slaughtering?" They said, "No, the children are going to see this." I said, "Whose children? Really be honest and say, 'My bloody white children would not understand that.'" I said that it is time that you teach your children to see it from a different perspective. It is high time. We had to stop the filming.

ATM: Wow! You made a courageous stand. You being there at that moment made a difference. That is an excellent example of how the arts can challenge conventional thinking.

MT: How many kids—just outside the SABC [South African Broadcasting Corporation studio]—are hungry? There was a cultural disconnect there. When I was interviewed by one of the Sunday newspapers, I said, "White people will always love their dogs and their cats before they love a black child." I also said, "One of the things I want to do with my art is instill self-love." We need that sense of dignity.

ATM: As I was walking with you today, I can see the high regard that people have for you and how you take time and task with people. I don't think that would happen with a celebrity in the U.S.

MT: I like [being] myself. I know that a lot of young people admire me, and it's really about standing my ground, fighting for dignity, and showing that you don't have to do anything that will make you less of a human being to [accomplish your goals].

ATM: Is that what brought you to the next stage, which is writing your own work and using your own words and voice to say that?

MT: Yes! I've been fortunate because producers and directors have always respected me. They know.

ATM: So they don't come at you with certain expectations or stereotypes.

MT: When I did *Yizo Yizo* [a popular television show], I would not strip for anybody. There was a sex scene, of course, and as an artist and professional, it is your work. There are certain things that you will feel are right for your character. At some point, I'm sure they should see her in bed with some man. There has to be a way to do that. I want to show the dignity of the black woman. If I have to fight for it, I will.

ATM: You are working on a one-woman play. What is it about?

MT: Yes, I'm still trying to get money. It's based on many things. A black woman allegedly kills her husband—and I say allegedly because I'm not sure if I want her to have killed him. The husband was a bloody pig and a womanizer who had lots of enemies. Because of the husband's high profile—a rich man-about-town—the abuses and everything else were just slipped underneath the covers. There is the question of AIDS, also. I've been questioning how our society is dealing with the issues of rape, child abuse, and wife abuse. I sat down and looked at our society and asked, "What went wrong?" I grew up in a community that protected its children. I grew up where elders were respected by all.

ATM: You are raising important questions that lurk beneath the surface, as the arts should. These problems exist, but do people want to face them—especially if art is now viewed superficially as only entertainment?

MT: I'm saying we have to go back to correct our values. I use a lot of proverbs in the play because I grew up hearing and listening to ones like, "The mother of a child holds the sharp end of the knife; the father of the child [confronts] the midwife and the lioness." These show the risks that parents take to protect their children. So what happened? What changed? Why are mothers now silent? Some mothers know that their husbands are sleeping with their children. They are silent because they are sitting in these mansions they don't want to lose. I'm saying, "For God's sake, where is that thing that made you who are?"

ATM: Your play is a social critique and a call-to-arms, a wake-up for your country.

MT: I'm questioning the justice system and media's role, too. I've seen how the media is driven by the lowest elements and profit. A lot of the things that I use in the play are real. I have not made up anything. I raise questions about how the justice system [responds] when a man is killed because a woman defends herself after many years of abuse because she has reached that point. I'm questioning all those things.

ATM: What's the title of the play?

MT: The title—I've never had any other one—is *Shwele Bawo.*

ATM: What does it mean?

MT: Shwele Bawo—it's a combination of Zulu and Xhosa languages. *Bawo* is the power, the spirit of God. It also depends on your interpretation, but it has to do with the highest spirit. If I say, "Shwele Bawo" to you, what would it mean? Yesterday, I asked somebody else, and she said, "Prayer." Prayer. So that's what it is.

ATM: Who is the central character?

MT: The center of the play is the wife of the dead guy, and that's me for now!

ATM: Gotta be you!

MT: I am not nervous, but, look, I'm opening a whole can of worms for my people and society in general, but I'm ready! You know, I was working on another popular series *Madam and Eve.* I don't know if you have heard of it—

ATM: —oh yes, it gained some notice in the States—the comic strip and the television series—because it was considered a breakthrough.

MT: The strip, yes. I did the first television series. I played Eve, and I remember during the time we were filming, white policemen set dogs on these black guys. Some my white friends didn't know what to say. They wanted me to start the dialogue, and I did not. I just stayed quiet. Then, my dear friend who is playing Madam finally said, "Oh gosh, did you see [what happened]?" I was so angry because if reconciliation is a distance of one hundred kilometers, one would imagine we'd probably have to meet each other at the fifty-kilometer mark. But, no, blacks are expected to go sixty to seventy to eighty, even ninety kilometers.

ATM: The issue of reconciliation and other pressing social ills can inspire artists but also infuse the production of that art. When blacks and whites meet on a so-called level plane, [bad feelings] are bound to erupt, despite the calming rhetoric. It is never really possible to separate art from real life.

MT: No way! I am an artist, but I am also a black South African woman who is sometimes angry with white South Africans. I feel you can't say, "Oh, we must forgive and forget." Yes, we've forgiven, but we'll never forget. Healing this country is going to be a lot of work for all of us.

MOTSHABI TYELELE is an award-winning, highly regarded actor who performs on stage and television. She trained in speech and drama at the University of Cape Town and at the Royal National Theatre Company in London. Tyelele is identified with several groundbreaking television series, including the popular *Suburban Bliss* and *Madam and Eve.* She is also an accomplished writer who tackled the controversial subject of violence against women in a play that she produced called *Shwele Bawo: A Grave Injustice* premiered in October 2004. Tyelele won the award for best performance by an actor in a lead role at the Naledi Theatre Awards in 2004.

ACTING CREDITS (PARTIAL)

***Friends* (1993).** Tyelele portrays Thembi.
***Suburban Bliss* (1996).** Tyelele is Thando.
***Madam and Eve* (2000).** Tyelele plays Eve.
***Yizo Yizo* (2002).**
***Soul City* (2003).** The actress portrays Cecile.
***Shwele Bawo: A Grave Injustice* (2004).**Tyelele wrote, produced, and performed the part of Dikeledi in this play that addresses the controversial subject of violence against women.
***Takalani Sesame*.** Tylele plays Ma' Dimpho.
***Nothing but the Truth* (2007).** In this play by John Kani, Tyelele plays Thando.

Partial List of Theatrical and Other Selected Releases in South Africa, 1994–2008

(Includes joint productions with other countries)

1994

Accused #1: Nelson Mandela
In a Time of Violence
Memories of Rain
Soweto Green

1995

Axe, The
Cry, the Beloved Country
Encounters: The Mysterious Disappearance of Boiki Majestic Tlhapi [Encounters: Episode 4]
Encounters: The President and the Prosecutor [Encounters: Episode 1]
Encounters: Episode 2
Encounters: Apartheid's Foot Soldier [Encounters: Episode 3]
Of Courage and Consequence
Ordinary People: A Day with the President
Out in South Africa
Prime Time South Africa
To Walk Naked [Uku Hamba 'Ze]
Voices from Robben Island

1996

Deadline, The
Domestic Differences
Mandela [Mandela: Son of Africa, Father of a Nation]
Masai in the Modern World: Kenya
New South Africa, The: A Personal Journey
Riches of the Elephants, The: Zimbabwe
Somebody's Children
Virus That Has No Cure, The: Zambia

1997

Fools
Foreigner, The
Gerrie and Louise
Iindawo Zikathixo: In God's Places
Mamlambo
Mandela, Son of Africa
Saints, Sinners and Settlers
Salvation
Walk in the Night, A

You Can't Eat Potential: Breaking Africa's Cycle of Poverty

1998

Apartheid's Last Stand
Christmas with Granny
Life and Times of Sara Baartman, The—"The Hottentot Venus"
Old Wives' Tale, An
Paljas
Silent Killer, The: AIDS in South Africa

1999

Aces
Chikin Biznis: The Whole Story
Home Sweet Home
Portrait of a Young Man Drowning
Where True Lies

2000

Boesman & Lena
Bubbles and Me
Facing Death . . . Facing Life
Hijack Stories
Isibande
Long Run, The
Moon in My Pocket, The
On Tip Toe: Gentle Steps to Freedom
Question of Madness, A: The Furiousus
Righteous Man, A: Nelson Mandela and the Jews of South Africa
Takalani Sesame
White Girl in Search of the Party

2001

Body and Soul
Born Free and Equal
Dispel Your Attitudes
Dreadlock Rasta in the Nyabingi
Dreams of a Good Life
Gotta Give
Guguletu Seven, The
Guilty
Heavy Traffic
Herbs and Muti in South African Religions
Home to Lupemba
Incense Treatment
It's My Life
Judgment Day
Kings Crown, The
Let's Talk about It
Looking for Busi
Love in a Time of Sickness
Miner's Tale, A
Moment, The
Mother to Child
Of Ochre and Water
Poetic Conversations
Red Ribbon around My House, A
Religious Symbolism and Ritual Use of Water
Simon and I
Sky in Her Eyes, The
South Africa A–Z: A Commentary on Post Apartheid South Africa in 2001
Struggle Continues, The [Luta Continua, A]
Traditional Markings and Cuttings

2002

Amandla! A Revolution in Four-part Harmony
Black Sushi
Cosmic Africa
Everything Must Come to Light
God Is African
Guguletu Ballet
Lion's Trail, A
Promised Land
Shooting Bokkie
Shouting Silent
Simon and I
Strong Enough
Tsoga
Ubuntu's Wounds

Uno's World
Waiting for Valdez
When the War Is Over
Zion Youth Crew

2003

Beat the Drum
Between Joyce and Remembrance
Casa de la Musica
Critical Assignment
Deafening Echoes
Ethiopia: A Journey with Michael Buerk
Everything Must Come to Light
Fisherman's Tale, A
Four Rent Boys and a Sangoma
I Am a Rebel
Karoo Kitaar Blues
Memories of Rain [Szenen aus dem Untergrund]
Philip Tabane
Proteus
Return of Sara Baartman, The
Soldiers of the Rock
Sophiatown: Blues for Mandela
South Africa: Chicken and Eggs
Stander
Transit Café
W'an Wina
Wooden Camera, The
Yu Chi Chan Club

2004

Art of Survival
Ask Me, I Am Positive
Being Pavarotti
Belonging
Blast!
Born into Struggle
Boy Called Twist, The
Cape in Fear: The Gang War in South Africa
Cape of Good Hope
Cinderella of the Cape Flats
Country of My Skull
Delmas—The Passion . . . the Pain
Don't Fuck with Me, I Have Fifty-one Brothers and Sisters
Drum
Forgiveness
Freedom Is a Personal Journey
Goniwe's Sacrifice
Hotel Rwanda
Hot Wax
Ikhaya
Max and Mona: The King of Tears
Meaning of the Buffalo, The
Mix
Nabantwa Bam (With My Children)
Orphans of Nkandla
Project 10: Cinderella of the Cape Flats
Project 10: My Yeoville
Red Dust
7 Up
South African Love Story, A—Walter and Albertina Sisulu
Spirits of the Uhadi
Story of a Beautiful Country, The
Story of an African Farm, The
Umgidi
Winter Is July
With My Children [Nabantwa Bam]
Yesterday
Zulu Love Letter

2005

Confusion
Conversation on a Sunday Afternoon
Crazy Monkey Presents Straight Outta Benoni
Enraged by a Picture
Flyer, The
In My Country
Lord of War
Mama Africa
Max and Mona
Morris Fynn Goes Native

Rape for Who I Am
Rifle Road
South Africa: Land of Beauty and Diversity
34 South
Tsotsi
Ubuntu's Wounds
U-Carmen e-Khaylista
Vuwani
Wah Wah
We Remember Differently
Uno's World

2006

Drive thru South Africa
Gathering of Scattered Cousins, A
i MIKE what i LIKE
Sibahle
We Are Together (Thina Simunye)

2007

Angel in the Dust
Footskating
Goodbye, Bafana
Jerusalema
21 Up South Africa: Mandela's Children

2008

Hansie
KwaMashu
Life Penalty

Bibliography

"African Renaissance: Interviews." In Nuttall and Michael, *Senses of Culture,* 107–26.

Balseiro, Isabel, and Ntongela Masilela, eds. *To Change Reels: Film and Film Culture in South Africa.* Detroit: Wayne State University Press, 2003.

Botha, Martin P. "New Directing Voices in South African Cinema: Graduates from Film Schools." *Kinema,* May 8, 2005. www.kinema.uwaterloo.ca/botha051.htm.

Chanan, Michael. "The Changing Geography of Third Cinema." *Screen* 38, no. 4 (1997): 372–88.

Davis, Peter. *In Darkest Hollywood: Exploring the Jungle of Cinema's South Africa.* Athens, Ohio: Ohio University Press, 1996.

Gerima, Haile. "'Afterword': Future Directions in South African Cinema." In Balseiro and Masilela, *To Change Reels,* 201–30.

Gilroy, Paul. "Cosmopolitanism Contested: What South Africa's Recent History Offers to a World in Which Solidarity Has Become Suspect." Keynote lecture, Celebrating Ten Years of Democracy, Wiser Conference. University of Witwatersrand, Johannesburg, May 10, 2004.

Givanni, June, ed. *Symbolic Narratives/African Cinema: Audiences, Theory and the Moving Image.* London: BFI, 2000.

Hess, Edwin. "The Birth of a Nation: Contextualizing *De Voortrekkers* (1916)." In Balseiro and Masilela, *To Change Reels,* 49–69.

Jameson, Fredric. "Third World Literature in the Era of Multinational Capitalism." *Social Text* 15 (1986): 65–68.

Kellner, Douglas. "Habermas, The Public Sphere, and Democracy: A Critical Intervention." Douglas Kellner's home page, Faculty, University of California Los Angeles. http://www.qseis.ucla.edu/faculty/kellner/kellner.html.

Kriedemann, Kevin. "Controversial Report on South African Film Industry." IAfrica.com, http://writersclub.iafrica.com/kevink/publicity/413186.htm.

Magogodi, Kgafela oa. "Sexuality, Power, and the Black Body in *Mapantsula* and *Fools.*" In Balseiro and Masilela, *To Change Reels,* 187–200.

Masilela, Ntongela. "The New African Movement and the Beginning of Film Culture in South Africa." In Balseiro and Masilela, *To Change Reels,* 15–30.

Mbalo, Eddie. "Why South Africans Should Celebrate the Success of the Film Industry," *Culture and Development.* http://topics.developmentgateway.org/culture/rc/Item-Detail.do~1005507.

Nixon, Bob. *Homelands, Harlem and Hollywood: South African Culture and the World Beyond.* London: Routledge, 1994.

Nuttall, Sarah, and Cheryl-Ann Michael. "Introduction: Imaging the Present." In Nuttall and Michael, *Senses of Culture,* 1–14.

——, eds. *Senses of Culture: South African Cultural Studies.* New York: Oxford University Press, 2002.

Ntuli, Dingi, and Maganthrie Pillay. "Audience Development Study: Strategies for Growth and Sustainability." Cape Town, South Africa: Cape Film Commission, June 2004.

Peterson, Bhekizizwe. "Politics of Leisure during the Early Days of South African Cinema." In Balseiro and Masilela, *To Change Reels,* 31–48.

Posel, Deborah, and Graeme Simpson, eds. *Commissioning the Past: Understanding South Africa's Truth and Reconciliation Commission.* Johannesburg: Witwatersrand University Press, 2002.

Silver, L. *A Guide to Political Censorship in South Africa.* Johannesburg: Witwatersrand Centre for Applied Legal Studies, 1984.

Solanos, Fernando, and Octavio Getino. "Towards a Third Cinema Movement." In *Movies and Methods: An Anthology,* edited by Bill Nichols, 44–64. Berkeley: University of California Press, 1974.

Tomaselli, Keyan. *The Cinema of Apartheid: Race and Class in South African Film.* New York: Smyrna/Lake View Press, 1988.

Ukadike, Nwachukwu Frank. *Black African Cinema.* Berkeley: University of California Press, 1994.

Walser, John. "The Film Industry in South Africa." International Market Insight, U.S. Department of State, Foreign and Commercial Service, Travel and Tourism Sector. http://strategis.ic.gc.ca/epic/internet/inimr-ri.nsf/en/gr126o4o2.html.

Wa Thiong'o, Ngugi. "Is the Colonialisation of the Mind a Prerequisite for the Independence of Thought and the Creative Practice of African Cinema?" In Givanni, *Symbolic Narrative/African Cinema.*

Wynter, Sylvia. "Africa, the West, and the Analogy of Culture: The Cinematic Text after Man." In Givanni, *Symbolic Narratives/African Cinema.*

Index

AUDREY THOMAS MCCLUSKEY, former director of the Black Film Center/Archive at Indiana University, is a professor of African American and African Diaspora Studies and current director of the Neal-Marshall Black Culture Center at IU. Her recent publications include *Richard Pryor: The Life and Legacy of a "Crazy" Black Man* and *Frame by Frame III: A Filmography of the African Diasporan Image.*

The University of Illinois Press
is a founding member of the
Association of American University Presses.

Composed in 10.5/13 Adobe Minion Pro
with Meta display
by Jim Proefrock
at the University of Illinois Press
Designed by Copenhaver Cumpston
Manufactured by Sheridan Books, Inc.

University of Illinois Press
1325 South Oak Street
Champaign, IL 61820-6903
www.press.uillinois.edu